SANTA BARBARA

A Guide to El Pueblo Viejo

By
Rebecca Conard
and Christopher H. Nelson

Introduction by
David Gebhard

Published by
The City of Santa Barbara
Under the Auspices of
The Landmarks Committee

CAPRA PRESS
1986

Copyright ©1986 City of Santa Barbara, California
All rights reserved.

LIBRARY OF CONGRESS CATALOGING IN PUBLICATION DATA
Conard, Rebecca.
Santa Barbara: a guide to El Pueblo Viejo.
"Published by the city of Santa Barbara under the auspices of the Landmarks Committee."
Bibliography: p.   Includes index.
1. Architecture—California—Santa Barbara—Guide-books.
2. Santa Barbara (Calif.)—Buildings—Guide-books.
I. Nelson, Christopher H.   II. Days, Mary Louise.   III. Title.
NA735.842C66   1985   720'.9794'91   84-72199   ISBN 0-88496-225-3 (pbk.)

Community Development Department
of the City of Santa Barbara

Capra Press
Post Office Box 2068
Santa Barbara, California 93120

TABLE OF CONTENTS

Explanatory Note 7
Introduction, *David Gebhard* 9
Oceanfront 27
State Street Plaza 61
Presidio and Pueblo 103
    East of State (No. 108) 114
    West of State (No. 194) 152
Mission 171
Santa Barbara's Survey of Architectural and
    Historic Resources, *Mary Louise Days* 187
Street Name Glossary, *Mary Louise Days* 190
Bibliography 199
Special Photographs and Illustrations 206
Biographies 207
Index 209

DEDICATION

This book is dedicated with affection and respect to the memory of Miss Pearl Chase, who, from 1920 to 1979, was instrumental in preserving and beautifying the El Pueblo Viejo area of Santa Barbara, and who inspired a community to recognize and protect its architectural and landscape heritage.

Financial assistance for production of this publication was provided by the City Council of the City of Santa Barbara; a bequest from Miss Pearl Chase to the City of Santa Barbara Planning Division, Community Development Department; Eduardo and Judith Orias; the Santa Barbara Trust for Historic Preservation, and contributions to the City's Pearl Chase Fund for Historical Publications.

CREDITS

Design: Frederick A. Usher
Maps: Henry Lenny
Photography: Hal Boucher, Tom Boucher, Alexandra Cole, Rebecca Conard, William B. Dewey, David Gebhard, Ernest Jones, Christopher H. Nelson, Harriet Von Breton.

SANTA BARBARA CITY COUNCIL

Sheila Lodge, Mayor
Hal Conklin   Lyle G. Reynolds
Gerry DeWitt   Tom Rogers
Jeanne Graffy   Sidney J. Smith

CITY LANDMARKS COMMITTEE

Betty Gordon, Chairman
Louise Boucher   Robert E. Johnson, A.I.A.
David Gebhard   Henry Lenny, A.I.A.
Thomas R. Giordano   James E. Morris, A.I.A.
Frederick A. Usher   Isabelle C. Greene

MEMBERS EMERITUS

Patrick J. Maher   Pearl Chase (1888-1979)
Lutah Maria Riggs, F.A.I.A. (1896-1984)

SURVEY AND BOOK SUBCOMMITTEE

Louise Boucher, Chairman   James E. Morris
David Gebhard   Mary Louise Days, Staff

ACKNOWLEDGEMENTS

We wish to thank the following individuals and organizations for their generous assistance during the preparation of this book.

American Institute of Architects, Santa Barbara Chapter, Plan File Room, Kenneth C. Kruger, F.A.I.A., chairman
Isaac A. Bonilla
Joy Tenney Bonilla
Rochelle Bookspan
Craig Buzzell
Carolyn Reed Chapman
John Chase
Edward Comport, A.S.L.A.
Hortensia Castro Cuellar
Alex D'Alfonso
Anthony O. Days
Virginia R. Days
William B. Dewey
Virginia Dibblee
Nick and Lina Dumas
Laura Feller, National Park Service History Division, Washington, D.C.
Rebecca G. Forsyth
Jaime Hernandez
Robert Ingle Hoyt, F.A.I.A.
Dee Travis Hudson
Eric P. Hvolboll
Rev. Mel Jurisich, O.F.M.
Paula M. Kammer
Lisa Kemp
Prof. Harold Kirker
Christine Linda Kraft
Leonard Kummer
Marjorie Low and Ashleigh and Dorothy Brilliant
Paul Mills
Lloyd F. Monk
David F. Myrick
Office of Historic Preservation, Department of Parks and Recreation, State of California
Prof. Richard Oglesby
Eduardo and Judith Orias
Tom Owen, California Room, Los Angeles Public Library
Ada Moro Pool
Judith Pritikin Savage
Debbie Randolph
Lily Rossi
Catherine Rudolph
Russell A. Ruiz
Dorothy Poole Russell
Santa Barbara Historical Society: Michael Redmon, Robert Miller, and Sylvia Griffiths
Santa Barbara Trust for Historic Preservation: Phyllis Moore, Alice Rypins, Heather Bryden, Gloria Forsyth, Jeremy Hass, John Hass, Vivian Obern
Clifton F. Smith
Walker A. Tompkins
University of California, Santa Barbara, Library
Richard S. Whitehead
Marilyn Zubler
Mayor and City Council, City of Santa Barbara, their committees and employees
Personnel of the City Community Development Department
Offices of the Santa Barbara County Assessor, Auditor, and Recorder

AN EXPLANATORY NOTE TO USERS

The buildings and sites described in this guide are located in El Pueblo Viejo ("the old town") Landmark District plus a limited geographical area outside the district boundaries. El Pueblo Viejo's irregular boundaries extend through the downtown, along the oceanfront, and discontiguously include the Santa Barbara Mission. Entries contained herein are arranged so as to divide this large district into smaller sections that can easily be covered on foot if the reader chooses to use the book as a walking tour guide.

Brief historical overviews introduce each of four areas: the Oceanfront, State Street Plaza, the Presidio, and the Mission. The State Street Plaza and Presidio represent the downtown section of El Pueblo Viejo, further divided into two subsections: East of State and West of State.

Construction dates for listed buildings are given as determined from available source materials. Where it has not been possible to ascertain an exact date, the abbreviation "c." is given in front of an approximate date.

In any given entry, the historic name (usually the building name when built or name of original client) appears first; if the current common name is different, it appears in parentheses below the historic name. Names of the architect or designer, if known at the time of this writing, are given on the same line as the date of construction.

If a building has been designated officially as a historic place, the appropriate designation appears in abbreviated form.

NHL	National Historic Landmark
NR	National Register of Historic Places
CHL	California Historic Landmark
L	City of Santa Barbara Landmark
SoM	City Structure of Merit

Please note that many private residences have been included in this book. Their inclusion here does not give the viewer permission to trespass on private property. Retail businesses, museums, and public buildings are open to visitors at regularly established hours.

"To restore a building is not just to preserve it, to repair it, and to remodel it, it is to reinstate it in a complete state such as it may never have been in at any given moment."

—Eugene Viollet le Duc
Dictionaire raisonne de l'architecture francaise

Introduction

"Beautiful buildings surrounded by ugliness partake of the ugliness and their beauty is impaired. So it is with all American cities where there is no architectural control," so noted Herbert Hoover in 1931.[1] Mr. Hoover, then President of the United States, was a frequent visitor to Santa Barbara and had often spoken with warmth, understanding and approval of the community's effort, not only to control its architecture, but to create a specific image by adhering to the architectural forms associated with its factual and mythical Hispanic past. Considering its relative remoteness, and smallness, it is surprising how important a position Santa Barbara has occupied within the history of twentieth century American planning and architecture.

It was, as Thomas W. MacKesey of the American Institute of Planners pointed out in 1939, the first community in America, to set up a municipal Board of Architectural Review by law.[2] It was also among the earliest of the American cities to press for a uniform architectural expression; and finally it is one of the regrettably small number of American communities which has continually sought to control closely its planning and architecture for well over half a century. While it would be admitted that those fifty-plus years of architectural controls in Santa Barbara have experienced blemishes and flaws, still it is a remarkable record when one takes into account not only the tremendous social and economic changes which have occurred in these decades, but also the appreciable shifts which have come about in planning and architecture.

We tend to look back to the 1920s exclusively in terms of its enthusiastic commitment to laissez faireism, of Calvin Coolidge's "The business of America is business"; but the twenties was as well the decade during which the professional planning of American cities really began to take place.[3] Planning and architectural controls though could only be realized after the ground had been prepared so that there was a consensus that a community should be carefully planned. Here too, the Santa Barbara experience looms large in the history of American planning. Many American communities have experienced intense but brief sallies into well thought out planning schemes, and even into the more difficult areas of architectural controls. Most of these have ended up as an ideal, not as a realized fact; for most were never allowed to leave the printed pages of a planning document. And for those that did, their effective life has, in most instances, been all too brief.

Santa Barbara has frequently been cited as the one community which prepared the ground for planning, architectural controls, and preservation, and once these concepts had been initiated, concerted effort was made to continue the education processes so that there would (hopefully) always be a broad basis of support.[4] Santa Barbara's experience with planning and architectural control pointedly indicates that a consensus of support can seldom if ever be the result of governmental activities. No professional planner or elected public body can create, let alone maintain, such a unanimity of purpose. To establish a long-lasting continuity of community support for planning, the urge must come from the citizens themselves. Santa Barbara's decades of affirmative results in architectural control narrow down, as we should expect, to the biographies of a number of its dedicated citizens. But it would be a mistake to see the maintenance of community support for planning and architectural controls in Santa Barbara solely in terms of the activities of its few dedicated women and men. The crucial questions are: How has it been possible to carry on this effective continuity of community involvement and support for over half a century? Is there something in this process which could be applied to other American communities, or is this phenomenon so special to Santa Barbara that it would be difficult to realize elsewhere?

At least a suggestion of answers to these and other questions can be provided by seeing what Santa Barbara was seeking to accomplish through planning and architectural controls, to understand how this was accomplished, and finally to appraise its successes and failures.

The effort to preserve and enhance Santa Barbara's Hispanic tradition was not an exclusive invention of the 1920s. As early as 1874, the editor of the Santa Barbara *Daily Press* noted, "The old landmarks and the most charming characteristics of Santa Barbara are disappearing before the march of 'improvements,' and though our practical people cannot move mountains, nor change scenes, nor spoil climate, they are doing all they can to despoil the quaint beauty of the place and make it just [another] commonplace American town."[5] Though such concerns were voiced on and off in the years that followed, it was in the twenties that a concerted effort was made to halt the unbridled "improvements" that were despoiling the city's character.

The planner, Charles H. Cheney, who was early involved in the initial steps of planning and architectural control in Santa Barbara in the early 1920s, set down what was first needed: "Plan for individual character. Every city, county or region has something of its very own, of life and subtle character, individuality. This is most precious. Its presentation and enhancement is the prime duty of every planner."[6] To translate this ideal into a readable physical artifact was, of course, the next step. The design of cities, of gardens, and of buildings are realized through readable agreed-upon images. A special sense of place can be most readily recognized by the unusual features of its natural physical environment, and by the imagery utilized in its planning schemes, its landscape architecture, and in the design of its buildings. The way in which we manipulate the latter can, as we are all aware, enhance or destroy the former. Mountains and hills, rivers and bays may remain, but carelessness can minimize or obliterate their contributions to the sense of the uniqueness of place.

From the early 1890s on Southern Californians became increasingly concerned with the question of enhancing an environment which should be distinct from the rest of the United States. Caroline L. Overman indicates the self-consciousness of Californians when she wrote, "...that whatever architecture in the semi-arid region is destined to become, it will not be commonplace and it will not follow the fashion set by other portions of the country."[7] What was distinct about California, in addition to its climate and natural environment, was its Hispanic tradition, expressed especially through its nineteenth century adobe houses, its renowned mission churches, and its receptivity to luscious tropical and semi-tropical horticulture. Out of these ingredients evolved one of America's first major regional architectural styles, that of the Mission Revival.[8] This romantic sense of historic continuity was then the device which was openly used in California to suggest that this was a special geographic environment which fulfilled Cheney's dictum, that it has "...something of its own, of life and subtle character, individuality."

Bit by bit the Hispanic language of adobes and of the mission churches was enriched by landscape and architectural images inspired by Mexico, Spain, Moorish North Africa, and of the Mediterranean shores of France and Italy. With its strong Hispanic inheritance it should not be a surprise that the city of Santa Barbara fully participated in this regional desire to create a distinct geographic personality. For Santa Barbarans, though, the question was not only how the city might contribute to the regional quality of Southern California, but how the community itself could emerge with its own distinct personality. From the beginning it was seen that this goal could become reality only if it were initiated and sustained by private individuals and organizations, who would on the one hand educate the citizenry and on the other would work closely with the elected and appointed officials of local government. It was also seen from the beginning that this goal could only come about if planning, landscape architecture, and architecture were approached as a single unified problem. The city itself was to be the designed artifact. Streets, parks, gardens, and buildings were individual components whose task was to contribute to the cityscape. By 1931 Cheney could look back and comment, "Santa Barbara is another instance where cooperation of minds and efforts toward preserving the early Spanish style of architecture already possessed by the city, is giving beauty and individuality to a community that seemed just a few years ago destined to be just another ordinary city."[9].

Although Santa Barbara's historic borrowings of the twenties and later were as diverse and catholic as the rest of Southern California, still in the end there was a marked difference; for the dominant theme of its urban and suburban architecture was inspired by the vernacular buildings and gardens of Spain's rural environment and small towns, supplemented by similar examples from Mexico. This reliance upon simplicity of volumes and surfaces accounts not only for the initial success of the Spanish Colonial Revival in Santa Barbara during the 1920s, but it also explains why this historic interpretation was able to weather the ins and outs of architectural fashion, from the 1930s to the present. These "painterly" Hispanic buildings of Santa Barbara provided a connection between high and low art, and between the traditional and the then newly emerging Modern. Santa Barbara's abstract version of the Hispanic had a remarkable variety of advantages ranging from economy of cost to the importance of landscaping as a foil for these simple forms.

The earliest of Santa Barbara's efforts to establish a distinct image dates from 1909, when a group of its citizens formed the Civic League, and engaged the nationally known planner Charles Mulford Robinson.[10] At the beginning of his report Robinson pointed out that since "...there is no manufacturing section to be developed, and catered to, at whatever sacrifice to aesthetic charm...," that the community could concentrate on "...the enhancement of the city's attractiveness." While Robinson did not directly discuss architectural controls in his *Report*, he did indicate that regulations should be adopted which would establish guidelines for design of commercial and residential streets, the accompanying landscaping, setbacks, etc. He was emphatic that public and private landscaping should be one of the principal devices to enhance the unique physical setting of this community.

It was the half dozen years after 1919 that planning and architecture in Santa Barbara reached fruition. The process was at the beginning a private one initiated in 1920 by the Santa Barbara Community Arts Association.[11] The individuals who organized and directed this private organization pursued a thoughtful, but low-keyed planned program. The three elements in this program were: to formulate specific proposals which could serve as the basis for legislative action by the City and the County; to bring about through education a solid consensus of its citizens; and finally to prevail upon the City and County governments to enact the needed legislation.[12] From the beginning it was realized that all three of these goals must be cultivated simultaneously, and that with the growth Santa Barbara was experiencing in the early 1920s it was imperative that planning and architectural controls be established as soon as possible. At the beginning Bernhard Hoffmann, Pearl Chase and their associates had "...been carefully educating the public to the need and values of architectural control, had set up an advisory committee of architects to pass on plans when voluntarily submitted, and had even persuaded the banks and lending agencies not to make loans except on plans approved by this committee..."[13] The Community Arts Association, through its Plans and Planting Committee, engaged Charles Cheney (Olmsted and Olmsted) to prepare the needed building and zoning ordinances; then to provide a plan for the crucial waterfront area of Santa Barbara; and finally to suggest the rationale and mechanisms needed to create architectural controls.[14]

Their choice of Charles Cheney was fortunate, for not only was he one of America's most respected professional city planners, he was a strong advocate of architectural controls as an essential planning device. Like other planners practicing in the 1920s, Cheney had to assume a realistic posture as to the legal basis for public architectural controls. While he was willing to mention begrudgingly the economic advantages for a community in adapting architectural controls, the substance of his argument rested on his belief that no city could be well planned without a mechanism to control its architecture. He continually returned to this theme in his writings. "Plan architectural control of all buildings, signs and physical appearances. The general architecture, mass, appearance of all buildings, private as well as public, is essentially a matter of public concern: "....Plan to maintain the 'town picture'.... The city needs protection from disfigurement, and the preservation of old buildings, of natural beauty, and architectural monuments."[15]

Cheney's position was that laissez-faireism in architecture and planning must be replaced by community considerations. Though a professional planner, he did not feel that architectural controls should be administered by a governmental bureaucracy or by elected officials. Instead he envisaged that both the public planning and architectural processes would serve as a point of contact between the public and private sectors. Planning commissions and architectural boards of review should be composed of private citizens. Ideally, the membership of such bodies should strike a balance between those private citizens with direct expertise, i.e. architects, landscape architects, engineers and others, and those whose basic credentials were a sense of civic obligation. Like other planners, Cheney pointed out that these public review bodies would be able to fulfill their duty only if they saw themselves as a bridge between the past and the future.[16]

If we glance back into Santa Barbara's history, especially that of the late nineteenth and early twentieth centuries, it should not be a surprise that the Spanish/Mediterranean tradition of architecture was seized upon as the image which would provide a linkage between the past, present, and the future. The community had been one of the principal early Spanish towns of Alta California and, like Monterey, the town possessed several renowned and striking examples of early nineteenth century Spanish and Mexican architecture. The Mission Church overlooking the city and the adobe dwellings clustered around the former Presidio lent a sense of old world age which was unusual for an American community west of the Mississippi. Nineteenth century "Victorian" architecture ranging from the Italianate to the Eastlake and Queen Anne was looked upon in the teens and twenties as a subject of embarrassment. Coupled with this negative reaction to the late nineteenth century architecture was the dream that Southern California would emerge as a new Mediterranean coast of North America.

Immediately after the First World War Santa Barbara began its concerted effort to revamp its visual image, so that past and present would symbolically merge as one. Bertram G. Goodhue, who had designed the Panama-California Exposition of 1915 in San Diego in the Spanish Churrigueresque mode was engaged to plan an entire commercial streetscape in the Hispanic/Mediterranean mode in Santa Barbara. "These buildings will not follow ordinarily commercial lines, but will be set back of the street line and will have patios, corridors and covered walks."[17] Shortly afterwards, in 1919, a competition was held for the design of a new combined courthouse and city hall for Santa Barbara County, and for the City of Santa Barbara.[18] The program for the competition required that a Hispanic/Mediterranean design be provided. Both Edgar Mathews' winning design, and the second prize design by Mooser and Simpson fulfilled this dictum. In looking over these designs it is easy to see why Mathews' scheme was selected, for it best summed up Santa Barbara's desire to create a special Hispanic image for itself—an image which would provide a visual linkage between its own late eighteenth/early nineteenth century provincially charming architecture, and the vernacular traditions of Spain and Mexico.

Next to actually constructing buildings and groups of buildings to convey architectural and planning ideas, is the public exhibition of architectural drawings and models. Goodhue's scheme for an entire street and the courthouse competition were presented via the display of drawings. Those were followed by a wide variety of suggested "Spanish Improvements" for Santa Barbara, all conveyed by the exhibition of drawings. James Osborne Craig and George Washington Smith (with drawings by Lutah Maria Riggs) suggested how De La Guerra Plaza (1921-22) could be replanned so that the buildings of the past (in this case the De La Guerra Adobe and the Yorba-Abadie Adobe) would be joined by a group of new Hispanic buildings, the total assemblage of which would create a distinct sense of the moment as well as of the past.[19] Smith (via drawings prepared by Lutah Maria Riggs) went on to indicate how other sections of the city including the beach front (1922) could be transformed into the Hispanic.

Between 1923 and 1925 the architects of Santa Barbara and the Community Drafting Room, together with the Allied Architectural Association of Los Angeles, demonstrated through the public exhibition of drawings, how individual blocks of State Street could be rebuilt within a unifying Hispanic architectural imagery.[20]

The step from concept to reality occurred first in the planning of the El Paseo complex. Here, in miniature, the architect James Osborne Craig (between 1921-22) created the Hispanic town which was the goal of the Community Arts Association.[23] El Paseo provided the perfect ingredients for such an exposé. The De La Guerra Adobe and eventually the Oreña Adobes down the street constituted the balance points of the past. The Street in Spain, the patio-oriented El Paseo Restaurant, the central courtyard, and the numerous passages and open spaces effectively demonstrated what could be accomplished through a unified Hispanic approach to planning, architectural landscape and architecture. El Paseo effectively brought the lesson home to a broad public in a way which could never have been accomplished through the gradual construction of individual buildings, or by the display of drawings, models, or the written word.

Looking west on Plaza de la Guerra; schematic drawing by Lutah Maria Riggs and George Washington Smith, 1922-23.

Other examples of how a homogeneous city would appear were put in place between 1922 and 1925. De La Guerra Plaza itself, as a part of the community's historic center, slowly began to assume an Hispanic flavor. A new City Hall was built (Lockard and Sauter, 1922-23) just north of the low one-story Yorba-Abadie Adobe; the Daily News (now the News-Press) building (George Washington Smith, 1922) was sited to close off the southern end of the Plaza, and the Plans and Planting Committee of the Community Arts Association prevailed upon the owners of the property on the west side of the plaza to remodel at least minimally the De La Guerra Plaza sides of their buildings.

As in the El Paseo complex, a play was created between the past and the present. The Yorba-Abadie Adobie with its adjacent California pepper trees and the De La Guerra Adobe to the north added the needed note of historic reality. Further down De La Guerra Street to the east, Bernhard Hoffmann accomplished a similar relationship in the Meridian Studios (George Washington Smith, 1922) where the nineteenth-century Lugo (Meridian) Adobe terminated a small courtyard, embraced on two sides by a story-and-a-half artist's studio.

Thus from the beginning it was recognized that the Hispanic tradition which Santa Barbara was seeking could not be realized by a scattering of individual buildings. The character of the smaller Hispanic cities of Andalusian Spain and of the provincial regions of central and northern Mexico was a result of the spaces between buildings, of variations in the way the buildings were related to the street and to one another; and above all in the variety and importance of horticulture. The site plan for the Lobero Theater, one of the city's major landmarks of the twenties (George Washington Smith, 1922-24), created a narrow winding paseo to the west; and a pepper tree-shrouded low-walled courtyard to the north. The north side of Carrillo Street, between State and Anacapa Streets, illustrated not only how the new and old could be developed into a picturesque street scene, but also how several small-scaled paseos could help to break up the visual rigidity of the gridiron streetscape. Vegetation—palms, citrus trees, olives and California pepper trees, plus semi-tropical flowers, shrubs and a profusion of vines hinted that the buildings were in part intruders into an Andalusian or Mexican arcadia.

The story of Santa Barbara's 1925 earthquake and the rebuilding of the community's downtown within the Hispanic architectural tradition has been told many times.[22] But as Pearl Chase, one of the key personages the Community Arts Association, noted, the quick enactment of legislation to create the architectural controls to bring this Hispanic image about would never have been possible without the preparations made by this private association.[23] By 1925 a consensus had been formed, an Architectural Advisory Committee was already in existence, and legislation needed for an ordinance to establish an Architectural Board of Review had been drawn up. "It should be noted here," wrote Bernhard Hoffmann in 1925, "that for some time the community consciousness as to its proper architectural expression had been becoming more definite and informed."[24] The remarkably rapid rebuilding of downtown Santa Barbara after the earthquake was of great and long-lasting value for those who argued for architectural image. The sudden, instant homogeneity of the commercial core of the city was impressive. At what seemed, like the touch from a fairy's wand, a humdrum (it could be anywhere in the U.S.A.) city had become something special. The abstraction of this idea, realized through a few individual examples, through drawings and writings, had become a reality. Santa Barbara's hoped-for transformation, which had commenced with El Paseo, was now there for everyone to see. Articles in newspapers, and popular as well as professional magazines glowingly extolled the results and went on to observe that here at last was a community where the ideals of civic controls outweighed the visual anarchy characteristic of most of America's cities.[25]

That architectural controls in Santa Barbara ultimately rested not upon officially appointed bodies, but upon community consensus, was pointedly illustrated in the approach taken to the design of the new Santa Barbara County Courthouse. The scheme proposed by the San Francisco firm of William Mooser and Co. was a variation on its earlier second prize design of 1919. Though this design was Hispanic, it was formal. A single building set in the middle of the block was decidedly out of scale with the Andalusian quality of the City. The County Board of Supervisors was prevailed upon to appoint a non-official architectural advisory body, which would advise the Mooser firm on the design of the building.[26] In a fashion traditional of Santa Barbara, this body consulted with members of the community's own architectural profession. Its earlier design was discarded and was replaced by an entirely different scheme designed by J. Wilmer Hersey. The new building was broken into four separate parts which were arranged in an informal "L" around a sunken courtyard; a courtyard which in its sunken portion symbolically designated the site of the nineteenth century courthouse. The scale and detailing of these four connected but visually separate buildings were no longer formal, overpowering and classical, but were now provincial and vernacular. Hints of public civic grandeur occurred here and there in individual elements—the great arched entrance (which leads one on only to a view of the hills and mountains beyond), the clock tower, and over-scaled balconies and loggias. What dominated the design, however, were the gleaming white stucco walls, posed behind extensive vegetation. The Courthouse, along with the stagehouse of the Lobero Theatre and the Fox-Arlington Theatre (now the Arlington Center for the Performing Arts; Edwards and Plunkett, 1929-30) were impressive case studies of how larger volumes could be maneuvered so that they added to rather than destroyed the provincial Andalusian scale of Santa Barbara.

The slight surge of building activities experienced in Santa Barbara at the end of the 1930s was reasonably controllable, though the aggressive advocates of the "Modern" were beginning to question the validity of Santa Barbara's cultivated Hispanic tradition. This was particularly apparent in the many remodelings of retail store fronts in the downtown area which occurred both before and after the

Second World War. In all but a few instances the Plans and Planning Committee was able to mellow the belligerent Modernism to the point where these new street level façades turned out to be mild background designs.

With the embracing of the Modern in the post-World-War-II years by a portion of the architectural profession as *the* one and only style, the visual homogeneity of Santa Barbara began to be compromised. But those who upheld traditionalism in Santa Barbara remained as determined and subtle in their battle with Modernism as they had been in these earlier efforts of the 1920s to Hispanize the city. In 1947 an official public Architectural Review Board was established by the City Council. In 1958 this board published a general statement of policy indicating the approach which it was taking towards architectural control. "The design of the buildings [in Santa Barbara] has been inspired chiefly by types developed under similar climatic conditions along the Mediterranean, in Mexico and in Southern California. The successful adaptation of these architectural forms, with ingenious variations to meet modern needs, using simple materials and soft colors, has resulted in the achievement of an architectural harmony that distinguishes Santa Barbara from other cities."[27]

The second area which demanded even more attention if Santa Barbara was to "...retain its charm and spirit...," had to do with planning considerations. The control of land use, of density and above all of building heights was rightly seen as a consideration which was as important as the design of individual buildings. If the city's low silhouette, devoid of high rise, could be maintained, then the sense of continuity of the Hispanic tradition would be assured. After the construction of the eight story Granada Building in 1922-1924 (A.B. Rosenthal) an ordinance was adopted (in 1924) which prohibited any commercial structures over six stories high, or residential buildings over three stories. On June 26, 1930, the first "comprehensive" Zoning Ordinance was adopted by the City. In this ordinance commercial and industrial buildings were even more severely limited to four stories (sixty feet in height), and multiple residential units were restricted to three stories (forty-five feet in height).

During the years 1967 through 1969, numerous proposals were made for exceptions to these height restrictions. In 1968-69, when a determined effort was made to destroy the concept of height limitation through the proposed construction of two eight-story towers on the El Mirasol Hotel site, this was correctly seen by the

Plans and Planting Committee and the Citizens Planning Association as a possible death blow to Santa Barbara's architectural tradition. The proposal was fought with great intensity in the courts and through a charter amendment, with the result that height limitations were taken out of the arena of politics, and placed within the safety of the City Charter itself.[28]

When in the early 1960s a general plan had been drawn up for the City by Eisner-Stewart and Associates, the City's unique Hispanic image was directly set forth and enshrined in the document.[29]

Just prior to Eisner's general plan studies, a quiet event took place which would eventually provide the public controls needed to nudge Santa Barbara back into its Hispanic tradition. This was the creating in 1960 by the City Council of a small obscure public body designated as the Advisory Landmark Committee. Notwithstanding its name, the principal task of this committee was to act as an historical design review body for the El Pueblo Viejo District which comprised the central core of the City, the sixteen blocks in and around the site of the historic late eighteenth century Presidio. Gradually, more stringent Hispanic architectural controls were reinstated, and the original sixteen block El Pueblo Viejo District was expanded, eventually including portions of the City as far away as the Mission itself. Simon Eisner wrote of these new efforts for preservation and architectural continuity: "The 'El Pueblo Viejo' ordinance represents a start toward the full statement in legislative terms of the desire of Santa Barbara to preserve its reputation as one of the nation's most attractive historic cities."[30]

In the decade of the 1960s the Plans and Planting Committee and Santa Barbara Beautiful were joined by two additional private organizations. These were the Citizens Planning Association of Santa Barbara County (founded in 1960), and the Santa Barbara Trust for Historic Preservation (founded in 1963). The first of these organizations concentrated its principal attention on planning, and of the politics of planning. The Santa Barbara Trust for Historic Preservation dedicated its major efforts to the full scale rebuilding of Santa Barbara's 1782 Presidio.

By the mid-1970s it was recognized that a more publicly visible body was necessary to administer the architecture of the city's historic core. A new committee was established in 1977, designated as the Landmarks Committee. The boundaries of the El Pueblo Viejo District were redrawn to include all of the business core of the city and the principal streets giving access to the city from the freeway (Highway 101). In conjunction with these changes, the City's

Architectural Board of Review adopted a policy for the edges of the El Pueblo Viejo District, so that new or remodeled structures adjacent to it would convey a sense of the Hispanic tradition.

The lesson which Santa Barbara provides is that the unique quality of its manmade environment rests upon a cultivated community concern and consensus. This common agreement or goal may be expressed through elected or appointed political bodies, but ultimately it remains as an affair outside of government itself. The Santa Barbara experience pointedly illustrates how elitism (the activity of the few) and democracy (popular consensus) can emerge as one. Santa Barbara's ideal was summed up in 1929 when Bernhard Hoffmann wrote, "The tempo of our age has been so speeded up with jazz, radio, the automobile and the aeroplane that now more than every before, it is necessary so to build and plan and execute so that simplicity, sincerity and beauty may not be overlooked or ignored in the mad rush."[31]

—DAVID GEBHARD

Proposed freeway bridge at U.S. Highway 101 and State Street, Freeway Advisory Committee drawing by Henry Lenny, 1985.

Notes

1. Quoted in Charles H. Cheney, "Architectural Controls," *The American Architect*, vol. 140, April, 1931, p. 23.
2. Thomas W. MacKesey, "Aesthetics and Zoning," *Journal of the American Institute of Planners*, vol. 5, no. 4, 1939, p. 98. Rollin L. McNitt, "Architectural Control Under the Police Power," *Community Builder*, vol. 1, January 1928, pp. 26-28.
3. Mel Scott, *American City Planning*, Berkeley: University of California Press, 1969, pp. 183-269.
4. David Gebhard, *Santa Barbara: The Creation of a New Spain in America*, University Art Museum, University of California, Santa Barbara, 1982. "Community Building in Santa Barbara," *Christian Science Monitor*, October 1, 1925. T.J. Franklin, "The Personality that is Santa Barbara," *Sunset*, vol. 57, July, 1926, pp. 42-43.
5. *Santa Barbara Daily Press*, January 3, 1874.
6. Charles H. Cheney, "Building for Permanency," *20th National Conference on City Planning*, Dallas, Texas, 1928, pp. 38-39.
7. Caroline L. Overman, "Modern Spanish Architecture in California," *The House Beautiful*, vol. 5, April, 1899, p. 33.
8. David Gebhard, "Architectural Imagery, The Mission and California," *Harvard Architectural Review*, vol. 1, Spring, 1980, pp. 137-145. Karen Weitze, *California's Mission Revival*, with a foreword by Harold Kirker, Los Angeles: Hennessey and Ingalls, 1983.
9. Charles H. Cheney, "California Cities Capitalize Natural Charm—A Symposium," *Western Architect*, vol. 40, March, 1931, pp. 11-12.
10. Charles Mulford Robinson. *The Report of Charles Mulford Robinson Regarding the Civic Affairs of Santa Barbara, California*, Santa Barbara: printed for the Civic League by the Independent, 1909.
11. M. Urmy Seares, "The Community Arts Association of Santa Barbara, California," *California Southland*, no. 60, vol. 6, December, 1928, pp. 12-13; 22; "Arts Association—Santa Barbara Plans and Planting Branch," *California Southland*, vol. 7, January, 1925, pp. 15-31. Edward Sajous, "How a Community Arts Association is Raising Architectural Standards," *American City*, vol. 29, July, 1923, p. 39.
12. Pearl Chase, "Bernhard Hoffmann—Community Builder," *Noticias*, vol. V, no. 2, Summer, 1959.
13. Charles H. Cheney, "Progress in Architectural Control," *Architect and Engineer*, vol. 90, August, 1927, p. 46.
14. "Charles H. Cheney will assist the Building Ordinance Committee of the Santa Barbara Chamber of Commerce in framing a new building code for the city," *Architect and Engineer*, vol. 75, November, 1923, p. 112. Olmsted and Olmsted, *Major Traffic Street Plan and Boulevard and Park System*, Santa Barbara: Plans and Planting Committee, 1924.
15. Charles H. Cheney, "Building for Permanency," *National Conference on City Planning*, Dallas, Texas, 1928, p. 39. Two later papers by Cheney on the subject are: "Architectural Control In America," *Proceeding, National Conference on Planning*, Chicago, 1940, pp. 125-129; "Architectural Control," *The Octagon*, February, 1940, pp. 18-19.
16. Charles H. Cheney, "Progress in Architectural Control," *Architect and Engineer*, vol. 90, August, 1927, pp. 45-46.
17. *Architect and Engineer*, vol. 58, September, 1919, p. 118.
18. "Competition for Santa Barbara County Court House and Memorial," *The Building Review*, vol. 18, November, 1919, pp. 85-87; 95.
19. Mary Osborne Craig, "The Heritage of All California," *California Southland*, No. 33, September, 1922, pp. 7-9. "When Santa Barbara's Dream of 'A Street in Spain' is called into being by Her Peoples" *Santa Barbara Daily News*, May 20, 1922, Special Photogravure Section; Irving F. Morrow, "A Step in California Architecture," *The Architect and Engineer*, vol. 70, August, 1922, pp. 46-103.
20. Irving F. Morrow, "New Santa Barbara," *The Architect and Engineer*, vol. 86, July, 1926, p. 46; illustration of drawings for

State Street, *Pacific Coast Architect*, vol. 28, November, 1925, pp. 35-36.
21. Harris Allen, "The 'Street of Spain,' Santa Barbara, California," *Pacific Coast Architect*, vol. 27, March, 1925, pp. 23-39. Henriette Boegkmann, "The Little Street of Spain," *International Studio*, vol. 81, June, 1925, pp. 184-188.
22. "Santa Barbara Earthquake Number," *Bulletin, Allied Architectural Association of Los Angeles*," vol. 1, no. 10, August 1, 1925; "The Santa Barbara, California, Earthquake," *The American Architect*, vol. 128, July 15, 1925, pp. 47-48; Winsor Soule, "Lessons of the Santa Barbara Earthquake," *The American Architect*, vol. 128, October 5, 1925, pp. 295-302; "What Earthquakes Cannot Destroy," *The Literary Digest*, vol. 86, August 1, 1925, pp. 29-30. Bernhard Hoffmann, "The Rebuilding of Santa Barbara," *Bulletin of the Seismological Society of America*, December, 1925, pp. 323-328. Pearl Chase, "Santa Barbara Resurgent," "The Reconstruction of State Street," (unpublished paper, Dept. History, University of California, Santa Barbara, 1970).
23. Pearl Chase, "Bernhard Hoffmann— Community Builder," *Noticias*, vol. V, no. 2, Summer, 1959, pp. 6-7.
24. Bernhard Hoffmann, "The Rebuilding of Santa Barbara," *Bulletin of the Seismological Society of America*, vol. 15, December, 1925, p. 325.
25. "Santa Barbara: The Case for a Unified Architecture," *Architectural Forum*, vol. 59, July, 1933. pp. 84-85. Edward F. Brown, "Does Beauty Pay?" *The American City Magazine*, vol. 30, February, 1924, pp. 165-166.
26. "The Santa Barbara County Courthouse," *California Southland*, no. 97, vol. 10, January, 1928, pp. 11-13.
27. *Policy for Architectural Control Adopted by the Architectural Board of Review of the City of Santa Barbara, California*, Santa Barbara, August, 1958.
28. The City Charter establishes a maximum height of sixty feet; commercial buildings are limited to four stories, and multiple residential buildings to three stories, according to zone.
29. Eisner-Stewart and Associates, *Santa Barbara, California: The General Plan*. South Pasadena: Eisner-Stewart and Associates, 1964, pp. ix, 9.
30. Ibid. p. 10.
31. Bernhard Hoffmann, "Architectural Aphorisms," *The Architect and Engineer*, vol. 96, March, 1929, p. 111.

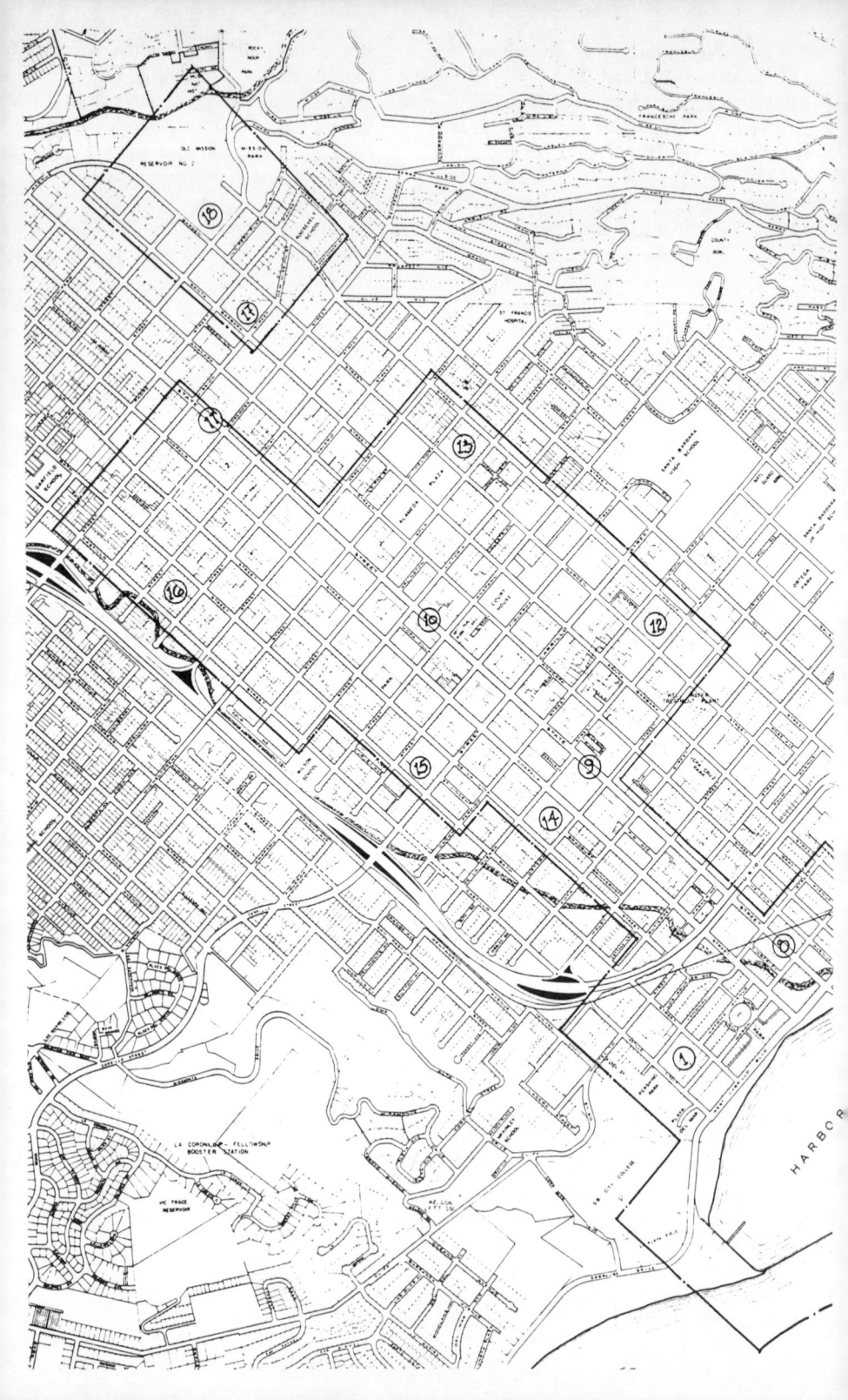

A February 1925 photograph of Plaza del Mar when it extended across West Cabrillo Boulevard and adjoined West Beach.

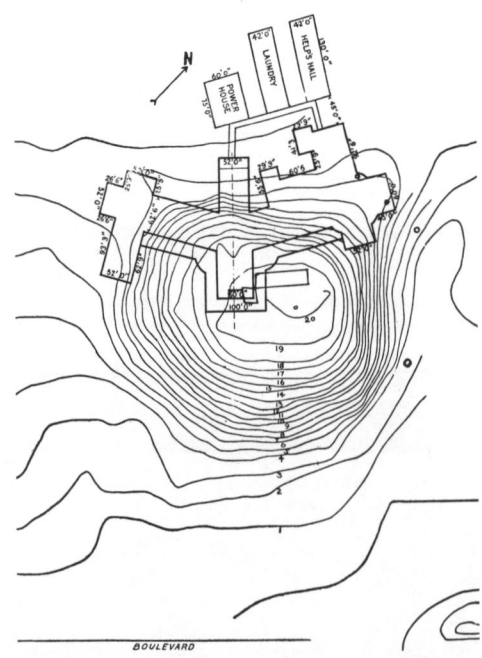

A site plan of the Potter Hotel superimposed on a contour map of Burton Mound probably prepared by J.K. Harrington in 1901.

OCEANFRONT

Until the Spanish colonists entered the Santa Barbara area during the 1780s, the oceanfront was the province of the Coastal Chumash. Cabrillo's 1542 account as well as later writings indicate that the Chumash lived in round, tule-covered houses arranged in rancherias, or villages. They hunted the inland range and fashioned clothing from animal skins. They also fished off the coast in dugout and plank canoes. Acorns, seeds, and a maize-like grain rounded out their varied diet. Mission records reveal that over 150 separate villages were once located within the present-day boundaries of Santa Barbara County.

Archaeologists have retrieved few weapons or warlike implements from any of the village sites which have been excavated. Thus, it would seem that the Chumash maintained a peaceful society. Various excavations have, however, uncovered many necklaces, bracelets, and earrings; inlaid wooden bowls, trays, and boxes; baskets and woven boxes; and carved pipes and other ornaments. Traditional Chumash lifestyles, technology, and arts virtually ended with European contact. After 1786, most of the coastal village inhabitants left their brush houses to live in adobe shelters near the Mission. Until the 1830s, the nearly deserted oceanfront, which now belonged to the Mission, was known as *el rancho de la playa*.

When the Mission lands were broken up in the early 1830s, title passed into the hands of many early day settlers, but the oceanfront area remained largely undeveloped until the turn of the twentieth century. The adobe on Burton Mound (1830s; entry #9), the Trussell-Winchester Adobe (1854; entry #1), the Santa Barbara Wharf at the foot of Chapala Street (1868-1878), Stearns Wharf (1872; entry #27), Bradley's Race Track (1873-1886), the pavilion (1886-1898) and race track (1886-ca. 1920) at the Agricultural Park, and the railroad (1887; entry #45) were the only prominent structures in the beach area throughout the nineteenth century. Almost all of them appeared after 1850.

Limited development did not mean, however, that development schemes were lacking or that the area was little used once Anglo-American settlement began. After Charles Nordhoff visited Santa Barbara in the winter of 1872 and then praised its "equable climate" in *California—A Book for Travelers and Settlers*, the oceanfront became a renowned health spa and recreational resort. Invalids, as they were called in Victorian-era parlance, flocked to the Santa Barbara coast, advertised widely as the "sanitorium of the Pacific," in hopes that the sulphur springs on Burton Mound and the sea air would cure their ailments. The Arlington Jockey Club, a group of wealthy, eastern-bred men, raced horses on the beach as well as at two tracks laid out in the East Beach area (see entry #37). A mule-drawn streetcar, established in 1876, carried residents and visitors to and from the bathhouses that dotted the area now known as West Beach. Crowds frequently gathered at the Agricultural Park to watch balloon ascensions, circuses, county fair events, and, of course, horse races. This popular spot would have had a resort hotel long before the Potter (1902; entry #9) except that the financiers known as the Seaside Hotel Company wisely decided not to risk building luxury accommodations so near the shoreline, which was subject to treacherous waves in stormy weather before the breakwater was constructed. The company members instead agreed on an inland location and proceeded to build the Arlington Hotel (1875; entry #94).

By the turn of the twentieth century, Santa Barbarans fully realized the inherent commercial as well as aesthetic values in nature's bounty. The decades since then have witnessed a series of confrontations and compromises between those who would exploit the area's full revenue potential as a tourist and fishing spot and those who have sought to enhance the area's natural beauty. The result has been gradual development balanced between competing commercial and aesthetic interests.

Initial preservation efforts came from the local business community, whose concern lay foremost with preserving what we now call "open space," not with preserving the cultural remnants of the past. The Chamber of Commerce, in particular, spearheaded efforts between 1899 and 1913 to raise money in order to buy oceanfront land. The Chamber was openly motivated by a desire to create a scenic waterfront that would continue to attract a wealthy tourist class. Many of those wealthy seasonal visitors so attracted to the area were likewise attracted to the business community's idea; and they continued land-syndicate purchases as well as other philanthropic civic projects throughout the 1920s and 1930s. These early twentieth century businessmen, although concerned with matters economic, nevertheless launched a preservation movement locally, the concerns of which have been broadly conceived to include the natural physical setting as well as the built environment.

As a result of privately initiated land acquisition projects, by 1920

The second public bathhouse (1915-1937, Russel Ray, architect) faced northeast along Cabrillo Boulevard from Plaza del Mar in this February 1925 photograph.

the city owned several parcels of oceanfront land, although few efforts had been made to realize their potential as scenic areas. The East Boulevard Improvement Association set about to change the situation in 1924, three years after the Ambassador (Potter) Hotel had burned. Upon learning that out-of-town developers were eyeing the East Beach area, the Association arose to stop these developers from building "undesirable amusement and cheap store programs" similar to those "being carried out on the old Ambassador Hotel grounds."

Working with the Chamber of Commerce, the Association engaged Charles Cheney of the firm Olmsted and Olmsted to plan an oceanfront parkway that would be Santa Barbara's counterpart to New York's Central Park and San Francisco's Golden Gate Park. These two groups then embarked on an ambitious plan to secure the rest of the beach property necessary to implement Cheney's plan, adopted by the city in late 1924. Although they made great strides toward their goal, by 1930 citizens at large seemed unwilling to pass the bond issues necessary to finance Cheney's plan through to completion.

During the late 1920s, moreover, another vision of Santa Barbara emerged to compete with the one established earlier. Its adherents envisioned the oceanfront not as a rural-like park, but as a bustling port of entry for freighters and passenger ships. The new, commercial-oriented image reflected some deeper changes in the character of the city. The heyday of wealthy part-time residents was on the wane. Tourists continued to come to Santa Barbara, but the automobile and middle-class affluence transformed the city from a winter retreat into a short-term vacation spot. The population, moreover, increased steadily until the early 1930s, when it stabilized at about 35,000. With this transformation came the threat of losing the economic ballast of eastern capital. Eschewing the idea of an industrial-based local economy, Santa Barbara leaders turned their attention to developing a city which would appeal to this new tourist clientele.

The Great Depression, followed by World War II, intervened, however, to slow both the economy and development. Nevertheless, by the late 1930s, the city had acquired the extensive park system now dressing the oceanfront, thanks to the efforts of many seemingly tireless citizens. Private benefactions and New Deal relief funds allowed the city also to build, acquire, or improve several recreational facilities. Population growth resumed after the war, spurring considerable building activity in the oceanfront as well as throughout the city. Many West Beach motels were built in the late 1940s or 1950s, and the surrounding residential neighborhood developed fully in the post-war years. Since then, the oceanfront has supported a compatible mix of residential, commercial-industrial, and recreational use. It is this continuing balance between protected open space and ever-changing mixed use that gives the oceanfront much of its distinctive character.

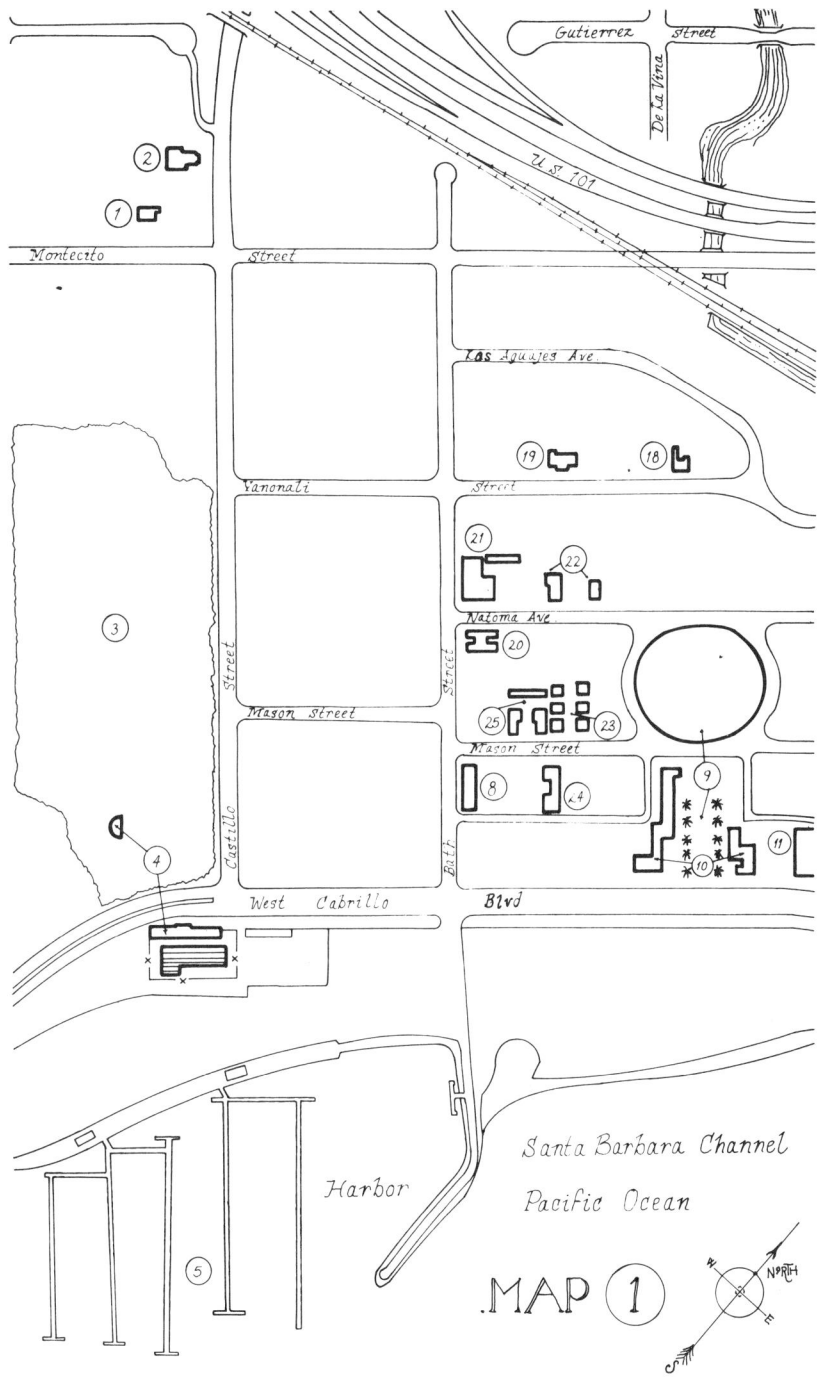

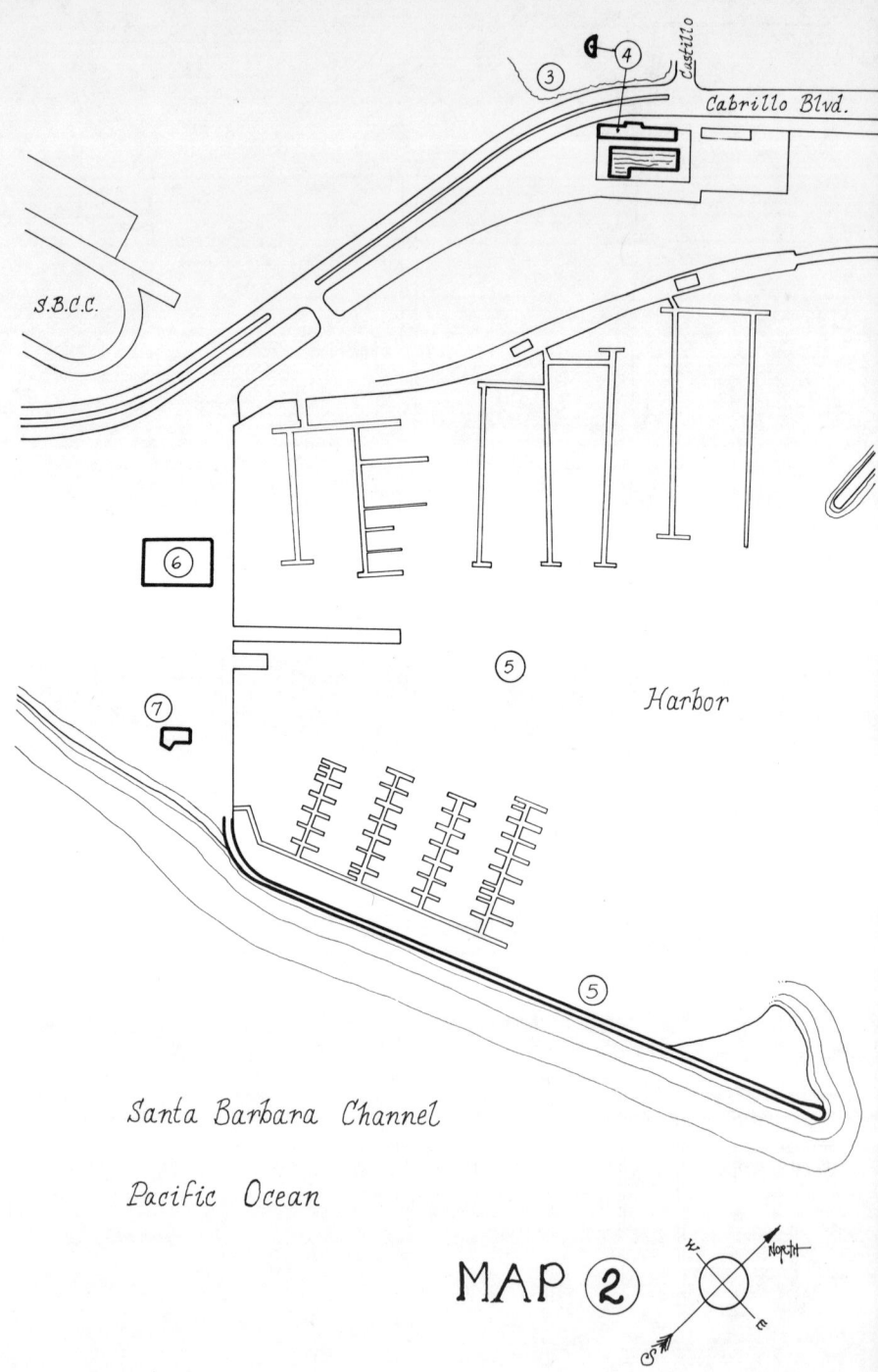

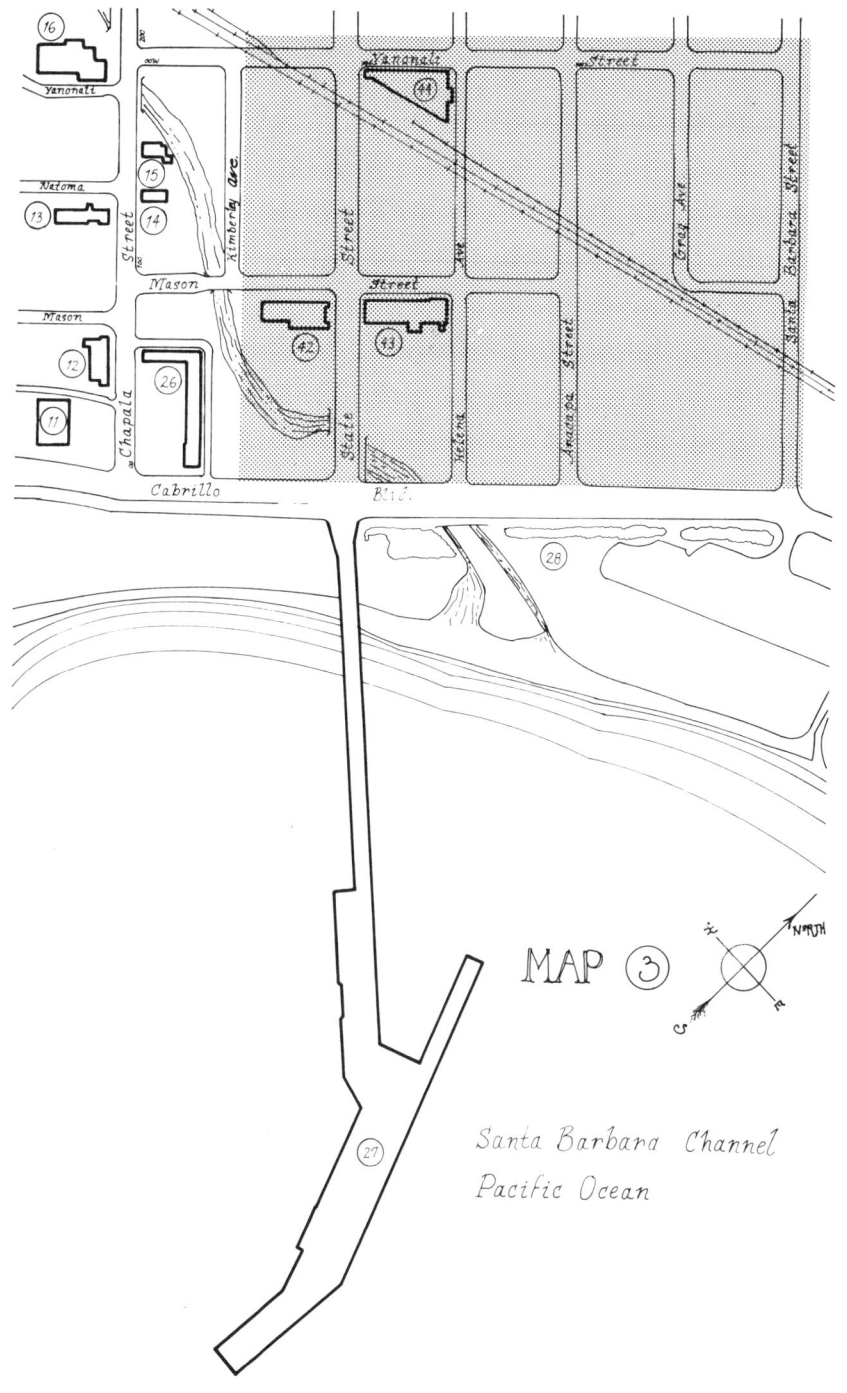

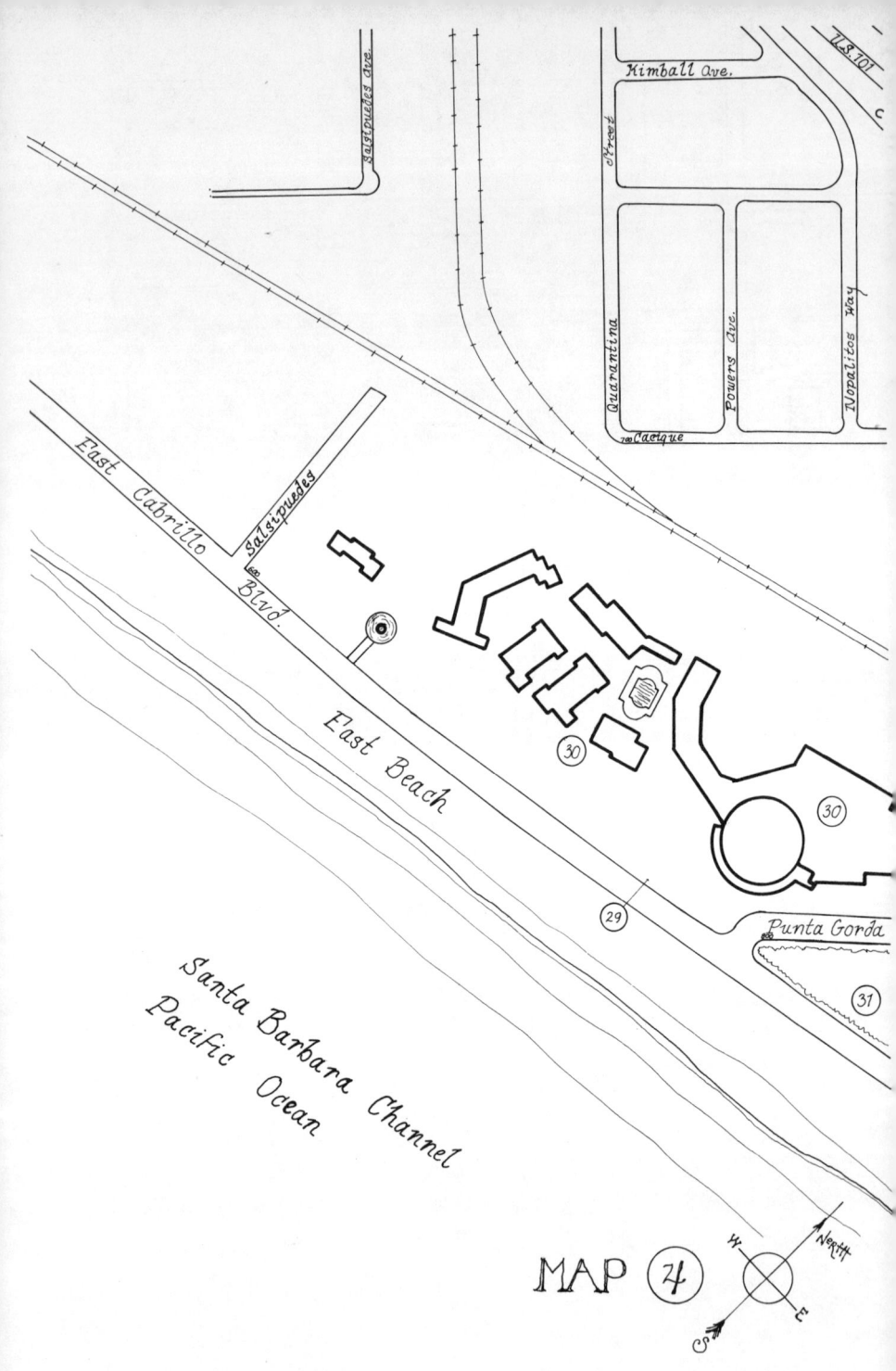

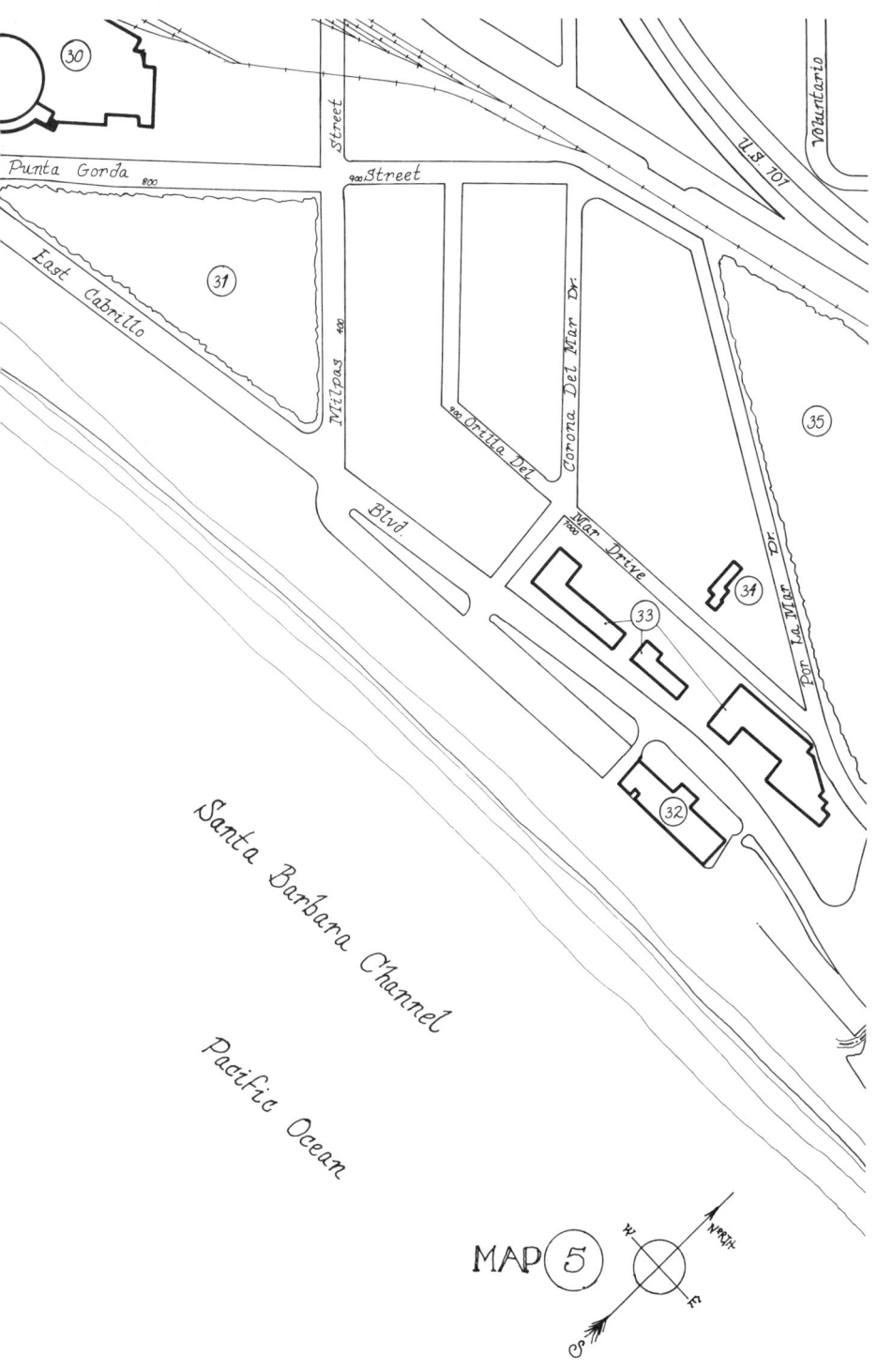

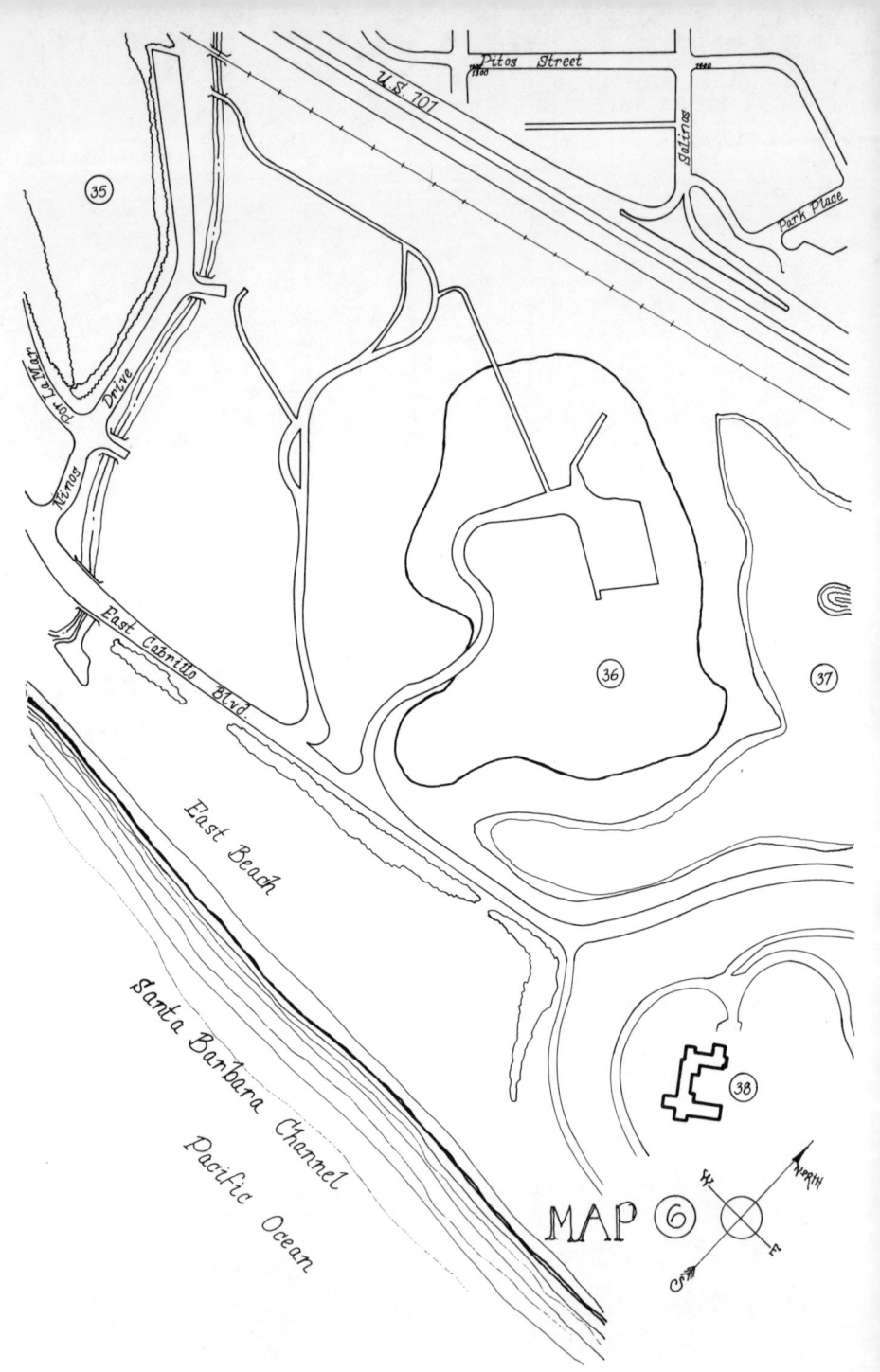

1.
Trussell-Winchester Adobe
412 W. Montecito St.
1854   L, CHL

Reflective perhaps of Captain Horatio Gates Trussell's eastern background, this clapboarded and shuttered adobe suggests the single-story Monterey Greek Revival style. A seafarer, Capt. Trussell took much of the timber used in constructing the adobe from the ship "Winfield Scott," wrecked on Anacapa Island in 1853. In 1881, Miss Sarah Winchester, a local school teacher, purchased the adobe, and the Winchester family continued to occupy it for several decades. The adobe, a City Landmark, is owned by the Santa Barbara Historical Society, which operates it as a house museum, open to the public on Sunday from 2-4 p.m.

Just west of the adobe on Montecito St. are two late 19th-century houses. The Italianate side hall house with an Eastlake porch, at 430 W. Montecito, was built ca. 1878.

2.
Fernald House
414 W. Montecito St.
(behind Trussell-Winchester adobe)
1862; attributed to Roswell Forbush
1880 remodeled and enlarged; Thomas Nixon
                                                 L

Eclectic in its overall design, this 19th-century dwelling is a combination of Gothic Revival with Eastlake, Queen Anne, and even Craftsman details. First located at 422 Santa Barbara St., the house with its landscaped surroundings occupied nearly an entire city block. The family of Judge Charles and Hannah Hobbs Fernald lived there continuously for over 80 years. In 1959 the Santa Barbara Historical Society acquired the house and moved it to the present location. A City Landmark, the house is now a museum, open to the public on Sunday from 2-4 p.m.

3. Pershing Park

Castillo St. between Yanonali and Mason Sts.
ca. 5 acres; acquired by the city 1926-27

A news item from August 5, 1939, boasts that, "They booted calves out of the chutes at Pershing Park yesterday. Los Vaqueros whirled the kinks out of their riatas....It was the day of stock horse competition that is becoming a highlight of the Old Spanish Days celebration." For many years after World War I, the National Horse Show was held at Pershing Park. The park continued to host various horse shows and rodeos until 1958, when the arena was demolished. This area also was the site of barns that housed the streetcars which were in city-wide use through the early 1920s. The park, in addition, has been used as an athletic field from pre-World War I days to the present.

During the 1960s and early 1970s the park's physical environment changed considerably as aging structures were removed, lighted athletic facilities were added, and the Old Spanish Days Carriage Museum was constructed. The museum, located at the north end, houses a wide variety of pre-automotive vehicles and is open to the public on Sundays from 2-4 p.m.

4. Los Baños del Mar and Plaza del Mar

corner Castillo St. and W. Cabrillo Blvd.
ca. 7.5 acres; acquired by the city in 1899, 1900, 1934
1938 pool; Associated Architects

Before Cabrillo Blvd. was extended westward in 1943, these two parks constituted a beachfront plaza surrounding a municipal swimming pool. Since the 1870s, in fact, Santa Barbarans and tourists have been coming to this spot to swim, stroll, picnic, and generally relax. As early as 1873 privately owned bathhouses accommodated ocean bathers, but in 1891 the city designated part of the area as a "public garden." By the turn of the century, the plaza had been improved with lawns, benches, palm trees, and walkways. The first Los Baños del Mar, built in 1901, contained, in addition to its heated indoor pool, a bowling alley, billiard parlor, roof deck, and outdoor bandstand. The bathhouse burned in 1913 and was replaced in 1915 by a new facility built by Edison Electric Co., whose streetcar line terminated at the plaza. When the 1925 earthquake damaged the second pool and building, they were temporarily closed. Later the city purchased the facilities, which were demolished in 1937. After several years of lobbying in Washington, D.C. for Depression-era work relief projects, the city was awarded PWA funds in 1937 to assist in the construction of the present-day Los Baños del Mar. In 1920, the concrete shell in Plaza del Mar was built for a Community Arts Association-sponsored play, which was part of the Primavera (precursor of Fiesta) festivities that summer. This park includes Moreton Bay and Rustyleaf fig trees as well as three types of eucalyptus not found elsewhere in Santa Barbara. Dr. A.B. Doremus, longtime volunteer park superintendent, was in charge of the original planting and had hoped to establish a grove of Montezuma Bald Cypress, the famous "Council Tree of Mexico City." Only one survived.

5.
Breakwater and Harbor
west of Stearns Wharf
1927-1930

Santa Barbara's manmade harbor owes its environmentally fragile existence to decades of dreamers, the philanthropy of Max C. Fleischmann, heir to the Fleischmann Yeast Co., and the generosity of U.S. taxpayers. As early as 1850 development-minded Santa Barbarans petitioned the federal government for funds to create a harbor. Repeated petitions were consistently rejected by the government, and it was not until the 1920s that local citizens appeared willing to finance such an expensive undertaking. Harbor proponents, however, disagreed on the site: some advocated dredging the estero that is now the Andree Clark Bird Refuge; others proposed digging out the Goleta slough; and still others advocated constructing a breakwater west of Stearns Wharf. The 1925 earthquake temporarily diverted attention from the municipal harbor project, but in 1926 Fleischmann offered the city $200,000 if the city would match that amount so that the project could go forward. Construction of the riprap breakwater proved more costly than estimated, however, and Fleischmann later donated another large sum to help see the project through to completion. No one, moreover, foresaw entirely the immense effect this artificial barrier would have on natural wave action and the littoral sand drift. For several years after the breakwater was completed, sand accumulated in the new harbor, while beaches further down the coast gradually eroded because the current no longer brought replenishing sand. The federal government, which had for so long rejected requests for funds to build a harbor, now came to the rescue. After the breakwater created a harbor, the city qualified for federal funds under the maintenance provisions of the 1935 Rivers and Harbors Act. Federal funds to maintain a constant dredging operation and several modifications to the breakwater since 1935 have helped to keep the sand accumulation problem within manageable limits. The severe 1982-83 winter storms damaged the breakwater area and Stearns Wharf. Problems notwithstanding, the harbor provides small seagoing vessels an official port of refuge in a strategic coastal location.

6.
Naval Reserve Armory
(Naval Reserve Training Center)
Shoreline Dr. at the Marina
1941; Winsor Soule; WPA supervising
   engineer: L.J. Seckels

During World War II the harbor was virtually closed to recreational use. Military patrol vessels had priority use from 1941 to 1945, and the U.S. Navy provided maintenance and logistical support. The Naval Reserve Armory was quickly constructed in order to accommodate these emergency operations, with major financial assistance coming from the WPA. Aesthetics were not sacrificed to necessity, however, as the Hispanic image is still in evidence—with a federal touch, to be sure, but still in keeping with the dominant theme in Santa Barbara architecture.

7.
Santa Barbara Yacht Club
    Marina, west of the breakwater
    1966; Cooke-Frost-Greer and Schmandt,
      design architects; Richard Bliss Nelson,
      supervising architect

When this clubhouse was christened in December 1966, it marked the end of nearly three decades of transiency for the Yacht Club. Organized in 1877, the club built its first meeting place at the foot of Stearns Wharf. After a devastating storm destroyed the building in the mid-1920s, members rebuilt their clubhouse, in 1929, on the city-owned wharf. Financial difficulties and internal strife, however, plagued the club for the next several years; and in 1938 the city finally invited the club to leave the wharf. From then until the early 1950s the club met in members' homes or in rented quarters. In 1951 the club remodeled the old Union Oil office building, in the harbor area, which it used until 1966, when the new building was constructed. A sweeping ocean view was most certainly the essential quality to be incorporated into the design, as the building proper sits behind two wrap-around decks.

8.
Sand Castle Motor Lodge
    18 Bath St.
    1945
    1952 additions and remodel; Owen King

One of several intimately scaled Hispanic style guest lodges in West Beach, the Twin Palms, as it was first known, began as a dwelling. By 1952, two guest rooms had been added. In that same year, an extensive addition and some redesigning by Owen King transformed the building into a substantial motel to lodge ever-increasing numbers of tourists. Both the original house and the later addition were built by well-known local contractor Charles Urton.

9.
Ambassador Park/Burton Mound
(site of Potter Hotel)
100-200 block of W. Cabrillo Blvd.
and W. Mason St.
.53 acres; acquired by the city 1924
1902 Potter Hotel; John Austin

CHL

The double row of Phoenix canariensis palm trees which border this small park reputedly framed the promenade that led to the entrance of a luxury resort hotel, which was built in 1902 on top of Santa Barbara's most important archaeological site, Burton Mound.

Early written accounts reveal that this manmade mound was an important Chumash village, Syukhtun (meaning "where the two trails run"), and burial site. At one time, the mound rose 30' above sea level and measured 600' long and 500' wide. An 1883 account describes the mound as "one grand catacomb...covered with immense quantities of sea shells."

In the late 18th and early 19th centuries the site was considered part of the Mission lands. Title went through many hands in the 19th century, including those of fur trader and early-day settler, Lewis T. Burton. Among other things, Burton was elected Santa Barbara's first American mayor in 1850. Although he was neither the first nor the last to own the land, the archaeological site came to bear his name. A large single-floor adobe, measuring 80' X 20' with a veranda on three sides, was located on the mound throughout much of the 19th century. It also came to be known as the Burton Adobe, although it was probably built in the 1830s by Joseph Chapman and enlarged by Thomas Robbins, owners who preceded Burton.

Milo M. Potter disturbed the prehistoric site considerably when he built his hotel in 1902. The Potter was one of several opulent resorts dotting the Pacific coastline in the early 20th century. Los Angeles architect John Austin designed the Islamic-influenced Mission Revival style hotel. Its amenities included a telephone in every one of its several hundred rooms and dinner served on Limoges china of a custom design bearing the hotel's crest, a mission bell. Potter sold the hotel shortly before World War I, and its name was changed to the Belvedere. Again sold in 1919, it was renamed the Ambassador, hence the name of the park and nearby residential area. In 1921, a fire completely destroyed the hotel, ravaging the several-story building in less than two hours.

Although many mourned the loss of the hotel, its passing also provided archaeologists an opportunity to excavate the site in 1923. The surrounding area was subdivided for residential use in 1924. This small park plot was deeded to the people of Santa Barbara for use as a public area. The mound itself remained vacant for another three decades.

The sturdy palms on this portion of the boulevard are California Fan Palms (Washington filifera).

10.
Ambassador by-the-Sea and Pacific Park Motels
202 W. Cabrillo Blvd., 122 W. Cabrillo Blvd.
1951; Owen King

Defining Ambassador Park's western and eastern boundaries are these early 1950s versions of the Spanish Colonial Revival style. As with most examples of this period, they combine post-World War II Modern with some Hispanic elements. King's successful designs both enhance and are enhanced by the park's quiet coziness.

11.
Veterans' Memorial Building
112 W. Cabrillo Blvd.
1927; Soule and Murphy   SoM

In the early 1920s, a group of Santa Barbara architects proposed designs for several buildings along Cabrillo Blvd. in the West Beach area; this, however, is the only one that was ever built. Particularly noteworthy is the pedestrian loggia, a feature the architects envisioned for buildings throughout the business district.

Constructed by well-known local contractors Snook and Kenyon, the building was known first as the Ambassador Ball Room, later as the Vista del Mar Ball Room. Its name was changed to Veterans' Memorial Hall in 1935, but it remained in use as a dance hall for many years after that. During World War II, when the U.S. Army maintained a redistribution center in the oceanfront area, the building was an important recreation spot. It is now owned and maintained by the county, serving as a veterans' services office and meeting place for veterans' organizations.

12.
Villa Rosa

15 Chapala St.
1930-31; George M. Thomas Studio

This complex, originally named Belvedere Apartments, forms an extensive streetscape of Spanish Colonial Revival architecture. Although the building sits close to the street, the fully landscaped surroundings suggest a garden setting, an image that was depicted in many drawings of Santa Barbara architecture during the 1920s and 1930s.

13.
La Ronda Apartments

103-107 Natoma Ave.
1930; E. Keith Lockard

Built at about the same time as the nearby Belvedere Apartments at 15 Chapala St., the landscape architecture of this Hispanic complex also suggests a garden setting. The architect, E. Keith Lockard, was one of Santa Barbara's major practitioners of the Spanish Colonial Revival style in the 1920s. Here is a large specimen of a Cork Oak (Quercus suber).

14.
Gledhill Studios

114 Chapala St.
1907; Augustus B. Higginson

The eclectic design of this building includes elements of Mission Revival and Craftsman styles, both of which were popular in the first decade of this century. Its proximity to the Potter Hotel no doubt influenced its original use: from 1908 to 1916 the lower floor housed various fine arts galleries, and in 1912 the building was called the Potter Art Gallery. The noted muralist and portrait painter, Albert Herter, had his studio here at one time; and from 1926 to the mid-1940s, Carolyn and Edwin Gledhill, well-known local portrait photographers, had their studios here.

15.
Hollander Buildings

118 and 120 Chapala St.
1911; 1912

Without its rooftop sun deck and garden, 118 Chapala St. is a rare Santa Barbara example of stripped classicism design, popular in World War I-era architecture. Constructed by local contractor J.C.F. Miller for Frederick E. Junior, the building was first used as a ladies' fine clothing store, L.P. Hollander and Co., whose clientele no doubt included guests at the Potter Hotel. The building was later converted into a single-family residence and, in the mid-1920s, remodeled into two apartments. Its neighbor at 120 Chapala St., similar in design, was built about a year later, at which time L.P. Hollander and Co. switched locations. The shop remained here until the hotel burned in 1921; after that it was converted into a private residence.

16.
Chase Commercial Building
(Offices)
203 Chapala St.
ca. 1924
1940 remodeling and additions;
  Edwards and Plunkett
1974 office additions; Gilbert Garcia

From 1924 until the early 1930s, this Spanish Colonial Revival commercial building was used as a bakery, garage, and service station. It represents the small-scale commercial development that took place simultaneously with residential building in the 1920s, after the Potter Hotel burned. In 1940, Edwards and Plunkett redesigned the front façade and added the tower for the 7-Up Bottling Company, which used the building as a bottling plant for many years after 1937. Intimate in scale, the building exemplifies the way in which mixed residential and commercial use is enhanced by harmonious architectural design.

17.
Moreton Bay Fig Tree
Chapala St. at Hwy. 101
.38 acres; acquired by the city 1976   L

This majestic Moreton Bay Fig (Ficus macrophylla), perhaps second only to the Mission as a visitor attraction, is rumored to have come from its indigenous Australia by ship. It was planted in about 1874 near State and Montecito Sts. and transplanted, in 1877, to its present location by Alonzo and Charles Crabb. Nearly a century later, in 1970, the city designated it a "tree of notable historic interest"; and in November 1976, the Southern Pacific Transportation Company deeded to the city the small parcel upon which it sits. It was designated a City Landmark in January 1982.

For Railroad Station, 209 State St., see State Street section.

18.
Van Horn House
136 W. Yanonali St.
1924

Although the design of this house is within the Spanish Colonial Revival tradition, the composition is remarkably formal, almost monumental. The original owner was J.A. Van Horn, the proprietor of an auto accessory shop on lower State St. As a small business owner, he was typical of the middle-income residents who gave this neighborhood its distinctive identity for several decades.

The house was constructed by Way and Morgan, builders of a number of Ambassador tract houses.

19.
Letsch Duplex
216-218 W. Yanonali St.
1937

Even this outstanding example of Streamline Moderne includes Hispanic elements, indicating that the Spanish Colonial Revival tradition was thoroughly integrated into Santa Barbara architecture in the 1930s. The designer, whose identity is unknown, successfully designed the duplex to suggest a single-family house. By 1940, shortly after the duplex was built for original owner Beulah Letsch, the West Beach had become a recognizable community of mixed commercial and residential use, locally referred to as the Ambassador District.

The Floss-Silk trees (Chorisia speciosa) in this block are distinguished by the stout thorns on their dark green bark. Pink to maroon flowers bloom in September and are followed by oval fruits which eventually burst into balls of fluffy silk cotton.

20.
Potter Hotel Annex
116-118 Bath St.
1920; possibly John Austin

Built after the hotel proper, this annex reportedly was used the first time for visiting royalty and entourage, and later for visiting high officials and their servants. Wealthy families who brought with them tutors and governesses for their children also stayed in this building. Since it sat some distance from the main building, the annex escaped the disastrous 1921 fire. It and the double row of palm trees that line Ambassador Park are the only remains of this great resort hotel. The building was later converted to apartments.

21.
Motel
232 Natoma Ave.
1929; E.H. Seiferle

This large Spanish Colonial Revival building, known for many years as the Natoma Apartments, was constructed by owner-builder C. Cicero, who also built the La Ronda Apartments at 103-105 Natoma Ave. The cast stone ornamentation, a common feature of the style, was used rather sparsely in Santa Barbara during the 1920s. Pointed arched doorways, reflective of Moorish architecture, are also rare in Santa Barbara. Construction of this apartment building, in the late 1920s, signaled the beginning of attractively designed, high density residential buildings in the area.

22.
Hunstable Houses
212 and 216 Natoma Ave.
1936 (212), 1939 (216); E.E. Hunstable

The Spanish Colonial Revival tradition continued with great vigor into the 1930s, although there was a tendency for the Hispanic imagery to become increasingly abstract, as is evident in these similarly designed duplexes. Here the emerging Modern and Moderne styles are integrated into the older tradition. Extant design sketches indicate that the owner-builder, Edward E. Hunstable, a salesman by occupation, also designed the buildings.

23.
Ambassador Bungalows
210-220 W. Mason St.
1924-25

After the Potter Hotel burned in 1921, the area returned, for a few short years, to an open field dotted with scattered houses. This bungalow court was among the first single and multiple-family residences that began to appear in the mid-1920s. Here the image of the middle class single-family residence is reduced to the smallest possible size.

24.
La Playa Motel
211 W. Mason St.
1936-37; Alex D'Alfonso

Comfortably nestled on a quieter side street, this lovely Spanish styled motel was designed and built by Alex D'Alfonso. It was first used as an apartment building and later converted to serve vacationers.

25.
Mason Apartments
226-232 W. Mason St.
1946; Howell and Arendt

In contrast to the prevailing Spanish Colonial Revival architecture in the oceanfront area, and especially to the Ambassador Court which sits adjacent to it, this complex presents a near-perfect example of pre-World War II Bay Tradition which continued on through the late 1940s and into the 1950s.

26.
La Casa del Mar Motel
(Harbor View Inn)
22 and 28 W. Cabrillo Blvd.
1947-49; R.H. Pitman
1983-84; Lenvik and Minor
  Cunningham Design Inc.,
  landscape architecture

The original section of this motel, that to the west, was built shortly after the end of the Second World War. Its two-story design, with an arcaded lower floor and a wood balcony above, illustrates the vigor of Santa Barbara's Hispanic tradition, even during a period when the Modern was close to universal in acceptance. The new section, to the east, is a carefully thought-out design which is sensitively related to the original building.

27.
Stearns Wharf

Cabrillo Blvd. at State St.
1872

The same entrepreneurs who hoped, in 1850, to see a harbor off Santa Barbara's shores also endeavored to develop port facilities to accommodate commercial and passenger ships. It was not until two decades later, however, in 1871, that the city authorized John P. Stearns to build a wharf to fulfill that vision. Completed in September 1872, this waterfront addition not only encouraged tourism—thousands disembarked here in the heyday of passenger steamers—but changed the course of the city's development, as real estate values soared and cargo-carrying ships deposited precious lumber to sustain the Victorian era construction boom.

The wharf's utility began to change with the advent of motoring tourists after World War I and the 1921 demise of the Potter Hotel. Commercial usage continued, of course, but when the old Yacht Club building was converted into the Harbor Restaurant in 1941, the wharf itself became a tourist attraction. By the mid-1950s, the wharf housed many of the establishments that some present-day visitors may remember—gift shops, a boat rental, a bait-and-tackle shop, a sport fishing concern, The Galley and Moby Dick coffee shops, and the legendary Harbor Restaurant, which perished in a 1973 fire. The wharf was closed to the public shortly after that and remained so until 1979, when the city began extensive repairs and reconstruction. Barry Architectural Design Group designed the wharf reconstruction master plan as well as the buildings erected in 1980-81 and a 1984 coffee shop addition. James J. Zimmerman designed the new Harbor Restaurant. In style, they are reminiscent of Colonial New England. Edwards-Pitman designed the two 1984 structures on the dog leg: the Nature Conservancy building and the Santa Barbara Museum of Natural History Sea Life Center. Sharpe, Mahan and Associates designed the steel-wall kiosk at the wharf entrance.

28.
Chase Palm Park, East Beach, and E. Cabrillo Blvd.

Stearns Wharf east to the Clark Estate acquired by the city 1891-1931

The genesis of this scenic boulevard and oceanfront promenade dates to 1891, when voters approved a $70,000 bond issue to finance construction of the western section. Architect Peter J. Barber, mayor at that time, is said to have planned the palm tree-lined drive (species Washington robusta) after seeing tree-lined boulevards in Geneva during an 1887 European trip.

Acquisition of the parkway between the boulevard and the ocean began in 1903 when a city ordinance authorized the condemnation of privately owned land. In the decades that followed, public-spirited wealthy citizens gradually purchased much of the condemned beachfront property. The East Boulevard Improvement Association was formed in the early 1920s for this express purpose. Its members, who consisted primarily of local businessmen, planning advocates, and philanthropists, were fearful that "cheap amusements" would be built in the oceanfront by less refined but no less entrepreneurial developers. The association engaged Charles Cheney of Olmsted and Olmsted to draw up plans for an expansive oceanfront park, plans which inspired them to purchase and hold land for that purpose. After voters approved park bond issues in 1925 and 1927, the association sold its parcels to the city at cost plus interest. The last parcel to be acquired was the old lumber yard located at the foot of Stearns Wharf, purchased by the city for $200,000 in 1931 after voters approved an additional bond issue, albeit a hotly contested one because of the Great Depression. In 1926-27, when Cabrillo Blvd. was reconstructed and slightly rerouted, the park strip buffer between Santa Barbara St. and Por la Mar Dr. was planted to screen from view the adjacent railroad and industrial area to the north.

"Chase" was added to Palm Park's name in 1978 to honor Harold S. Chase and his sister, Pearl, who were instrumental in its acquisition. A plaque, located at the foot of Santa Barbara St. and dedicated in November 1982, memorializes the Chases for their leadership in Santa Barbara's community development and conservation efforts.

29.
Southern Pacific Roundhouse Site

Juncture of Punta Gorda St. and E. Cabrillo Blvd.
1926; A Mr. Christie of Southern Pacific, in consultation with the Community Drafting Room; E.C. Nichols, assistant engineer; G.W. Corrigan, division engineer

When an earlier brick roundhouse was severely damaged in the 1925 earthquake, the Plans and Planting Committee of the city's Community Arts Association urged representatives of Southern Pacific to design the new roundhouse in keeping with the Spanish Colonial Revival style. Legend has it that Pearl Chase, a member of the committee, displayed to Southern Pacific representatives a postcard depicting a bullring in Seville, Spain, as a suitable design idea; and, in fact, the rebuilt structure bore a striking resemblance to its legendary origin. From 1926 to 1961 the roundhouse served steam locomotives of the Southern Pacific line. When S.P. converted to diesel equipment, the roundhouse was substantially altered and leased as a warehouse. It was demolished in September, 1982, to make way for Fess Parker's convention center-hotel complex.

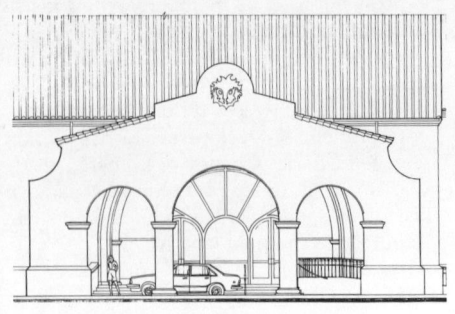

30.
Fess Parker's Hotel

E. Cabrillo Blvd. at Punta Gorda St.
1985-; Edwards-Pitman
   Hoffman Associates, landscape architecture

In the late 1970s and earlier, various proposals were made for the location of a major hotel facing onto East Beach. Out of these proposals evolved the present design, which carries on the Hispanic architectural and landscape tradition of Santa Barbara. The Cabrillo Blvd. side of the group of buildings is dominated by a symbolic re-creation of the circular form of the earlier Southern Pacific Roundhouse. Toward the north and the mountains is the enclosed auto court with an entrance which successfully looks back toward both the turn-of-the-century Mission Revival and to the Spanish Colonial Revival of the 1970s. The separate wings of the building and the principal courtyard with its pool relate the new hotel to that of the 1927 Biltmore Hotel in nearby Montecito.

31.
Cabrillo Ball Park

E. Cabrillo Blvd. between
   Punta Gorda and Milpas Sts.
5 acres; acquired by the city 1925-27

This small park was acquired in five pieces after a 1925 city ordinance designated that the property be used for a public park. The condemned property included part of an area known as Shore Acres, a subdivision containing some substantial bungalows which were moved in 1927. Voter-approved bond funds were used to purchase the property from the East Boulevard Improvement Association, which purchased and held the land for the city in the interim. The park, later improved with a baseball diamond, was used extensively by recuperating servicemen during World War II.

32. Cabrillo Pavilion

1118 E. Cabrillo Blvd.
1926; Roland F. Sauter and
E. Keith Lockard

When the old Plaza del Mar bathhouse was closed in 1925 because of earthquake damage, David and Martha Platt Gray (vice president of Ford Motor Co.) offered the city $100,000 to build a new pavilion and bathhouse at the opposite end of the oceanfront, on the condition that the city would furnish it. The city failed to do so, but the Grays built and furnished it anyway, then gave the building to the city in 1927. The visible fruits of their persistence did not go unnoticed. "It was after the completion of the breakwater and the Gray Pavilion," according to former mayor Patrick Maher, "that people really began to see the possibilities for developing the waterfront and harbor into the recreational area it is today."

During World War II, Army Redistribution Headquarters and medical aid stations were located in the top floor, while the first floor bathhouse remained open to public use. During the mid-1950s, the Mar Monte Hotel leased the facility from the city and used it as a convention center. It is now a cultural arts facility and bathhouse operated by the City Recreation Department.

33. Vista Mar Monte Hotel

(Sheraton Santa Barbara Hotel and Spa)
1121 E. Cabrillo Blvd.
1927-30; Walker and Eisen, Los Angeles
1935 remodeling; Walker and Eisen
1956 swimming pool area; Richard B. Taylor
1977 remodeling and additions; Richard Bliss Nelson
1982-83; Sharpe, Mahan & Associates

Construction on the Vista Mar Monte began shortly after the Cabrillo Pavilion was finished. When it opened in 1931, after three years of building at a cost of $5 million, Santa Barbara had a new resort hotel to replace the Potter and the Arlington. The architecture of the new beachfront hotel conformed to the Spanish Colonial Revival image. The two grand old hotels accommodated patrician lifestyles from 1875 to 1925; the Mar Monte attracted famed Hollywood stars and other celebrities during the 1930s and 1940s. During World War II, the Mar Monte, as well as the nearby Biltmore and Miramar Hotels, was used exclusively for 18 months as part of the Army's Redistribution Center. Here Pacific combat soldiers relaxed before being relocated. Recent additions and alterations now accommodate an ever-increasing number of short-term visitors.

34.
Los Patios

1015-1023 Orilla Del Mar
1930; William Mooser Co. SoM

Los Patios was one of the first multiple residential buildings to appear in East Beach. Original owner Sam E. Kramer engaged the firm of William Mooser Co. to design this many-angled Hispanic building for use as an apartment building. It was converted to a motel in 1952, and later reconverted back to apartments.

The design centerpiece of this two-story garden apartment is the large arched opening leading to the courtyard. This building, plus the Eastern Star Home in Brentwood in West Los Angeles, (1930; 11725 Sunset Blvd.) provide a good indication of this San Francisco-based firm's approach to Hispanic imagery.

35.
Dwight Murphy Field

E. Cabrillo Blvd. between
Por la Mar Dr. and Niños Dr.
10.5 acres; acquired by the city 1925

The city purchased this acreage, as it did much of the oceanfront park land, from the East Boulevard Improvement Association. Always a popular soccer field, the park was first known as the Municipal Soccer Field. Depression-era federal funds were used to improve the field further; and in 1933 it was dedicated and renamed in honor of Dwight Murphy, internationally known Palomino horse breeder, who presided over the city's Park Commission from 1927-1931.

36.
A Child's Estate
1300 E. Cabrillo Blvd.
16 acres; acquired by the city 1953

The name of this popular spot reflects its history as much as its present-day use. Like Burton Mound, this spot originally was the site of a Chumash village which dates back 5,000-7,000 years. The estate is best remembered, however, for Vega Mar, meaning "meadow by the sea." Vega Mar was a rambling Mission Revival mansion featuring a very high central tower, which Easterner John Beale, a retired tea and coffee merchant, built on the knoll in 1897. When Beale died in 1914, his widow, Lillian, married John Howard Child; and the Beale Estate (Vega Mar) became the Child Estate. Mrs. Child gained local notoriety in the 1930s when she allowed transients to construct a hobo village on her property. In 1947, she gave the estate to the Santa Barbara Foundation, which, after her death, turned it over to the city. During the 1950s the mansion was used as a caretaker's residence and later as a fraternity house; it was burned by the city in 1959. In 1961 the Child's Estate Foundation was formed; and after the city leased the property to the foundation, the Junior Chamber of Commerce spearheaded a volunteer effort to develop the estate into a park and zoological gardens and a children's zoo.

37.
Andree Clark Bird Refuge
E. Cabrillo Blvd., east of
A Child's Estate
42.42 acres; acquired by the city 1909

Originally a tidal marsh, or estero, the bird refuge is one of man's more successful efforts to recreate nature within the 18th-century English landscape garden tradition. In the 1870s, Bradley's Race Track ringed the Salt Pond, as it was then known, and horses raced and trained there daily when the track was dry. Bradley's remained a favorite gathering place for racing enthusiasts until 1886, when competitors, collectively known as the Santa Barbara Land and Improvement Co., built the Estero Race Track and Agricultural Park slightly west of here, roughly in the area that lies between Santa Barbara and Salsipuedes ("get out if you can") Sts. In the early-20th century, when citizens turned their attention and efforts toward securing oceanfront land for public use, 60 people donated $100 each in order to purchase the old Salt Pond. They later sold the land to the city. Many of these subscribers envisioned that the city would turn the marsh into a municipal harbor, but that dream never became reality. In 1928, Huguette M. Clark donated $50,000 as a memorial to her deceased sister, Andree, so that the pond could be dredged to create a shallow freshwater lake surrounded by walkways and bridle paths.

38.
Clark Estate
1407 E. Cabrillo Blvd.
1932-36; Reginald D. Johnson;
Don Shugart, structural engineer

Bellosguardo, or "beautiful lookout," is a rambling 22-acre estate obscured from street view (but not from the beach or from A Child's Estate) by a high sandstone wall. It became a summer residence for the family of William A. Clark (U.S. Senator from Montana 1901-07), who purchased the Graham estate (the original house of which is gone) in the early 1920s. In keeping with its intended use, the architectural style of the main house, late 18th-century French, has the feeling of a country estate rather than a townhouse. The Clarks, whose wealth came from mining and railroad interests, were representative of the affluent seasonal visitors who were drawn to Santa Barbara's beauty and climate. They, as did others, brought some of the East with them, in this case the library and dining room from their New York house, which were incorporated into the interior design.

39.
Watering Trough and Fountain
E. Cabrillo Blvd. and Channel Dr.
1911; Francis W. Wilson   L

This beautiful stone drinking fountain for man and beast, of classical Beaux Arts design, was donated to the city by Dr. Charles Caldwell Park, a local physician, in memory of his two deceased sons. The Parks were a prominent Montecito family, and Dr. Park also served as president of Santa Barbara Associated Charities. Several fountains were donated to the city during the early-20th century; this is one of the few that remain, and it has been designated a City Landmark.

40-a.
(Former) State of California Department of Motor Vehicles
>40 Los Patos Way
>1936; Chester Carjola

The thick walls and deeply recessed windows of this wood frame and stucco building create a feeling of the Hispanic adobe tradition. Built in 1936 for the California Highway Patrol, the building was originally located at 928 Rancheria St. (later renamed Hollister Ave.). It was used by the Department of Motor Vehicles until 1961. In the same year it was moved to its present site, and for many years after that it was used as a restaurant.

40-b.
Patio de las Aves
>1801 East Cabrillo Blvd.
>1984; James J. Zimmerman Cunningham Design, Inc., landscape architecture

A one- and two-story complex of stores and restaurants which carefully reflect the Monterey aspect of Santa Barbara's architectural tradition, these buildings are arranged around a central court. The new structures replace an earlier Spanish Colonial Revival Standard Oil service station designed in the mid-1920s by Edwards, Plunkett & Howell.

41.
Johnson House
>50 Los Patos Way
>ca. 1872

This story-and-a-half French Second Empire building is the larger section of a dwelling originally located at 812 De la Vina St. The other, smaller section is now situated at 810 De la Vina St. where it is used as an antique shop. The original owner, W.H. Johnson, a sea captain, built the house out of redwood lumber presumably unloaded at the newly completed Stearns Wharf. The mansard roof is covered with slate. When the house was condemned to make room for a parking lot in 1962, the owner moved this portion to its present location, restored and added to it, and converted the house for commercial use.

In 1887 part of the east side of the 800 block of State Street looked like this.

Here is how it looked in 1926.

STATE STREET PLAZA

One of Santa Barbara's most striking and unusual features is the way the city's streets are laid out on the basis of a roughly northeast-southwest diagonal rather than the rigid north-south system incorporated into national land policy by Thomas Jefferson in the 1780s and prevalent virtually everywhere in the United States west of the Appalachians. This quirk is a result of local geography and of the area's original settlers, the Chumash, who followed the constraints of the land. In Santa Barbara's case it is two fault zones that have determined the geography—the Mesa zone to the west and the Mission zone to the north and east. The area between these two, the present City of Santa Barbara, was filled in by erosion, creating an alluvial basin. The main Chumash trail basically bisected this basin, running from the village of Syukhtun at the mouth of Mission Creek past a smaller village near the Presidio area northwest to the village at Mission Canyon. Thus geography, and the use of the land that it imposes, early determined the general location of what would later become Santa Barbara's main thoroughfare.

When the Spanish settlers arrived in 1782, they were almost as dependent on the land and its resources as were the Chumash. The land determined the location of the Presidio, the Mission and, of course, the harbor. Linking these three was the old Chumash trail. With minor variations it became the main path for the Spanish and subsequent Mexican settlement. Along its length, adobe dwellings were constructed, including Casa de la Guerra (entry #64) near the center of the alluvial basin, the Orella adobe (entry #78) on the northern fringe of the pueblo and, in the 1830s, the two-story Monterey-style adobe of Alpheus Thompson (entry #65). This last represented the brief fusion of Hispanic culture (as represented by the masonry adobe tradition) with the rising Anglo-American culture (here exemplified by the use of wood and a central plan) not only along State Street but more generally in Santa Barbara and California as well.

With the United States' victory over Mexico in 1848 came the victory also of Anglo-American ideas over Hispanic traditions. The most readily apparent of these new ideas, at least in city planning, was the imposition of a right-angled grid system upon the land, buildings, and ownership patterns. Rigid Yankee logic usually imposed this grid system regardless of local conditions; in Santa

Barbara, however, the grid was adjusted to the contours of the land and harbor and basically oriented on the axis of the former trail from the oceanfront to the Mission. This was the first step in eliminating the previous picturesque irregularity and replacing it with a system more efficient for transportation, property ownership and development.

The grid, however, existed only on plat maps until State Street was built and aligned in the 1860s and 1870s. In 1875 a streetcar line was constructed linking the oceanfront with the Arlington Hotel and bisecting the growing commercial district on lower State Street. North and south, two-and three-story false-front wooden buildings were erected (see Pierce Block entry #54 and the Orella Building entry #59), covered sidewalks were constructed, and the street paved. As commerce increased, larger buildings were put up by the now dominant Yankee entrepreneurs. These include, from south to north, the Fithian Building (entry #56), the Upper Clock Building (entry #73), W.W. Hollister's Santa Barbara College (entry #84), and the Lower Hawley Building (entry #86). Although these buildings were designed in a variety of imported eastern architectural styles—the French Second Empire being only the most popular—they all shared the Anglo-American concern for general symmetry, right-angledness, and basic modular construction; that is, they reflected vertically what the street grid represented horizontally. Because of this, by the early twentieth century State Street, in its rigid commercial logic, resembled any American small town Main Street.

Although there were earlier attempts to Hispanicize State Street, it was not until 1925 and the earthquake that the opportunity arose to remake Santa Barbara's main thoroughfare. The destruction was so extensive that plans were drawn up to reconstruct virtually the entire street in a consistent Hispanic or Spanish Colonial Revival style. Even the name of the street was briefly changed from State to Estado, although this, unlike the Hispanic architectural mode, never caught on. Of course, the logic of the grid continued to dominate the town and especially State Street, but attempts were made to break from it even if only minimally. Instead of a uniform façade line abutting the sidewalk, it was recommended that some buildings be set back to create patios (Copper Coffee Pot, entry #78) and that others have projecting pedestrian arcades (Pier One, entry #71).

The Depression and World War II severely restricted new construction and, after the war, architectural fashion and the Santa

Barbara economy dramatically changed. Architects employed elements of the Spanish Colonial Revival idiom (Restaurants, entry #96), but in most cases new buildings and alterations to existing buildings were in the International Style of architecture. The other factor that influenced State Street in the 1950s and 1960s was the enormous expansion in automobile traffic. This had a particularly large impact on the 400-700 blocks of the street. There, car-related businesses proliferated, some which had been established as early as the 1910s. They brought with them a decline in more people-oriented businesses and an increase in visual and even social chaos. By the late 1960s State Street faced the same potential for urban decay prevalent throughout the country.

In an attempt to combat this, the city in 1969 transformed six blocks of State Street into a beautifully landscaped Hispanic drive-through plaza. Robert Ingle Hoyt was architect and John Robert Russell was landscape architect. In 1982 the plaza was extended another block south. Richard B. Taylor was the architect and landscape architect. Contemporaneously, architects, through the encouragement of the Landmarks Committee, again began to rediscover the city's Hispanic tradition. Many commercial buildings are either being restored to their earlier architectural style (St. Vincent's School, entry #209) or remodeled along Spanish Colonial Revival lines (Hitchcock Building, entry #86) and new construction on State Street, as elsewhere in downtown Santa Barbara, is generally being carried out within the city's Hispanic tradition.

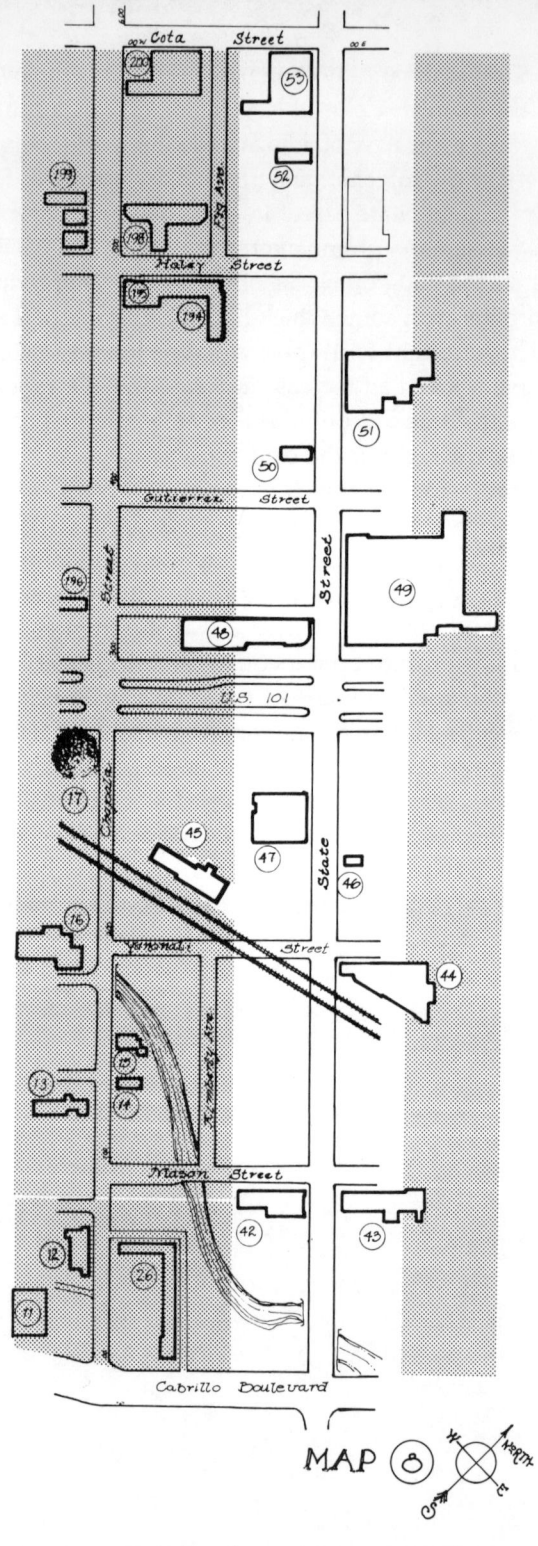

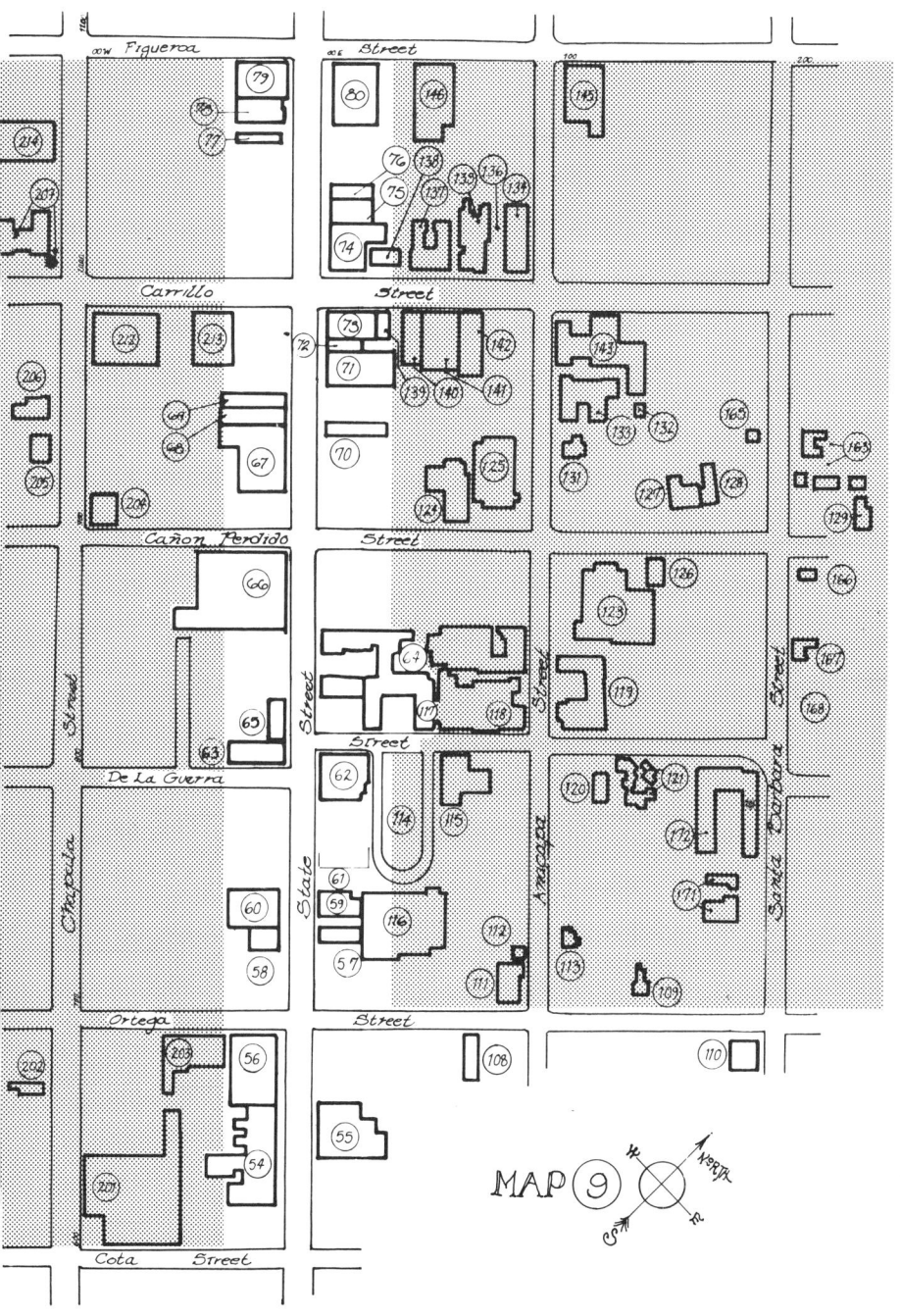

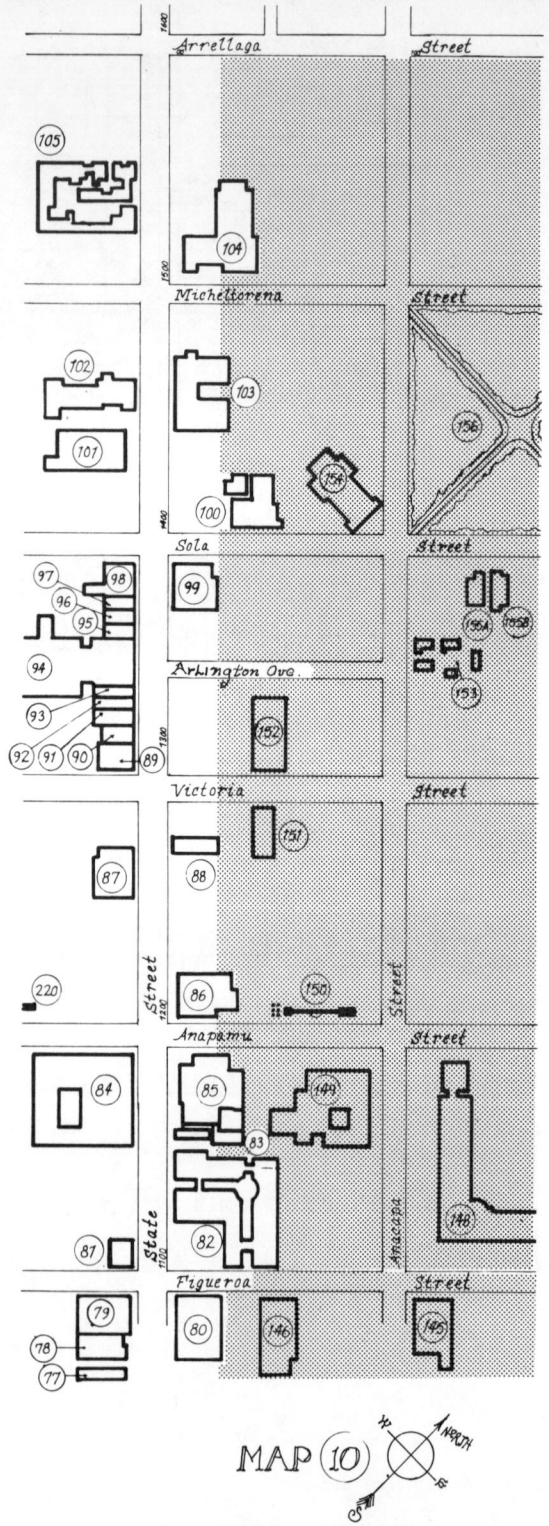

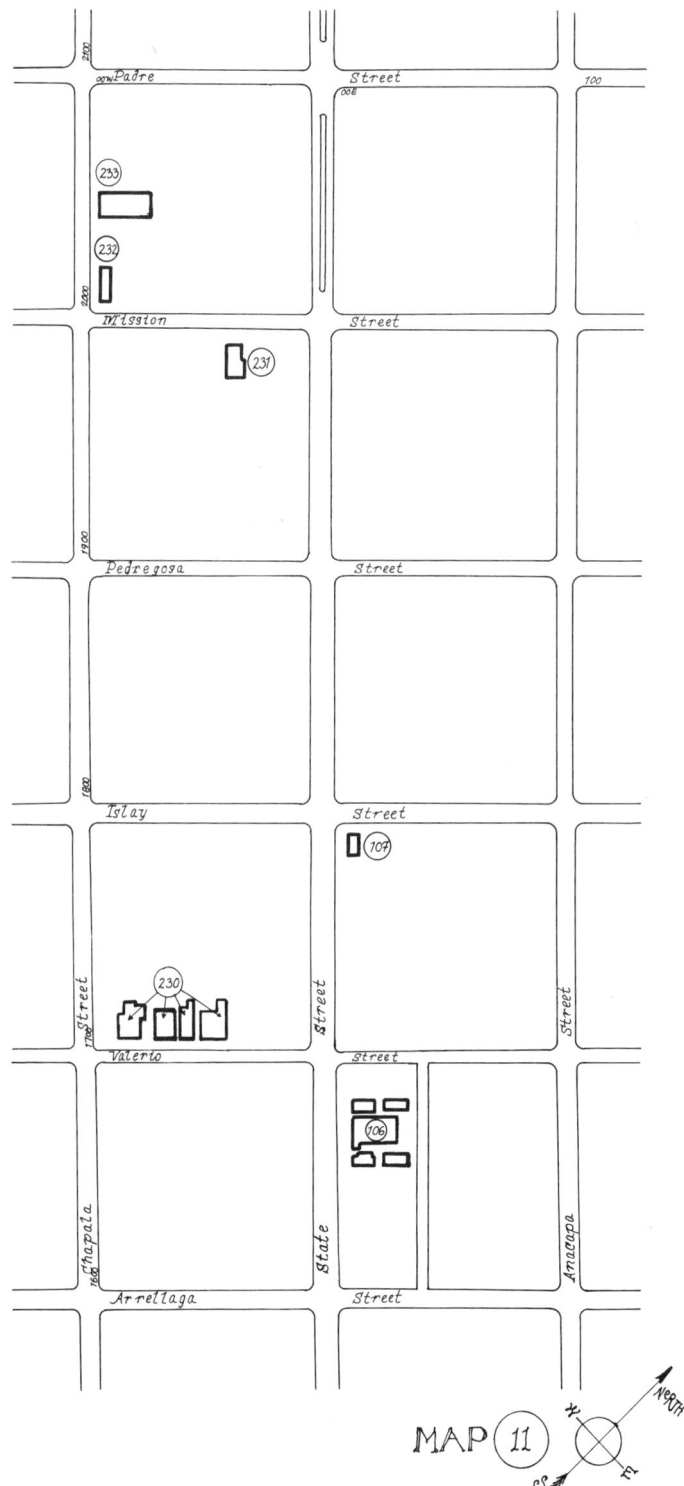

42.
Hotel Californian
35 State St.
1925; F.S. Ward
1926; Architectural Advisory Committee

This building was originally completed only four days before the infamous earthquake of June 1925. The hotel owners were forced to curtail operations when the outside walls crumbled, exposing a honeycomb of rooms. It reopened several months later after $50,000 worth of repairs were made. The façade, a handsome example of 1920s Spanish Colonial Revival architecture, is particularly noteworthy for its arcade, a feature echoed by the arcades of the Santa Barbara Datsun building at 36 State St. and the Channel Islands Surfboards building at 136 State St.

Across the street and to the north of the hotel once stood the building where Allen and Malcolm Loughead first built the F-1, a ten-passenger airplane. The Lougheads operated their Santa Barbara factory at 101 State St. from 1916 to 1921, after which time the operation was moved to Burbank and renamed Lockheed Aviation Company. The building was irreparably damaged by fire in 1979.

43.
Hitchcock Motor Company

(Santa Barbara Datsun)
36 State St.
1922
1925 alterations; supervised by
Community Drafting Room

A two-story garage built on this site in 1922 was one of the many buildings damaged in the 1925 earthquake. The structure was rebuilt according to the suggestions of the Architectural Advisory Committee, as the arcaded façade indicates, with the Community Drafting Room of the Community Arts Association, Plans and Planting Committee, supervising the design and execution. Hitchcock Motors, one of Santa Barbara's first and most prominent automobile (Packard) dealers, located here from 1922 to 1940.

44.
Crane Company

(Channel Islands Surfboards)
136 State St.
1926; Soule, Murphy & Hastings

Soule, Murphy & Hastings designed this Hispanic building in keeping with the 1920s plans for arcaded shops in the commercial district. The building originally was used as a display room and warehouse for plumbing fixtures and supplies. In 1944, the city council granted the U.S. Coast Guard's petition to use the building as a "pistol range."

45.
Southern Pacific Railroad Depot
(Amtrak Station)
209 State St.
1905; Francis W. Wilson   L

After Southern Pacific completed the Coast Line in 1901, making it possible for passengers to travel uninterrupted from Los Angeles to San Francisco, rail excursions became quite popular. The increased rail traffic, however, necessitated larger facilities in Santa Barbara; and when Southern Pacific realigned its local tracks in 1905, the company also built a new passenger depot, the fourth depot to be built in the city since 1887, when the railroad first arrived. Francis W. Wilson, a local architect active here from the 1890s to the early years of this century, was engaged to design the new building. The Mission Revival style was selected so that the depot would "conform in general style to the Mission Architecture so appropriate and so popular in Southern California." The station was sited to allow passengers and their escorts easy arrival and departure by way of State or Chapala Sts. For over five decades an attractive lawn area, known as Depot Park, lined the access driveway between the depot and State St.

In 1980 the depot was declared a City Landmark. It is one of but a few remaining Mission Revival buildings in Santa Barbara. It is also one of only a small collection of Mission Revival railroad stations remaining in California.

46.
Larco Fish Market
(Andria's Seafood Restaurant)
214 State St.
1911; William Poole

This tiny sandstone building was constructed by stonemason Peter Poole as a market for one of Santa Barbara's most prominent early-day fish dealers. Andrea Larco migrated here from San Francisco in 1876. A decade later he and his son, Sebastian, were leaders among the prospering fishermen who regularly shipped lobster to San Francisco in addition to supplying the local market with the catch of the day. Larco moved to this location in about 1905 from his previous location at 122 State St. Between 1918 and 1931, several processing and storage facilities were added. The market operated in the stone building from the time it was built, in 1911, to 1943 when the site was sold to Farallone Fisheries. In 1982 it was reopened as a fresh fish market. The restaurant opened in 1983.

47.
Hotel Neal
217 State St.
1905-06; J.W. Bagley
1925; Sauter and Lockard
1979; Contract Design Limited

No sooner had the new Southern Pacific depot been finished than developer and hotel man Neal Callahan built this Mission Revival hotel to serve the increasing number of rail passengers and visitors. The restaurant located on the ground floor rear, was, in fact, first called the Southern Pacific Eating House. Substantial repairs were made to the building following the earthquake. By Santa Barbara standards the Neal was a modest hotel; as late as 1935 the single room rate was $1.00 per night, while the much newer and larger Hotel Californian at 35 State St. charged $2.00 and the luxurious Mar Monte at 1121 E. Cabrillo Blvd. charged $3.50-$6.50 per room. In 1980 the hotel was remodeled into a restaurant. Its neighbor at 225 State St., originally a commercial laundry building (1909), was transformed into a restaurant in 1977.

48.
V.E. Wood Auto Building
(Gregg Motors Ltd.)
315 State St.
1922
1946; Harold John Vaile

This automobile showroom combines Spanish Colonial Revival elements, such as the first-story piers, the deeply recessed second-story windows, and a low pitched red tile roof, with a curving Art Deco corner—thus combining two of the popular architectural styles of the 1920s.

Vincent E. Wood became the area's Buick dealer in 1912, continuing until 1955. This building was constructed for the business by J.Y. Parker, a brickyard proprietor who owned several lots in this vicinity, and for whom Parker Way is named.

49.
Auto Show Rooms and Seaside Oil Company Building
(Work Inc. and shops)
318-330 State St.
1911; 1913; J. Corbley Pool
1917; Russel Ray, attributed
1926 alterations; Lionel Pries
1937 addition; Carleton M. Winslow and R.H. Pitman   SoM

Henry Bothin of Montecito and San Francisco had this group of buildings constructed for the El Camino Motor Car Company. The original 1911-17 nondescript auto show room buildings were severely damaged in the 1925 earthquake, and it was Lionel Pries who provided the romantic brick and stucco Moorish arcaded street front. Seaside Oil Company, a local corporation, established its headquarters at 330 State St. in 1937 and remained for 35 years. Winslow and Pitman added the three-arched loggia and its tower to the north in 1937. Though small in size this two-layered tower with its thin lantern is one of the really handsome tower designs in the city. A mildly streamlined Modern service station adjoined the tower to the north until the early 1970s. Wings for the Douglas Dauntless dive-bombers were manufactured at 322 State St. during World War II. The Bothin Helping Fund made the northwesterly section of the main building available to Work Inc., a non-profit training program for handicapped persons, in 1974.

Across the street, the Chinese Parasol tree (Sterculia platanifolia), also known as the Franceschi Flame Tree, marks the site of the Southern California Acclimatizing Association nursery established here in 1893.

50.
Faith Mission
(Savoy Hotel)
409 State St.
1888-89; Peter J. Barber, attributed   L, NR

When this building opened as the Faith Mission, its function was described as "reclaiming young men from their erring ways and pointing out to them the right path to follow to enable them to become good Christians and worthy members of society." By 1931, the structure had been converted into a hotel, and during World War II it was used by servicemen. Architecturally, the hotel is a significant example of the Italianate/Eastlake styles of architecture. The broadly projecting and heavily detailed cornices at the roof line and over the door and window openings gave the façade a three dimensional, almost sculptural appearance. They are formed of galvanized metal wired to the brick wall.

The 400 block of State St. has a history of automobile-related uses, such as the old Wood's Garage at 400 State, built 1910 and 1916, and the garages built for Henry Bothin's real estate company in 1915 through 1921 on the same side of the street. Across State St. at 415-419 State are two structures built by the 1890s for the Pierce Bros. furniture store. The combined two-story buildings remained in furniture use until 1977.

In the 500 block of State St. there are a number of small Hispanic-style structures which were remodeled or built new after the June 29, 1925, earthquake. Pleasant groupings are created, especially from the hotel at 524 State St. (1901) to the corner of Cota St. The Salvation Army building at 500 State St. was built after the earthquake as the Medico-Dental Arts Building. The building at 511 State St. has cast metal columns on the façade.

51.
Shops and Office

428-434 State St.
1884
1925; William A. Edwards   SoM

The de la Guerra family owned this property for approximately one hundred years, as the city's earliest maps show it in Francisco de la Guerra's name, and later records indicate that his grandnieces owned it until the 1940s. By 1884 a two-story brick commercial building had been constructed, housing shops on the first floor and a hotel on the second. The 1925 earthquake severely damaged the second story, so the Hotel Grand portion was removed, and William A. Edwards remodeled the front of the ground floor into a balanced four-bay structure with Moorish arches in the center section.

52.
Diedrich Auto Parts

515 State St.
1926-27; William Poole

On or near this site was the Santa Barbara *Herald Weekly* building in the 1880s. Its competitor, the *Morning Press*, was located next door. Later used as a meat market, the building was heavily damaged in the 1925 earthquake. A new structure, the present building, was constructed in the Spanish Colonial Revival style in 1926-27. Architecturally, the alternation between the three large arched window openings and the smaller infill arches is of interest.

53.
Neal Callahan Building
  527-535 State St.
  1926-27; Roland F. Sauter and
  E. Keith Lockard

The site of this large building has been occupied by hotels since 1856. That year, the two-story American House opened for business. In 1870, the hotel was burned and was rebuilt in 1872, and renamed the Occidental Hotel. This part of State St. was the hub of the Anglo-American commercial district at that time. At one time, the Occidental was the largest hotel in the city and boasted a telegraph office, barber salon, billiard hall, saloon, and two fine privies to the rear. For many years it was the Mascarel Hotel. Then, as the Hotel Barbara, it was demolished in the wake of the 1925 earthquake. The present structure was constructed in 1926-27 by Neal Callahan, a pioneer hotel man who had come to Santa Barbara in 1894. To avoid a repeat of the 1925 disaster, the hotel was built to be earthquake-proof with 13-inch reinforced concrete walls. The architectural style employed by Sauter and Lockard was, of course, the Spanish Colonial Revival. The plateresque detailing about the entrance is particularly impressive.

54.
Pierce Block
  607-621 State St.
  ca. 1874, 1886
  1925; Fitzhugh and Teal

Charles Pierce built the city's first lumberyard on the site of this building in about 1871. His office and residence were at 611 State St. adjacent to the Post Office building at 609 State, which he also owned. These buildings were expanded over the next several decades until they stretched from 607 to 621 State St. Architecturally, they were in the then-fashionable false-front commercial style. After the 1925 earthquake, the stores were joined and remodeled in the Spanish Colonial Revival style. The long façade arcade seen here was typical of much of the Hispanic architecture of the period.

Next door at 605 State St. is a ca. 1885 building with metal columns; it formerly had two stories.

55.
Mission Theatre
618 State St.
1911

This mildly Mission Revival theater building originally had two tiny mission towers on top of the façade. It had the distinction of featuring performers from the Keith-Orpheum Circuit as well as popular motion pictures. A 1913 guidebook stated: "As a rule the best pictures, clean and wholesome pictures, are to be found at the MISSION THEATRE." The marquee of the Warner Bros.-operated theater was remodeled in 1937. Other alterations took place in 1929 (J.L. Curletti) and 1963. By 1948 Spanish-language films were being shown, in addition to English-language, and a few years later the theater was showing only films made in Mexico. In 1983 Metropolitan Theatres began showing second run general release films. The Mission is the city's oldest existing movie house.

56.
Fithian Building
629 State St.
1895-96; Thomas Nixon
1925; Sauter and Lockard   SoM

When originally constructed by Civil War hero Major Joel Adams Fithian in 1895-96, this building was a three-and-a-half-story French Second Empire structure with a high clock tower. It was located at one of the city's busiest intersections and contained stores on the first floor, offices on the second, and a meeting hall on the third. Often called the "Lower Clock" building to distinguish it from Mortimer Cook's building farther up State St, it incorporated Benigno Gutierrez's brick drug store which was, until it went out of business in 1979, Southern California's oldest drug store. The Fithian Building suffered considerable damage in the 1925 earthquake, and the third story and clock tower were removed. The present Spanish Renaissance style appearance of this important building dates from Sauter and Lockard's remodeling of 1925 for its owner Dr. C.C. Park.

57.
Tomlinson Building
   714 State St.
   1925; Sauter and Lockard

This commercial building was constructed by George Tomlinson in 1925. It is representative of the small commercial buildings which transformed State St. through the use of the Spanish Colonial Revival following the 1925 earthquake. The dominating design element, as with 26 E. Ortega nearby, is the large arched window opening.

58.
Alexander Building
   (White House of Santa Barbara)
   717 State St.
   1896
   1925; Architectural Advisory Committee
   1934; Edwards and Plunkett

This is another example of a late 19th-century building which now reads as a Hispanic design. It was damaged in the 1925 earthquake, and was repaired with some changes which brought it closer to the Spanish tradition. The present arcaded design of the building is the result of the 1934 remodeling. Some additional changes were made to the front entrance and the adjoining storefront windows in 1976. There is an attractive painted design under the roof eaves. Eisenberg's clothing store, founded in 1898, and later called the White House, moved to this location in 1934.

59.
Orella Building

(Pure Gold Vintage Clothing)
718 State St.
ca. 1875
1925; Soule, Murphy & Hastings

Beneath the Spanish Colonial Revival exterior of this building is one of State St.'s oldest structures. Built in the 1870s, it was transformed to its present appearance following the 1925 earthquake. The arched first story and the shed tiled roof are typical of the architecture of the period.

60.
Parma Building

721-723 State St.
ca. 1880
1920

Before the Parma brothers remodeled this building in 1920, it had been occupied by the Portola Theatre and a confectionery store. The remodeling was for a grocery store, thus the Parma brothers continued the business G.B. Parma had begun with his fruit and variety store established in 1872. Originally, the prominent architectural feature consisted of an arcade "running lengthwise through the building with stores on each side and in the center," as one contemporary chronicler noted. The façade and the rear portion have since been altered. The soffit under the front eave has a painted design similar to the Alexander Building next door.

61. Storke Plaza
722-724 State St.
1973

From at least the 1870s until 1925, this property was commercially developed. Some years after the earthquake of 1925, Thomas M. Storke, founder and editor of the *Santa Barbara News-Press*, purchased the lot to allow access to the *News-Press* building from State St. It was offered to the city in 1972, the year after Storke's death. An adjacent three-foot section of the land had served as a public alley since 1868. It was popularly known as "Caesar's Alley" in honor of Caesar Lataillade, a councilman who once boasted he could deliver every Spanish-speaking voter in Santa Barbara to the candidate of his choice. In honor of the city's bicentennial in April, 1982, the government of Spain presented Santa Barbara with a statue of King Carlos III, who had directed that the Presidio be established two hundred years before. This statue, another casting of which is in Burgos, Spain, is located at the State St. end of the small city-owned plaza.

62. McKay Building
Bothin Building
(La Placita Building)
746 State St.
1903-04; Francis W. Wilson
1925-26; Lionel Pries

Although originally constructed in 1903-1904 by the Santa Barbara Improvement Company, the building did not achieve its present appearance until after the 1925 earthquake. Less than a month after that disaster, the Bothin Helping Fund of San Francisco announced that it would spend $300,000 to rebuild 12 large buildings, all of which would conform to the Spanish Colonial Revival style of architecture adopted by the city. This Bothin Building was considered one of the most important reconstructions "as its completion will remove the last vestige of 'Main Street' architecture from City Hall Plaza." It is on the site of the two-story Leyva (Leiba) Adobe which predated 1851 and was demolished in 1903. This adobe home and store building protruded into the original line of E. De la Guerra St. and is a reason why the present street is offset for two blocks.

63.
Las Tiendas Building
801 State St. and
4 W. De la Guerra St.
1925; A.C. Sanders

This Spanish style building was constructed in early 1925 on the site of the old Central Bank building. It is another of Santa Barbara's pre-earthquake Hispanic structures. Although the State St. side has been remodeled, the De la Guerra façade still shows the original arched first story and open-balconied second story, with some openings altered.

64-a.
El Paseo
808-818 State St.
(Entrances also on De la Guerra, Anacapa and Cañon Perdido Sts.)
1922-24; James Osborne Craig, Mary Craig
1928-29; Carleton M. Winslow   NR, L

El Paseo was the first major step in converting Santa Barbara's architecture from Anglo Main Street to Hispanic Pueblo. The personages responsible for much of the transformation were Bernhard and Irene Hoffmann, a wealthy eastern couple who were to become two of Santa Barbara's most influential citizens in the 1920s. They worked with the architect James Osborne Craig and, after Craig's death, with his wife, Mary Craig. The result was this charming complex with its famed Street in Spain, central fountained courtyard, an open-air patio, restaurant and quaint passageways, all of which partially encompass the historic De la Guerra Adobe. The enthusiasm for Hispanic architecture was reflected in one reporter's praise: "What a place the Paseo De la Guerra is to be! It fairly exudes the spirit and charm of an old-world plaza." Ever since, it has been a delight for both visitors and residents alike. The arcaded Anacapa St. façade with its own small courtyard was added in 1928-29 by Carleton M. Winslow. In the mid-1960s Lutah Maria Riggs remodeled the State St. entrance into El Paseo. Architects for the 1984 restaurant remodeling were Leifer-Marter. Its interior design was by Douglas Bartoli. Since 1971, the complex has been owned by the Santa Barbara Trust for Historic Preservation. Note also the carefully chosen planting with its many fruit-bearing trees.

64-b.
Casa de la Guerra
11-19 E. De la Guerra St.
1819-1827   NR, CHL, L

After the Mission and the Presidio, the De la Guerra Adobe is the most important surviving remnant of Santa Barbara's Spanish-Mexican heritage. The U-shaped adobe is not only significant because of its builder, José de la Guerra, but also for the prominent role it has played in the community's social life. The de la Guerras formed the most prominent family in Spanish and Mexican Santa Barbara, and José de la Guerra was its patriarch. He was, as well, the fifth comandante of the nearby Presidio. Festivities associated with the adobe begin with Richard Henry Dana's description of a wedding there in his *Two Years Before the Mast*, through the Festival Arts activities of the 1920s, to today's Old Spanish Days Fiesta. It was in the 1920s that the old adobe was incorporated into El Paseo complex. Now owned by the Santa Barbara Trust for Historic Preservation, this grand adobe's preservation is assured.

65.
Thompson Adobe Site
(Piccadilly Square)
813 State St.
1834-36

At 805-807 State St., now a part of the Piccadilly Square shopping complex, the Yankee trader Alpheus Thompson built in 1834 an impressive two-story adobe house for his bride, Francisca Carrillo. The building with its two-story porch was the first example in California of what would come to be known as the Monterey Style, exemplified to the north in Monterey by Thomas Oliver Larkin's 1835 adobe. From December 7, 1846, to January 3, 1847, Lieutenant Colonel John Fremont and his battalion stayed at the Thompson house. It is generally believed that it was on this site that the first American flag was raised in Santa Barbara. The old adobe was later used as the San Carlos Hotel. This landmark of early Anglo-American California history was, regrettably, torn down in 1913.

66.
Howard-Canfield Building
829-833 State St.
1903; John Parkinson

This building was originally constructed in a mildly Beaux Arts classical mode with projecting cornice, balustrade and pedimented entrance. All of this was stripped off in 1950 in an attempt to modernize it. From its construction, the building has housed several distinguished Santa Barbara stores. Diehl's Grocery Store, the city's most luxurious dry goods establishment, had the corner location until the 1930s. Trenwith's clothing store, one of Santa Barbara's oldest business establishments, was located here from 1904 until it went out of business in 1981.

67.
Bothin Building
903-911 State St.
1902; W.H. Aiken & J.V. Elliott
1925; Lionel Pries

The original Bothin Building, constructed in 1902 for W.H. Aiken, was a three-story brick building in a vaguely classical style. It was heavily damaged in the 1925 earthquake and reconstructed as an important two-story structure. This, as with 746 State St., was funded by the Bothin Helping Fund, which owned the building. The distinctive first story series of arches and the recessed second story balcony do much to set the tone for this part of State St. This is one of the really distinguished examples of the Spanish Colonial Revival in Santa Barbara.

68.
Levy Shoes
   913 State St.
   ca. 1885
   1919; J. Corbley Pool

This is one of the few buildings on State St. not in the Spanish Colonial Revival style. It is a quaint doll house-like structure with a partial mansard roof and pitched dormers. Since 1920, it has been the location of Levy Shoes and Hosiery. Prior to that, it housed a meat market and a Chinese restaurant. Michel Levy altered the building to its present style in late 1919.

69.
Osborne's Book Store
   921-925 State St.
   1914; J. Corbley Pool
   1925; H.L. Wass

This property has been the location of Osborne's Book Store since the turn of the century. The present building, however, was constructed for the widow and stepdaughter of Robert Louis Stevenson in 1914. The arcaded façade with central bullseye motif dates from 1925 when the building was remodeled after the earthquake.

70.
State Street Dry Goods Store
    (Nardo Building)
    922 State St.
    1887
    1925; Stanley Edwards, Architectural
        Advisory Committee

Although the first story of this building has been altered, the second story is relatively intact with a projecting wooden balcony in the Monterey Revival style of architecture. This is one of the buildings in which the short-lived Architectural Advisory Committee, a predecessor of today's Landmarks Committee, influenced the remodel design. Early in its existence the building housed a grocery store.

71.
Rogers Furniture Building
    (Pier One)
    928 State St.
    ca. 1885; 1890
    1925; Soule, Murphy & Hastings

When the 1925 earthquake struck Santa Barbara, destroying and damaging many buildings on State St., architects and planners reiterated an earlier proposal that, in the rebuilding, the "east side of State Street should be arcaded to protect the pedestrian and the glass display windows from the late afternoon sun." This building, built as two separate structures and remodeled, is significant in that it was one of the few to apply the concept. The others that did not were castigated in the literature of the period as having the "zealous conviction that business, to be effective, must be disagreeable."

    The Rogers Furniture company occupied this location from 1904 to 1968. It was founded by E.F. Rogers, member of a merchandising family residing here since 1874.

72.
Blyth, Eastman, Dillon & Co.
930 State St.
1927; Edwards, Plunkett & Howell

This simply designed building gains its distinction through the continuation of the recessed arcade motif of its neighbor to the south. The sound proportions, minimal decoration and Doric-columned arcade make this a classic example of Santa Barbara's "High Renaissance" phase of the Spanish Colonial Revival of the 1920s. It was built by Salisbury Field and Co. for Logan and Bryan, bond brokers.

73.
First Federal Savings Building
(Home Federal Savings)
936 State St.
1963; Melvin A. Rojko and
  Glenn Marchbanks, Jr.

This building is on the site of Mortimer Cook's three-story French Second Empire "Upper Clock Building" constructed in the 1870s. It was for many years the major landmark of this part of State St. and initiated the northward drift of the commercial center of Santa Barbara toward Carrillo St. Architecturally, the present building is of interest in that it represents the continuity of the Spanish Colonial Revival in Santa Barbara when it had all but disappeared in the late 1950s and early 1960s.

74.
County National Bank
(Bank of Montecito)
1000 State St.
1919-21; Myron Hunt

This basilica-like bank building occupies a prominent site in downtown Santa Barbara. Prior to the present structure, one of the earliest gas stations in the city was on this site. Originally the County Bank building, it was praised at the time of its construction as a design "unique and singularly beautiful in material, lines and coloring." Particularly noteworthy are the two Corinthian columns flanking the central arched entrance which are repeated in the interior.

75.
Santa Barbara Mutual Building
1008-1010 State St.
1924; Soule, Murphy & Hastings

This Hispanic Renaissance building has remained unaltered since it was built in the 1920s. The central portion with second story paired and balconied French doors and its large square first story opening are mirrored in the Chase building adjacent.

76.
Chase Building
1012 State St.
1917
1926; Soule, Murphy & Hastings

The Chase Building, although small in size and architecturally similar to its neighbor to the south, is rich historically in its association with the Chase family, important benefactors to Santa Barbara and its Spanish heritage. Hezekiah G. Chase founded the family real estate business elsewhere on State St., moving to this address in 1917. He, his son Harold Stuart Chase, and daughter Pearl Chase, were prime movers in the Spanish renaissance of the 1920s. The family name can still be seen above the entrance. This structure is the surviving portion of the Santa Barbara Abstract Co. building developed by E. Salisbury Field at 1012-1016 State St.

77.
Russ' Camera
1025 State St.
1916; William Poole
1983; Lisa Bregante

This one-story brick structure was built for Josefa Erro, a member of the Orella family, for many years owners of a large portion of this block. It began as a grocery store, then became the Goldfish Cafe in the 1920s. Later it was a dry goods store and an Oriental arts shop. In 1983 the building was sensitively remodeled in accordance with El Pueblo Viejo district guidelines.

78.
Orella Adobe
(Copper Coffee Pot)
1029 State St.
ca. 1859
1927; Edwards, Plunkett & Howell

The Copper Coffee Pot with its charming outdoor patio is of both architectural and historic interest. Encased in the south wall of the present building is a remnant of the original 19th century adobe. This adobe dwelling was probably constructed by Augustin Janssens, owner of La Purificación Rancho in the Santa Ynez Valley. The Orella family incorporated a portion of the adobe in the 1927 structure, as well as using some of the original red tiles for the roof. The restaurant is something of a Santa Barbara institution and gathering place, a function that dates back to its construction, as can be seen in the charming Fiesta photographs in the entrance.

79.
Santa Barbara Savings
1035 State St.
1930; Edwards & Plunkett

This building with its basilica plan and large arched entrance is similar to the Bank of Montecito a block to the south. Although its exterior is less decorated than the Bank of Montecito, the interior boasts Corinthian columns, a central nave, and side aisles reminiscent of early Christian churches.

80.
Elks Club Building
(Lloyd's Bank)
1036 State St.
1926; Parkinson & Parkinson

This building was originally constructed as the Santa Barbara Elks Club, with a retail store space on the ground floor. Since then it has been used for several purposes, notably the Montgomery Ward department store. The arcade on both State St. and East Figueroa St. continues a common Spanish Colonial Revival motif found along State St.

81.
Retail Store
1101 State St.
1931-32; H.A. Minton

Formerly the Owl Drug Store, this building has somewhat unusual stylized classical detailing at the corner and above the display windows.

82. La Arcada
1110 State St.
1926; John Cooper; Myron Hunt, consulting architect

La Arcada Court was constructed adjacent to the site of the mid-19th-century Our Lady of Sorrows Church. This large church was of adobe and brick construction, and not surprisingly, the brick towers fell and it was destroyed by the 1925 earthquake. It was the main downtown Catholic church, succeeding the original Presidio chapel.

This two-story Hispanic complex is organized around a T-shaped paseo system which connects to State St. to the west, Figueroa St. to the south, and the Art Museum/Public Library courtyard and paseo to the north. An open-air restaurant is used as the focus where the two axes join. The State St. front of the building is arcaded on the ground floor, occupied by retail stores, galleries and restaurants, while within the paseos there are enclosed bridges on the second floor to connect the office space units. At the northeast corner of State and Figueroa Sts. (site of the church), the architectural firm of Ketzel-Goodman in 1983 successfully remodeled a separate corner building so that it carries on the Spanish theme of the original La Arcada building.

83. Copeland Stationers
(Shops)
1124 State St.
1924

The prime interest of this small building is its triple arcade with free-standing and engaged attenuated Corinthian columns. The capitals accentuate the delicate, classical façade of this structure.

84.
San Marcos Building
1129-1133 State St.
1913-14; J. Corbley Pool
1925-26; Myron Hunt & H.C. Chambers

Originally on this site was Col. W.W. Hollister's Santa Barbara College (founded 1869), a two-and-a-half story Second Empire building with a three-and-a-half story curved mansard tower. This was the town's first secondary educational establishment and lasted only a few years. It was then coverted to a hotel. It was here that Col. Hollister died in 1886. By 1913, this use too was outmoded, and a new four-story office building was constructed by John Hawley. On June 29, 1925, the great Santa Barbara earthquake struck. The L-shaped building was caught in its powerful vise; the west section pounded against the north, and the corner portion collapsed, trapping in the rubble a dentist who had gone to work early. He was the first of 13 earthquake fatalities. Rebuilding of the structure was rapid. The top two floors were eliminated, and cast concrete Churrigueresque ornamentation was applied to the façade. Note also the paseo leading to the delightful central courtyard and patio, where the building's frieze features medallions of historical figures.

85.
Santa Barbara Museum of Art
1130 State St.
1914; Oscar Wenderoth, Francis W. Wilson
1941; David Adler, Chester L. Carjola
1983; Warner and Gray

Originally a federal post office, this building was one of several in California designed by the government which took into account the character of the community. Similar post offices were built in Pasadena and Berkeley. It was in a somewhat ornate Italian Renaissance design with central arcaded courtyard and exterior applied pilasters and decoration. After the post office was moved to its present location in the 1930s (see entry #123), the building was remodeled and converted into the Santa Barbara Museum of Art. The 1941 remodeling, by the Chicago architect David Adler, produced a design which was far more Hispanic than the original building. Internally, the central patio was transformed into a more delicate, almost Regency space.

In 1983 Paul Gray of Warner and Gray designed a new addition to the southeastern portion of the building. This new addition provided an entrance which faces out upon a courtyard connected to the block-long paseo system, and looks out directly upon Library Avenue, with its view of the Courthouse tower. The design of the new wing continues the Hispanic theme of the 1941 remodeling, and is as successful as that provided earlier by David Adler. A new Italian marble entrance, carrying on the theme of the State St. loggia of the museum, provides an invitation to a two-story interior space. Adjacent to the museum is a memorial to Lockwood de Forest, landscape architect who was responsible for much of the planting on this site. The hedge along the State St. frontage is an unusual dwarf Kei-Apple (Dovyalis [syn. Aberia] caffra).

86.
Lower Hawley Building
Hitchcock Building

(County Savings Bank)
1200-1204 State St.
1887
1926; Jose L. Curletti
1982; Donald E. Pedersen

This building was constructed by Walter N. Hawley, a San Francisco financier, for his carriage and hardware store, at about the same time as his building across the street and up the block (see entry #87). In many ways, Hawley continued the work of W.W. Hollister whose San Marcos Hotel was across the intersection. The Hawley-Hitchcock Building originally had a projecting cornice with brackets and a corner turret. All this was stripped off following the 1925 earthquake by the then owner, Mrs. Herbert R. Hitchcock, proprietor of a dry goods store. The structure was redesigned into Spanish Colonial Revival style during a substantial remodeling in 1982. It is now the headquarters of a savings and loan association.

87.
Upper Hawley Building in Victoria Court

1225-1233 State St.
1887; Peter J. Barber
1978; Designworks   SoM

As with 1200 State St., this building was the work of Walter N. Hawley. As architect, he chose Peter J. Barber, Santa Barbara's most famous 19th-century designer. The building originally had a balustrade at the edge of the roof, as well as a central mansard tower. These were removed following the 1925 earthquake and a more Spanish-style tile roof was put up in their place. The Upper Hawley building is a City Structure of Merit and was restored in 1978 during the formation of the Victoria Court complex from a group of existing buildings combined with new construction. An admirable feature of Victoria Court is the paseo system built into it.

88. Kerry's Restaurant
(Copeland's Sporting Goods)
1230-1232 State St.
1947; Roy W. Cheesman

Built for Reginald Kerry after World War II, this is an example of the handsome Spanish Colonial Revival buildings designed by Roy Cheesman. There are two others on this block frontage, 1220-1224 State St. and 1226-1228 State St. (both 1948). A sporting goods store moved into this building in 1974.

89. Christian Science Reading Room
(and shops)
1301, 1303, 1303A State St.
1950-51; Kem Weber and
  Roy W. Cheesman

Internationally known designer Kem Weber and architect Roy Cheesman successfully combined contemporary Spanish red tile and stucco with Streamline Moderne curves and angles in this building so that it forms a unit with the other Hispanic buildings along this block. Unity, in fact, was their chief goal, according to a statement Weber made to their clients, the First Church of Christ, Scientist, Santa Barbara: "As designer and architect, we have only one aim...and this is to get as complete a unity in the building, its planning and its materials as well as its execution." Toward that end, Weber designed the interior as well, which features a vaulted ceiling with exposed beams, clerestory windows, a garden room, black walnut paneled walls, and furniture designed by Herman Miller. A curved, cast concrete planter in front of the building was, regrettably, removed in 1981.

90.
Shop and office building

    1307 State St.
    1979; Michael Carmichael

The asymmetrical, dramatically styled arched entrance and towering stucco chimneys of this contemporary Hispanic building are echoed on the rear façade, which opens onto the Arlington paseo.

91.
Shop and office building

    (Lou Rose Annex)
    1309 State St.
    1934; Edwards and Plunkett
    1954 additions; Howell and Arendt

Although this building was designed specifically for commercial use, its patio setback, Monterey Colonial Revival style balcony, and partially exposed stairway combine to create the scale and appearance of a residence. The Arlington Silk Oak tree (Grevillea robusta) in the front courtyard has been designated a historic tree by the city. It was originally part of the Arlington Hotel gardens, and was singed in the 1909 fire which destroyed the first hotel.

92.
Shop
(Paul Bhalla's Restaurant)
1311 State St.
1931; Edwards and Plunkett
1936 remodeling; Schwartz and Feil

The Monterey Colonial Revival style balcony of this shop enhances and amplifies the intimate scaling of the building of 1309 State St. Gilchrist's jewelry store occupied the premises for a considerable period.

93.
Lou Rose
1315 State St.
1922 attributed; Arthur B. Benton
1926 addition; Edwards, Plunkett & Howell
1934 remodeling; Hunt and Chambers

This Spanish Colonial Revival shop was built for the Arlington Hotel Company. It was first leased by I. Magnin and Company and has been used as a women's clothing store ever since. In 1947 I. Magnin's moved to the next block, and in 1949 Lou Rose took over the location.

94.
Fox Arlington Theatre
(site of Arlington Hotels)
1317 State St.
(1875 Arlington Hotel; Peter J. Barber)
(1910 Arlington Hotel; Arthur B. Benton)
1930-31; Edwards and Plunkett
1976 restoration: Arendt, Mosher, Grant, Pedersen, and Phillips   L

The Fox Arlington Theatre stands on the site of two elegant and world-famous hotels, both of them named Arlington. The first hotel, a three-story Italianate wooden building, perished in a 1909 fire. The second, a hollow tile, concrete and brick four-story

building designed in the Mission Revival style, was damaged in the 1925 earthquake. A small stuccoed brick arch located behind the theater, near the corner of Sola and Chapala Sts., dates to the second, Mission Revival hotel. The arch and its gate formed part of a wall enclosing an extensive garden and deer park which surrounded the hotel.

In the late 1920s, when word got around that Fox West Coast Theatres was considering the site for a new movie house, Joseph Plunkett, one of Santa Barbara's outspoken advocates for rebuilding the city in the Spanish idiom, requested a meeting with Fox officials. Legend has it that Plunkett borrowed a pencil from a Fox executive and sketched the initial design on the paper liner from a hotel dresser drawer, using the drawer itself as a drafting surface. He apparently made such an inspired presentation that Fox immediately commissioned Edwards and Plunkett to design the new theater.

With its magnificent spire towering above the city, the theater was to have been the center of a full block of small shops connected by a cross-axis paseo. Although the full scheme was never realized because of the 1930s depression, a paseo parallel to the theater façade connects Victoria and Sola Sts., and a gracefully arched courtyard loggia links the entrance to State St., the latter an elegant reminder of what might have been. Inside the auditorium, a mock Spanish village runs along the walls and an elliptically vaulted, "star-studded" ceiling creates an illusory nighttime sky.

In 1976 the building was restored and converted into a community performing arts center. For this it received the Historic Preservation award from Santa Barbara Beautiful, Inc. For obvious reasons the Fox Arlington is considered to be one of the great monuments of the Spanish Colonial Revival in Santa Barbara. It was designated a City Landmark in 1975.

95.
Town House Restaurant
(The Village Fair)
1321 State St.
1926; A.C. Sanders

First known as the Town House Restaurant, this Hispanic building was later converted into a retail shop. Its small second story balcony contributes to the architectural unity of the block, as does the rustic tile roof on the adjacent building.

96.
Restaurants

1325 and 1327 State St.
1946; Soule and Murphy

The finials along the roof repeat details found on the Fox Arlington Theatre tower, thereby tying an otherwise plain façade into the Hispanic architecture of this block.

97.
Alpha Floral

(and Woman's World)
1329 and 1331 State St.
1940; Alex D'Alfonso

The simplified Spanish Colonial Revival design of this building, with its marble glass-framed windows which suggest Streamline Moderne, blends nicely into the understated Hispanic streetscape along this block. These two shops are located on the 1888-1892 site of the Arlington Hotel lawn tennis court.

98.
Gervasoni's My Florist and offices

1335 and 1345 State St.
1976; Stanley R. Riffle, Jr.

Although it is a recent addition to the Fox Arlington block, this multi-level-roofed building, with its Monterey Colonial Revival balcony and its hexagonal tower, is a fitting capstone to the block's architecture. The building won the New Small Business award from Santa Barbara Beautiful, Inc. in 1976 for its corner tower and two-story windows that "give a giant terrarium effect."

99.
Coast Federal Savings and Loan

1330 State St.
1980-81; Holewinski and Blevins in consultation with Edwards-Pitman

Similar in design to the financial institution at 1302 State St., the Spanish character of this building is established by the sculptured stucco massing, the arched windows, a curvilineal exterior stairway, and a red tile gable roof.

The 1300-1900 blocks of State St. boast rows of Queen Palms (Arecastrum romanzoffianum), a common Santa Barbara street tree and among the most beautiful. Many of these were planted by Dr. Doremus in 1912.

100.
Welch-Ryce-Haider Mortuary

1400 State St. and 15 E. Sola St.
1907; 1920
1956 additions and remodeling; Howell, Arendt, Mosher and Grant

In 1952, the Welch-Ryce Corporation purchased the existing buildings on this parcel, a Gothic Revival church structure, formerly part of the Congregational Church, which dates to 1907; and a funeral parlor (originally built to house an auto repair shop) which dates to 1920. A chapel and additional slumber rooms were added to these buildings in 1956. The architects chose a sedate Spanish Colonial Revival design for the building complex, the principal feature of which is a very modest loggia which opens onto the parking lot.

101.
I. Magnin and Company
1415 State St.
1946-47; Timothy L. Pfleuger

The understated lines of this stylish Regency building, designed by one of San Francisco's leading architects, allows it to meld quietly into the city's Hispanic streetscape. I. Magnin's presence in Santa Barbara goes back to 1912 when the San Francisco firm established its first out-of-the-city branch here in the old Potter Hotel at the beach. At the time, Santa Barbara was probably the natural location for such expansion as it was not uncommon in those early years for wealthy residents and visitors to spend several leisurely days riding a passenger steamer to and from San Francisco in order to shop for fashionable clothes and other amenities. In early 1923 I. Magnin relocated to 1315 State St.

102.
Santa Barbara Clinic
(offices)
1421 State St.
1920, 1927, 1929-30; Carleton M. Winslow
1978; Audax (Donald G. Sharpe) **SoM**

This elegant plateresque Spanish Colonial Revival building has been designated a Structure of Merit by the City because of its arcaded and ornamented two-story façade. The building's designer, Carleton M. Winslow, Sr., assisted Bertram G. Goodhue in the design of the 1915 San Diego Exhibition which helped to establish the Spanish Colonial Revival in Southern California. Winslow designed this building five years later, and many of its details reflect the exposition's influence. Originally constructed to house physicians' offices, the building was extensively remodeled behind its façade in 1978 and converted into general offices.

103.
Brinks Grocery
Jordanos' Market

(Home Savings and Loan)
1424 State St.
1933; Carleton M. Winslow
1972; Frank Homolka and Assoc.
 (alterations)
1982-83; Frank Homolka and Assoc.
 (additions)

The original Jordanos' Market portion of this building is the northern section with its gable tower. This market, which was almost but not quite Churrigueresque in design, was Santa Barbara's first supermarket, oriented to its south parking lot, rather than to the street. Designed by Winslow for Brinks Grocery, the 50' × 100' structure was constructed by local builder A.C. Jensen. From 1939 to 1957 Jordano Bros. operated a market here.

Changes were made in the building in 1972 to accommodate Home Savings and Loan, and the luxurious walled and fountained garden to the north was added at that time. The garden is an appropriate touch historically as well, since this was the site of the Verhelles' City Nursery during the first two decades of this century. The new 1982 wing more than doubles the original building. The low tower of the new wing conveys the atmosphere of the 1920s interpretation of the Spanish Colonial Revival.

104.
Trinity Church
1500 State St.
1912; Philip Hubert Frohman and Harold Martin

This stone veneer Gothic Revival church was the third church to be built by the Trinity Episcopal congregration, founded in 1867. After abandoning its first church when Southern Pacific laid tracks at a noisome distance, and after losing the second church, a redwood building, to fire in 1903, the congregation wisely decided to build its third church of native sandstone. Architect Philip Frohman, one of the designers of this English Perpendicular Gothic-influenced building, later gained national recognition as the chief architect of the Washington Cathedral.

Church records reveal that a sizable mortgage incurred to build this monumental, fireproof structure was speedily retired; in 1919, "the mortgage was burned with pomp, circumstance, and much celebrating." The 1925 earthquake, however, tried the congregation's patience once more, when the east and west gables caved in and the tower was nearly demolished. After a delay of almost a year, while Mr. Frohman revised the plans to include earthquake-resistant steel reinforcements, the church was reconstructed at a cost which exceeded that of the original. It is not known whether the congregation engaged in a revelrous mortgage-burning ceremony a second time.

105.
Moore Building
(Courtyard offices)
1513-1515 State St.
1906-1922; original buildings, most demolished since then
1927 additions and remodeling; Edwards, Plunkett & Howell
1933 and 1935 additions; Edwards and Plunkett

The village-like appearance of this Spanish Colonial Revival medical office complex is due to accretion as much as it is a result of conscious planning. Original owner Dr. Henry W. Moore, a dentist, built his residence and offices here between 1906 and 1922. In the 1920s and 1930s, the Moore Estate three times engaged well-known architects Edwards, Plunkett and Howell to make the major alterations and additions that give the complex its present look. The arcade, flagstone paseo, and interior courtyard with its corner stairway successfully open up the complex without diminishing its intimacy, a notable accomplishment by sensitive architects.

106.
Avery Garden Court
(Diamond Apartments)
1628 State St.
1923; A.H. Avery

A well-known local contractor, A.H. Avery, designed and built this complex in the 1920s, a decade when many apartment buildings and bungalow courts were built in Santa Barbara. This handsome Spanish Colonial Revival apartment is an unusual example of this building type, in that it consists of a two-story central unit of 16 apartments flanked to the north and south by pairs of single-story duplexes. The designer-builder initially equipped each unit with a dumbwaiter so that tradesmen could deliver purchases without inconveniencing the occupants, as well as with a conveyor that sent trash to a basement incinerator. The project was also known as Estado Court Apartments.

107.
Van Dyke House
1734-1736 State St.
1913-14
1941 remodeling; Edwards and Plunkett

This office building was originally the residence of rancher Sidney S. Van Dyke. Built in 1913-14, the house remained in the Van Dyke family until about 1940, when ownership passed to Walter H. Pinkham, a dentist. Pinkham engaged Edwards and Plunkett to remodel the house for office use. The original style was no doubt Craftsman, as some Craftsman-like elements remain, but the alteration design is a sensitive blending of the older style and the newer Hispanic idiom.

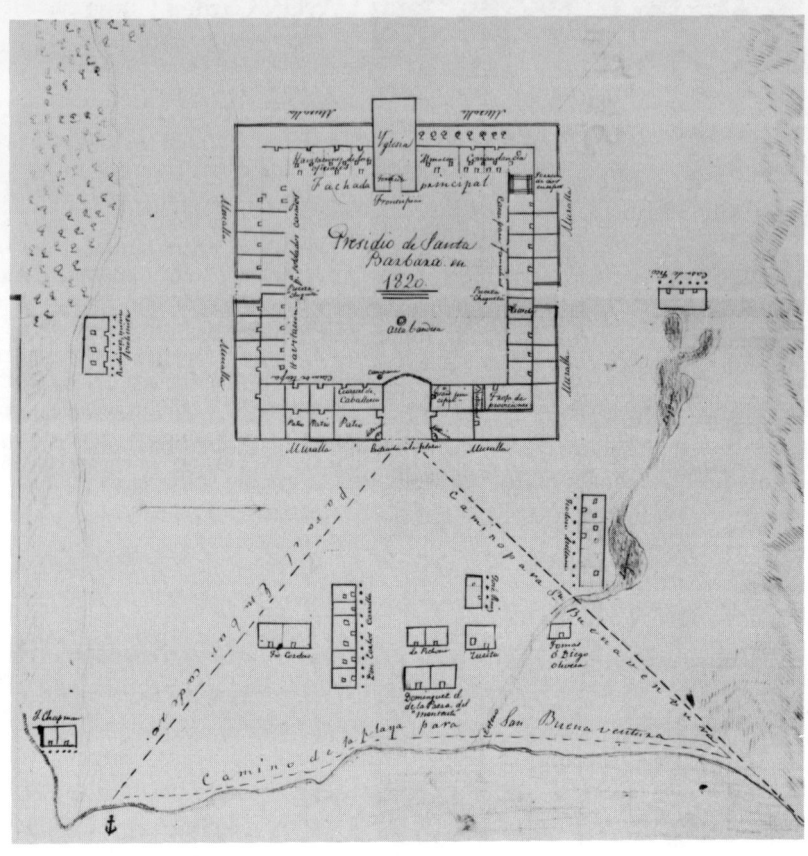

An 1820 drawing of the Santa Barbara Presidio showing uses of buildings, outlying adobe dwellings, and the roads coming into the community.

PRESIDIO AND PUEBLO

By the time José Francisco Ortega, Felipe de Neve, and Fr. Junipero Serra founded the Santa Barbara Presidio on April 21, 1782, the Spanish conquistadores had almost three centuries of frontier experience which they fully used in the plan and construction of the Presidio. They carefully selected the site with respect to the proximity of soil suitable for adobe bricks, trees for firewood and the wood portions of the building, stone, lime, fresh water, pasturage, an adequate harbor, and natives to Christianize. The structure's plan was based on similar forts built elsewhere in the Spanish empire. The resulting design, a square four hundred feet to the side enclosed in a nine-foot high defense wall with two diamond-shaped bastions located on the diagonal, theoretically would enable soldiers to protect the four sides of the fort with enfilading fire. Other standard features included a two-story high chapel opposite the main gate, and parallel rooms to the east and west with adjoining vegetable gardens for the soldiers and their families. The comandante, priest, and officers enjoyed somewhat larger quarters adjacent to the chapel. The whole was an entirely planned structure, one the Spanish had perfected over several centuries of frontier military experience.

The Presidio, however, was actually more a garrisoned outpost than it was a military fort. The outer walls may have been of four-foot thick adobe, but it is doubtful whether they were ever meant to withstand a hostile attack. The Presidio's location protected it from attack by enemy ships, but also prevented it from being able to defend the harbor, except for a primitive redoubt overlooking the anchorage. The Presidio served as a permanent camp located in a remote and difficultly accessible region. It provided housing for the governmental and military authority of the area. It showed the flag.

Unlike the Presidio, the pueblo of Santa Barbara appeared to be completely unplanned. As one early observer noted, houses were sited as if they had been blown out of a blunderbuss. Spain's "Royal Ordinances Concerning the Laying Out of New Towns" in the colonies of the Americas, promulgated in 1573, stated that the four corners of the plaza were to face the four points of the compass. The Presidio's plaza de armas was Santa Barbara's main plaza until the military abandoned the fortress. Shortly thereafter the streets were laid out at right angles to the newer plaza in front of Casa de la Guerra, not to the original civic plaza de armas.

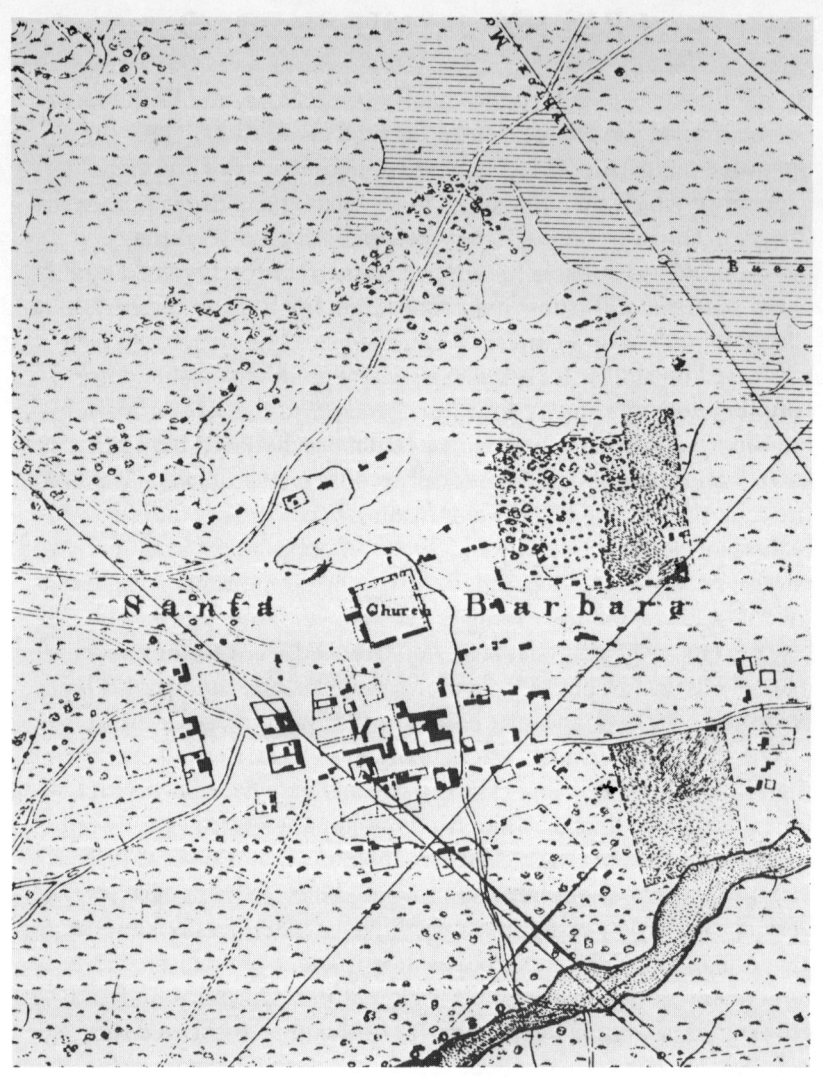

The 1854 United States Coast Survey map of Santa Barbara.

The village consisted, by 1850, of approximately one hundred of these haphazardly located adobes. The heaviest concentration was around Casa de la Guerra (entry #64) some five hundred feet west of the Presidio. The earliest ex-muros adobe was probably Casa Arrellanes constructed about 1795 to the south of the fort (entry #169). There were no improved streets within the village, although a main path led south to the oceanfront and north to the Mission. To the south were located two fruit and vegetable gardens, although these were probably later additions; the Mission provided food for the community before its secularization in 1833.

Architecturally, the town's adobes varied in size from the tiny one-room Buenaventura Pico adobe (entry #132) to the elaborate U-shaped De la Guerra mansion. This latter was hardly typical either in size or design, even though later during the Spanish Revival it would be cited as the prototypical architectural image of the colonial period. Very few other adobes followed this layout. Most were simple rectangles, one room wide, and varying in length from the twenty feet of the Pico adobe to the eighty-three feet of the Burton Mound adobe (entry #9). None had fireplaces or chimneys, very few had tile roofs. Instead, locally plentiful bitumen was used to waterproof structures. They were, all in all, rudimentary if picturesque structures not greatly superior in creature comforts to the tule dwellings of the Chumash.

Beginning in the 1830s with the arrival of the first Anglo-Americans, who brought with them commerce, civic orderliness, and much different standards of comfort, the pueblo began slowly to take on a quite different aspect. Increasingly, wood was substituted for adobe, streets for paths. Civil government functioned in distinct buildings (especially the first City Hall, entry #115, and the Barber-designed County Courthouse, entry #148), replacing the former relative informality of Spanish and Mexican semi-military rule as represented by the rapidly decaying Presidio. Commerce flourished on State Street and residential areas flanked the business district to the east and west. The Presidio area, however, never became an important or fashionable Anglo-American residential district except near its northern fringe about Sola Street. While there were occasional isolated residences such as the 224 E. Figueroa Street house (entry #147), this area remained the Hispanic part of town focused, appropriately, on the remains of the Presidio. And although the descendants of the original settlers adopted many Anglo-American traits, especially in the architecture of their houses, they continued to maintain a basically cohesive Hispanic culture until after World War II when the downtown area underwent rapid commercialization.

At the heart of the Hispanic community and near the former Presidio were located Santa Barbara's Japanese and Chinese immigrant communities. These two groups settled in the East Canon Perdido Street and Anacapa Street area and lived an almost entirely segregated existence with their own restaurants, joss houses (entry #124), groceries, and churches. As with the Hispanics, the Asian-Americans were almost entirely removed from the area by the dramatic changes which occurred during and following World War II.

The story of the Presidio area after the war is one of commercial expansion in which residences have been replaced by ever-larger office buildings. This continues to the present, notably on East Carrillo Street, one of the major axes of development in the downtown area (Towbes Building, entry #144). Simultaneously, however, the old Presidio, where today's Santa Barbara began, is being gradually and painstakingly restored, more than two hundred years after its founding.

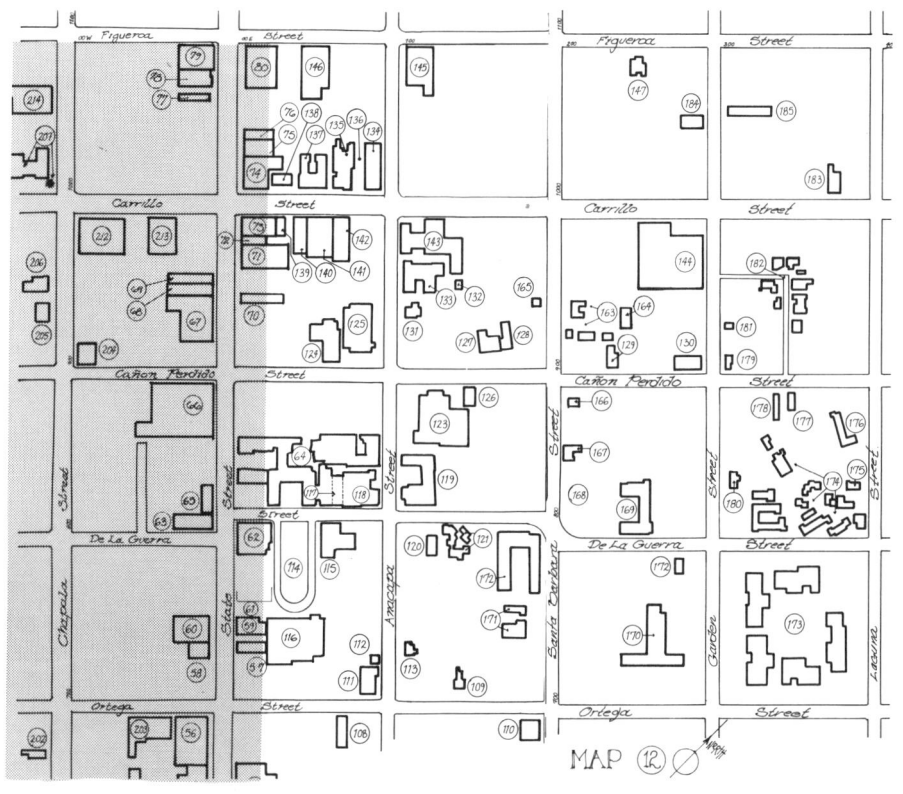

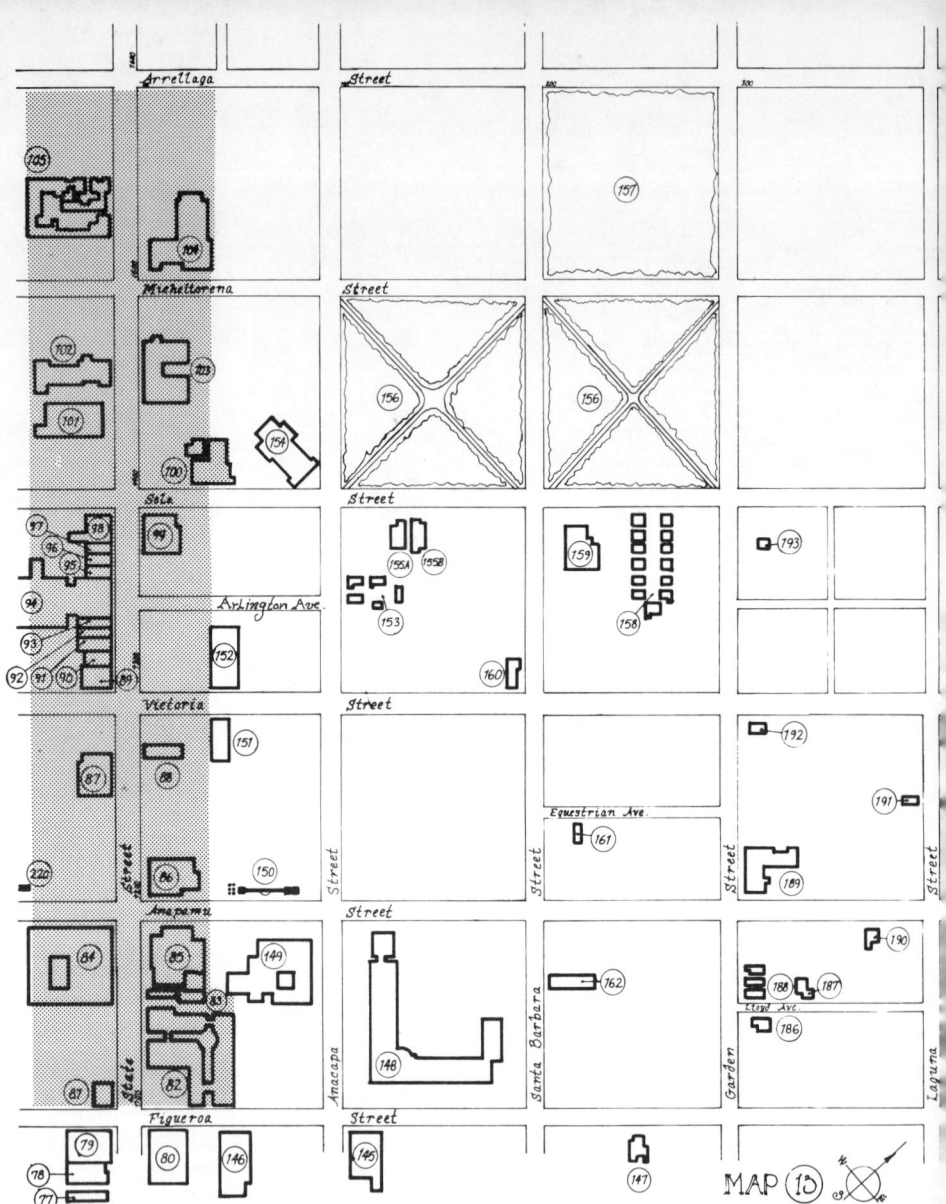

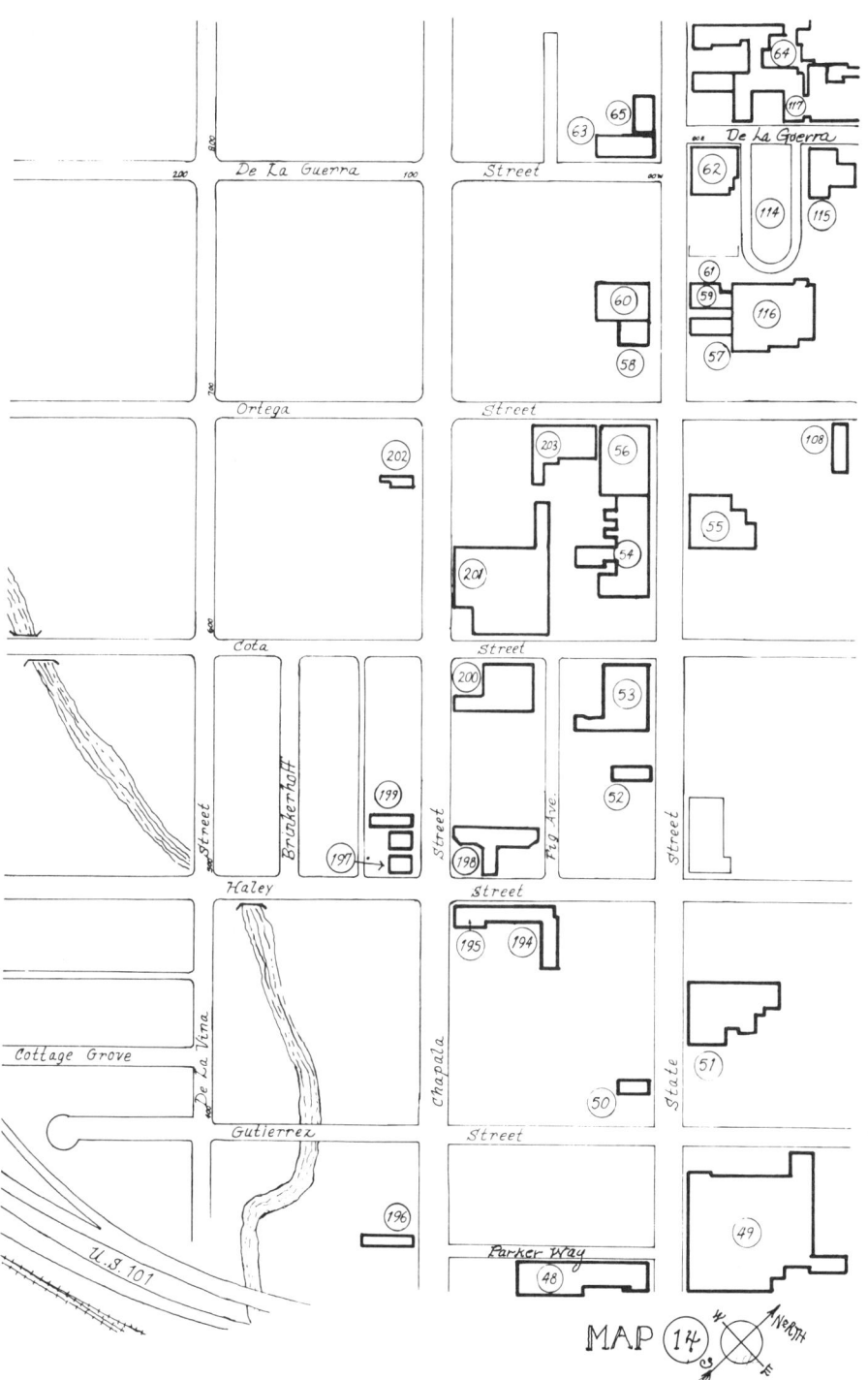

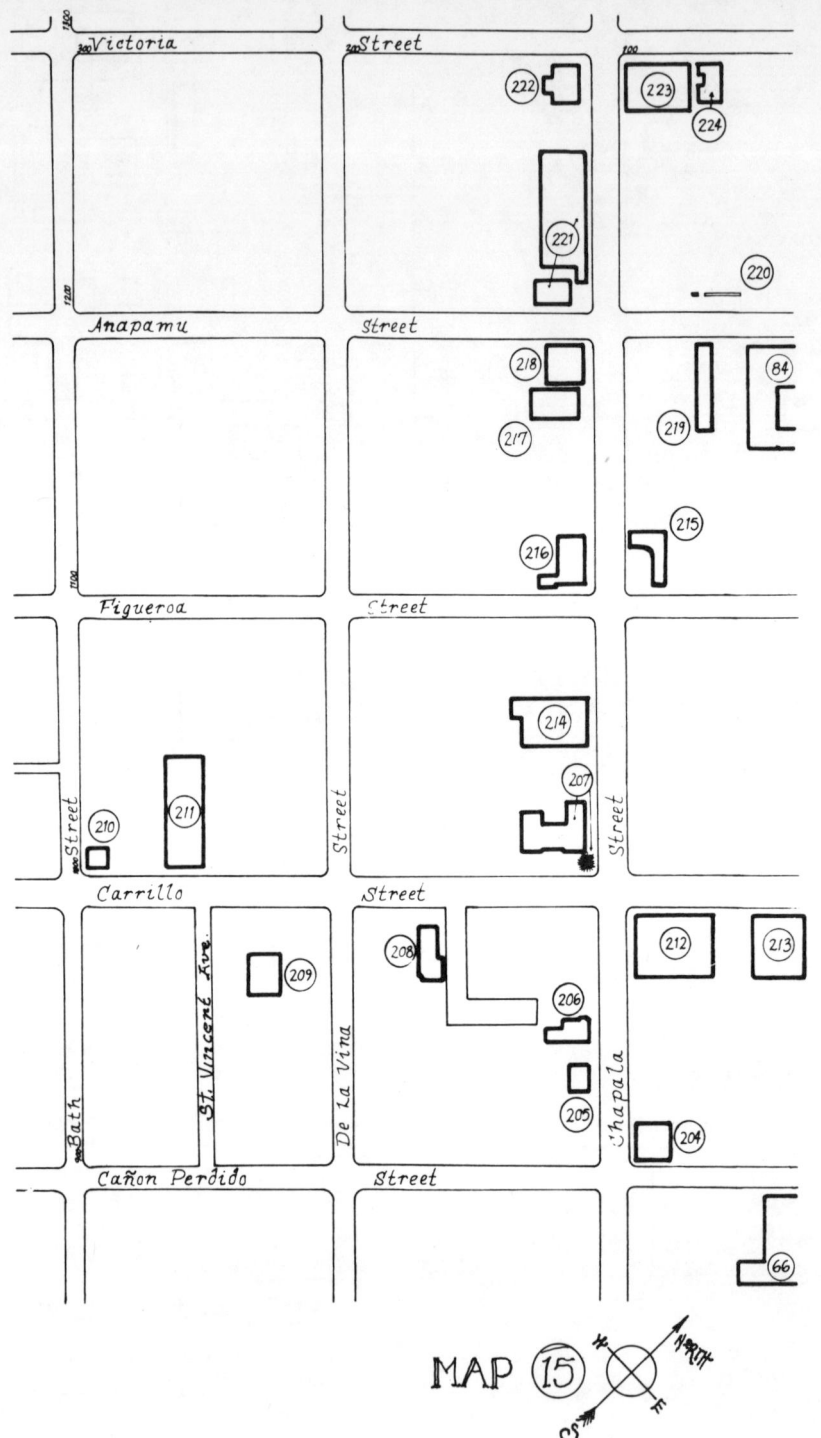

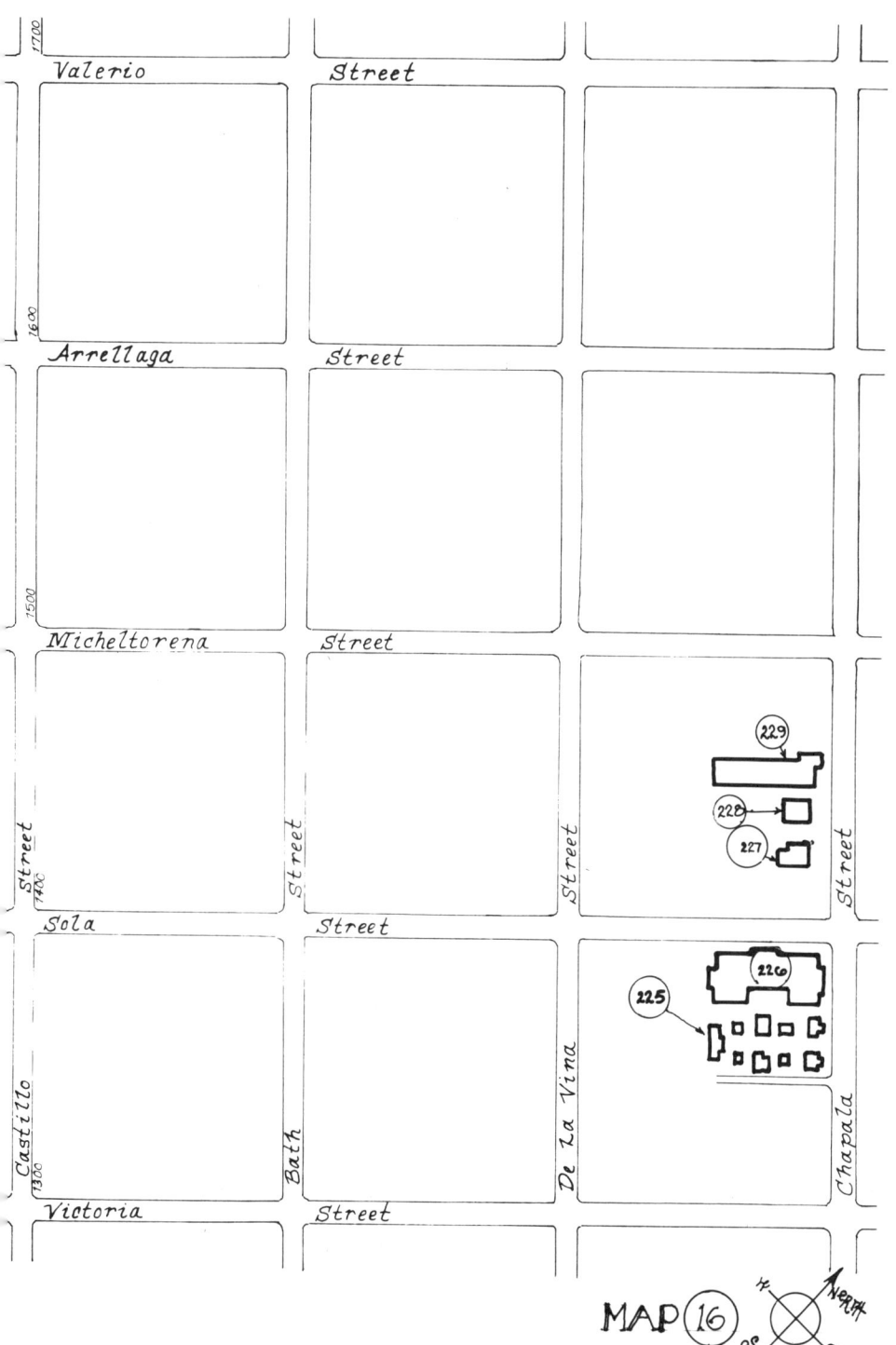

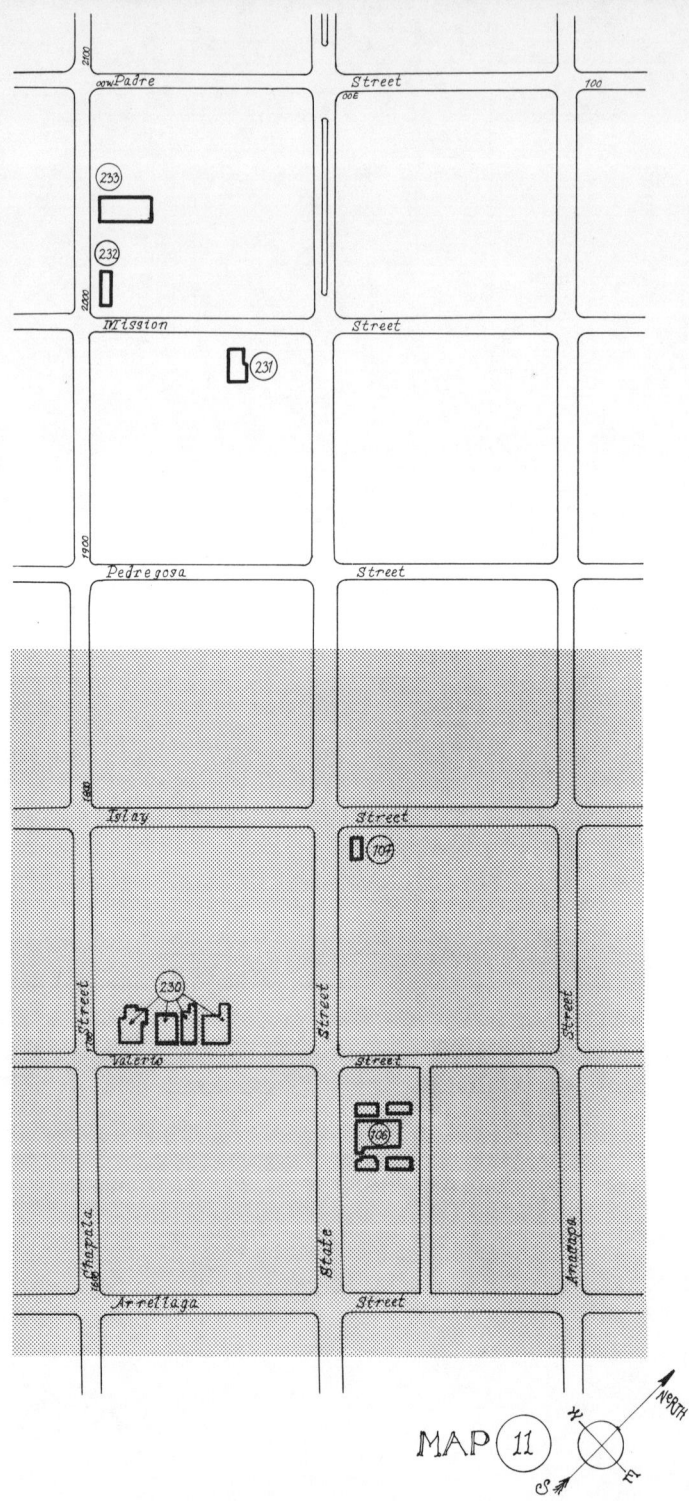

108.
Daily Independent
(Antique Market Place)
26 E. Ortega St.
1894
1926; William Poole

This small building is another example of a structure remodeled in the Spanish Colonial Revival style following the 1925 earthquake. It was constructed by William La Vies for his newspaper plant. An addition was made to the rear in 1926. Since then, it has seen a variety of uses including two iron works and a Chinese laundry. The façade with its large arched display window and smaller arched entrance is attached to an otherwise undistinguished shed.

109.
Garretson House
117 E. Ortega St.
1891

In a neighborhood now almost entirely commercial, this house is a close to unaltered survivor from the residential past of a century ago. Not only are all the main features of the house intact—the fishscale decorated gable in the otherwise hipped roof, decorative porch columns, balustrade, bay window and stained glass—but the site has also retained its integrity with the original planting and sandstone retaining wall.

J.M. Garretson built his family home the same year he constructed his grocery store next door (now gone).

110.
First Congregational Church Site
(California State Employment Building)
128-130 E. Ortega St.
1867
1952; A. Quincy Jones Jr.

This site derives its significance from having been the original location of one of the oldest Protestant churches to hold continuous services in Santa Barbara.

The existing State office building is a characteristic early 1950s modern design by one of Los Angeles' principal architects of the post World War II years.

111.
Los Arcos Antique Center
705-707 Anacapa St. and
35-37 E. Ortega St.
1925; Edwards, Plunkett & Howell

The present structure is near the site of the 19th-century Magdalena Cota Adobe which once served as the County Courthouse and jail. The 1925 Spanish Colonial Revival building is unusual architecturally because of the pointed arch arcade along Anacapa St., the corner tower and the single pointed arch on E. Ortega.

112.
The Adobe Antiques
711 Anacapa St.
ca. 1905

This tiny building is a late example of Santa Barbara's adobe tradition. Although partly constructed of wood, the building displays the scale and composition traditionally associated with adobe construction. The perimeter wall and garden fountain reflect Spanish landscaping concepts. Note also the large pepper tree and the palms in the yard.

113.
Gothic Cottage
710 Anacapa St.
1887

Although significantly altered and now surrounded by parking lots and commercial buildings, this quaint cottage exemplifies the middle class residential character of this area a century ago. The bargeboard in the gable ends and the steeply pitched roof establish its Carpenter Gothic character. Note also the fine sandstone wall in front.

114.
De La Guerra Plaza
De la Guerra Street between State and Anacapa Sts.
1855   CHL

This plaza was formally set aside as a park in 1855 by the City Council. Due to its location directly in front of the city's most important residence, the De la Guerra Adobe, it had previously been used as a gathering place and festival area since the 1820s. The plaza, however, remained a park only until 1874 when a typical brick city hall was constructed. The two tall Washingtonia palms once flanked the building's rear entrance. With the growing appreciation of the city's Hispanic heritage in the early 20th century, the city hall was remodeled in a Mission Revival style. It was torn down in 1924 after the completion of the present City Hall. The plaza remains today the ceremonial and civic center of Santa Barbara.

115.
City Hall

De la Guerra Plaza
1923; Sauter & Lockard

Constructed before the 1925 earthquake, the Santa Barbara City Hall is an early monument to the Spanish Colonial Revival. The removal of the previous city hall located on the plaza had been recommended as early as 1909 when it was described as the "incongruous red firehouse and city hall sticking into the Plaza like a sore thumb." The present building is distinguished by its graceful two-story arcade which faces onto the plaza. Note also the old pepper tree in front.

Just south of the City Hall is the site (now a parking lot) of the Yorba-Abadie Adobe. This adobe, which was built before 1826, was one of the most elaborately interior decorated adobes in early 19th-century Santa Barbara, having interior walls which were painted in a variety of colors and patterns. The structure was damaged in the 1925 earthquake and was eventually torn down in the 1940s to provide a few more parking spaces. A plaque commemorates its existence.

116.
News-Press Building

De la Guerra Plaza
1922; George Washington Smith
1951; Edwards & Wade

The News-Press building visually anchors the south side of De la Guerra Plaza and the De la Guerra Adobe anchors the north side. It was designed by the distinguished architect, George Washington Smith, in a simple, almost classical style. The tower and east wing were added in 1951. The building is also a monument to Thomas More Storke, the editor and publisher for more than 50 years of Southern California's oldest daily newspaper, the *Santa Barbara News-Press*. The architectural example set by the News-Press building and the adjacent City Hall did much to encourage redesign of the plaza area following the 1925 earthquake.

117.
Oreña Store
25 E. De la Guerra St.
ca. 1860   NR, L

This building is one of the earliest brick commercial structures still standing in Santa Barbara. It was constructed about 1860 in the Italianate style by Gaspar Oreña who also owned the adobes to the east (see #118). Used originally as a dry goods shop, it later served as a police courtroom, book shop, art goods store, and, from 1903 to 1913, as the *Daily News* office. From 1954 to the present, it has been used as an antique store. Architecturally, the building, with its symmetrical arched façade, contrasts with the early California adobe tradition of the adobes next door. In this, it is an early example of the Anglo-Americanization of the town as expressed through its architecture. This historic structure is owned by the Santa Barbara Trust for Historic Preservation.

118.
Oreña Adobes
27-29 and 39 E. De la Guerra St.
1849; 1858   L

The one-story adobe at 39 E. De la Guerra St. was constructed in 1849 by José de la Guerra, a comandante of the Santa Barbara Presidio. It was used at that time as a storehouse for merchandise purchased from ships visiting the harbor. It was later sold to Gaspar Oreña who constucted the adjacent story-and-a-half adobe at 27-29 E. De la Guerra. Although the Oreñas spent much of their time at one of their cattle ranches, most of their thirteen children were born here at their city residence. The adobes were restored in 1919-1920 under the direction of James Osborne Craig who, shortly afterwards, restored the De la Guerra Adobe and created El Paseo complex. These adobes are unusual in that their present owners are descendants of the Oreña family.

119.
El Presidio Building
802-812 Anacapa St.
1945-46; Joseph J. Plunkett

L (part); SoM (part)

Incorporated into this restaurant and office building are a portion of an adobe building, a replica of another, and a 1906 hotel. The Miranda Adobe and the guard house were located just to the rear of the present structure. This building is the last work of the designer Joseph Plunkett, who also was involved in the design of the great Fox Arlington Theatre (see entry #94). It is a post World War II example of the Spanish Colonial Revival and has many characteristic Plunkett features, most notable of which is the delightful former wedding chapel which has an octagonal tower and dome. With its central courtyard and fountain, it is a fitting neighbor to the El Paseo complex across the street. Presidio Avenue to the rear is generally considered Santa Barbara's oldest street. The two adobes mentioned above were located on this side of the building.

120.
Santiago De la Guerra Adobe
110 E. De la Guerra St.
ca. 1812   L

Though extensively altered, this single floor adobe was reputedly constructed as early as 1812, making it one of the city's oldest remaining adobes. It was centrally located across from the Presidio's Mexican-era guardhouse (see entry #119) and adjacent to the Lugo Adobe (see entry #121). Santiago de la Guerra, nephew of Antonio Maria de la Guerra, was a member of the all-Spanish-speaking "Lancers," a cavalry unit formed by Antonio Maria de la Guerra to fight with the Union forces in the Civil War. They got as far as Arizona before news reached them that the war was over.

121.
Lugo Adobe/Meridian Studios

112-116 E. De la Guerra St.
ca. 1830
1922
1923; George Washington Smith
1925; Carleton M. Winslow   L

The Meridian Studios consist of a grouping of five buildings of which the Lugo Adobe, located to the rear, dates to the early 19th century. This adobe, like so many of the period, was originally constructed by a Presidio soldier. It passed through the hands of a number of owners before Bernhard and Irene Hoffmann, important city benefactors, purchased the property and remodeled the adobe in 1922. The following year the couple commissioned George Washington Smith to design a master plan for the property and a studio building on the front of it. At this time the Hoffmanns were also building El Paseo a block to the west (see entry #64). In 1925 the complex was completed with a two-story shop and second studio structure designed by Carleton M. Winslow. Since its construction, the Meridian Studios have housed several well-known artists and architects, including Winslow, Ettore Cadorin (the sculptor of the "Spirit of the Ocean" at the Courthouse, entry #148), the painter Colin Campbell Cooper, and the architectural office of Edwards and Plunkett. Architecturally, the studios are distinguished by their pastel-colored stucco walls and the structures' diagonal siting. This creates a tranquil courtyard setting of color, flowers and fountain separated from the street by iron gates, thus recreating a bit of old Spain, or Mexico, in downtown Santa Barbara.

122.
Santa Barbara Historical Society Museum

136 E. De la Guerra St.
1964-65; Robert Ingle Hoyt

The Santa Barbara Historical Society, a significant force for preservation in the county for 50 years, was formed as a volunteer association in 1932. After occupying a wing of the Mission for a number of years, the Society constructed its headquarters in the heart of El Pueblo Viejo across from floor tiles, wrought iron, and wood detailing. Note also the authentic Hispanic-style landscaping to the front and in the courtyard of the building to the rear.

123.
United States Post Office
836 Anacapa St.
1936-37; Reginald D. Johnson

Prior to its present location, the post office occupied what is now the Santa Barbara Museum of Art (see entry #85). When the old building proved insufficient, Thomas M. Storke, among others, convinced the U.S. government to construct its new post office in an appropriately Spanish style. This was accomplished in the building's general massing and overall appearance. In detailing, however, the architect used a number of decorative motifs derived from the then-popular PWA Moderne.

124.
El Centro Building
21-27 E. Cañon Perdido St.
1929; Edwards, Plunkett & Howell

Architecturally, this Spanish Colonial Revival building successfully blends with the Lobero Theatre next door to the east. The building's balconies and the exterior brightly colored tile staircase are impressive aspects of its design. Historically, the site of the building was the location of a tong-controlled Chinese joss house, a Chinese Masonic Temple, and substandard housing for Chinese laboring families. This block of E. Cañon Perdido was the center for Santa Barbara's Chinese population. The wood building burned in the 1920s and was replaced by the present structure.

125.
Lobero Theatre
33 E. Cañon Perdido St.
1924; George Washington Smith

CHL, L

The Lobero Theatre is the oldest continuously operating theater in California. On this site in 1873, José Lobero, an Italian immigrant, opened Southern California's first opera house in a refurbished school building which was said to have been the largest adobe structure in the state. Although the exterior was relatively undistinguished, the interior was praised as "attractive and appropriate" and having an "air of quiet elegance." The opening night program consisted mainly of extracts from Italian operas but was marred, as one reporter noted, by "outrageous and hideous cat-calls, shrieks and noise of the half-grown boys at the concert." In spite of this, the opera house prospered through much of the 19th century. By the early 1920s, however, the old structure was dilapidated and the private Community Arts Association, after first considering renovation, decided ultimately to construct a new theater. The present building, with its graceful three-tiered design culminating in the 70-foot high stage house, is a work of the prominent Santa Barbara architect George Washington Smith (together with Lutah Maria Riggs). This Spanish-style design, along with the contemporaneous City Hall and News-Press Building, did much to further the Hispanization of Santa Barbara in the 1920s.

Note also the adobe walls behind the theater which were constructed from the bricks of the original theater on this site.

126.
El Cuartel
122 E. Cañon Perdido St.
ca. 1788

NR, CHL, L

El Cuartel is the oldest building in Santa Barbara, being a fragment of the Spanish Royal Presidio founded in 1782. Permanent buildings for soldiers' housing were begun a few years later under Felipe de Goycoechea, the second comandante of the Presidio. For many years El Cuartel housed José Jesus Valenzuela, the gate-keeper for the rapidly deteriorating fort during the Mexican period. In 1941, shortly after the adjacent post office was constructed, it was purchased by a group of public-spirited citizens and its preservation was assured. The structure now houses a state park gift shop and museum. It will eventually be incorporated into the Presidio reconstruction project. Note the modern Hispanic-style garden to the east.

127.
Cañedo-Whittaker Adobe
123 E. Cañon Perdido St.
ca. 1788   NR, CHL, L

Originally constructed as one of the residential units for noncommissioned officers at the Presidio, this adobe was later granted to José Maria Cañedo during the Mexican period. His son and subsequent owners occupied the house until 1920 when Elmer H. Whittaker of Montecito purchased the property. He added the part to the rear and altered the interior plan. The front portion of the adobe dates back to the old Presidio, with the exception of the four-panel door and double-hung windows, both improvements of the early American period. Now included in El Presidio de Santa Barbara State Historic Park, the adobe forms a part of the Presidio reconstruction, being joined to the newly reconstructed Padre's Quarters and Chapel to the east.

128.
Presidio Chapel and Padre's Quarters
125 E. Cañon Perdido St.
1788
1977-81; Frank D. Robinson
1982-84; Gilbert Sanchez

The Padre's Quarters is the first segment of El Presidio State Park to be reconstructed by the Santa Barbara Trust for Historic Preservation. To the east is the Chapel, thus the logic of this adobe serving as the padre's residence. The Chapel, the largest of the buildings of the Presidio, was the next unit of the old Presidio to be constructed. Both the Padre's Quarters and the two-story chapel have been rebuilt in adobe bricks reinforced with steel to meet seismic safety standards. Part of this site was once the location of a Buddhist temple built in 1923 when this part of East Cañon Perdido St. was the heart of Santa Barbara's Asian community.

129.
Studio Building

215 E. Cañon Perdido St.
1928; Soule, Murphy & Hastings

This Spanish-style building with its projecting wooden bay window was once a part of the Community Arts Association's Festival Arts School. The other, "temporary" wooden structures forming the complex (see entry #163) were meant to be replaced by permanent Spanish-style buildings such as this one, but the school foundered in the financial crisis of the 1930s.

130.
Brooks Building

233 E. Cañon Perdido St.
1982-84; Wahlquist, Lawrence, Richards Inc. and Clayton Brooks

This is a recent version of the Monterey cantilevered balcony style, which will within a few years easily be mistaken for one of Santa Barbara's adobes of the late 1830s.

131.
Cota-Knox Building

914-918 Anacapa St.
1871

Considered one of the oldest existing brick buildings in downtown Santa Barbara, the single floor, flat-roofed Cota-Knox building was constructed as a residence by José Lobero for the use of his mother-in-law, Francisca Cota, whose own adobe residence had been demolished when Anacapa St. was put through. Lobero, two years later, established a theater, the successor of which is still located across the street (see entry #125). A former Civil War surgeon, Dr. Samuel B.P. Knox, subsequently purchased the property. Architecturally, the house, with its brick construction and symmetrical façade, is an early example of the rapid Anglo-Americanization of the city in the 1870s. It originally had a small Eastlake porch.

132.
Pico Adobe
920 Anacapa St.
ca. 1820   L

This tiny gabled-roof adobe has remained relatively unaltered due to its location in the middle of the block just outside the old Presidio walls. Its original owner was the family of Santiago Pico, a Presidio soldier. Originally a one-room residence without the fireplace, it is a very good example of a modest adobe dwelling of the mid-19th century. Buenaventura and Anita Pico resided here in the second half of the 1800s.

133.
Margaret Baylor Inn
(Lobero Building)
924 Anacapa St.
1926-27; Julia Morgan

The Lobero Building is of interest both for its architect and its original use. Julia Morgan was the most important woman architect of her time, as well as the first woman to attend the prestigious École des Beaux Arts in Paris. She is thus an excellent example of the liberated women of the 1920s. It was precisely for them that this building was constructed, as a contemporary news account noted, "There is a proven need for a hotel in Santa Barbara for the use of business women." Architecturally, the building's strict symmetry and classical details reflect Julia Morgan's Beaux Arts education.

134.
City Commerce Bank
33 E. Carrillo St.
1975; Richard B. Taylor, Eldon C. Davis

Since this structure provides the eastern terminus for a block of historically significant Spanish-style buildings, it was important that it should sympathetically complement the adjoining buildings. It boasts such Hispanic architectural elements as adobe-like walls, second story projecting balconies, wrought iron detailing, and red tiled roof.

135.
Little Town Club

27 E. Carrillo St.
1885
1923-24; George Washington Smith
1928; Edwards, Plunkett & Howell
1936, 1937; Chester L. Carjola
1948; Harold John Vaile   SoM

In 1915, the Little Town Club purchased this lot and, located upon it, a one-story Italianate cottage dating to about 1885. The all-women club needed new quarters so its members, many of whom lived in Montecito, could continue to meet informally for lunch or to rest and visit with one another while shopping in town. Various building improvements were made in the next few years, but by 1923, members considered the clubhouse inadequate for their needs. Rather than seek out a new meeting place, the club engaged the masterful architect George Washington Smith to redesign the existing building; and, with the help of expert contractors, Snook and Kenyon, he transformed the "little white cottage into a stucco building and an artistic charming club house." In 1928, Martha (Mrs. David Sr.) Gray donated money to add a two-story wing to the rear and western side; Edwards, Plunkett & Howell designed this addition. When the existing dining hall was replaced (1948) by a one-story addition, the club dedicated the new hall to her. Chester Carjola designed a one-story dressing room addition to the rear (1936) as well as the library expansion and front wall extension (1937). Despite additions and alterations by several designers, this Hispanic building, with its adjacent walled courtyard, reflects a remarkable continuity of architectural design and detail.

The trees on these blocks are the Indian Laurel Figs (Ficus microcarpa), variety nitida, an evergreen tree much-planted recently.

136.
Aguirre Adobe Site

Approx. 21-33 E. Carrillo St.
1841

The Aguirre Adobe (1841-1884) was located on this site, making it of historical significance. José Antonio Aguirre, a wealthy merchant and landowner, constructed the palatial adobe for his bride, Francisca Estudillo. The quadrangle design, unique in California architecture, was centered around a courtyard with a 15' wooden-floored corridor onto which the 19 apartments opened. Although the family retained the property, the adobe was used as a permanent residence for less than a year. From 1843 until 1880 the adobe met various needs of the city and county of Santa Barbara. It functioned as military barracks, the county courthouse and jail, a school for the Sisters of Charity, the post office, and the meeting place for several church groups. The Aguirre Adobe was demolished in 1884 after years of neglect.

137.
Mihran Studio
17-21 E. Carrillo St.
1922; Robert W. Hyde   SoM

This Monterey Revival building with its projecting second story balcony is a worthy neighbor to the historic Hill-Carrillo Adobe next door to the west. So worthy, in fact, that it is often mistaken for a historic adobe itself. It is similar to the 1835 Pacific House in Monterey and resembles Santa Barbara's own Monterey-style Ortega-Masini Adobe in Montecito.

138.
Hill-Carrillo Adobe
11-15 E. Carrillo St.
1825-26   CHL, L

Daniel Hill, an early Yankee immigrant to Santa Barbara, built this adobe for his Spanish bride, Rafaela Luisa Ortega. It is said to have had the first wooden floor in the pueblo. In addition, the first child of Anglo-American parents to be born in Santa Barbara was born here to Rachel Holmes and Thomas Oliver Larkin. The subsequent owner, Captain John D. Wilson, was in the fur trade, and evidently not terribly literate as can be seen in the following from a letter to Larkin in 1842: "I recevud your Litter before I laft St Barbara regarden the otter skins thair is now one hundred & four Skins in St Barbara all good Blak ones inded the beast lot that has been got...." Wilson and his wife Ramona made their adobe one of the centers of social life in Mexican Santa Barbara. Later it served as a daguerrotype gallery, a make-shift City Council meeting room, and the residence of Guillermo and Joaquin Carrillo. In 1928, the adobe was to be demolished for a motion picture theater. Max C. Fleischmann, one of Santa Barbara's premier philanthropists, stepped in and assured the building's preservation. The adobe now houses the Santa Barbara Foundation. Note the old-fashioned street lamps along both sides of this block.

139.
Gidney Building
(Salisbury Field Building)
10 E. Carrillo St.
ca. 1900
1925; Edwards & Plunkett

As with so many other buildings in the downtown area, this store is a post-earthquake remodeling of an earlier structure. The balconied window and large arched entrance are characteristic of the Spanish-style architecture of the 1920s. The westerly portion was demolished in 1963 for the savings and loan building at 936 State St.

140.
Hunt's China Shop
12-14 E. Carrillo St.
1926-27; Associated Architects of Santa Barbara

The architectural style of this building is patterned after a 16th-century Spanish townhouse. It relates quite well to its more impressive neighbor to the east, designed in a loose version of a 17th-century Italian palazzo. The building is on the site of the city's first library, built in 1892 and designed by Peter J. Barber. The present structure is a sophisticated example of the Hispanic architecture of the 1920s. It was originally constructed for the Chamber of Commerce. The Hunt family commenced doing business in the city in 1871. Note the plaster medallion of Saint Barbara above the entrance.

141.
Masonic Temple
16 E. Carrillo St.
1923-24; Carl W. Werner

This building is a fine interpretation of late Northern Italian Renaissance architecture. The second and third floor loggia with pointed voussoir and applied decoration patterned after the Masonic Order's emblem is particularly impressive. Although the first floor has been altered on several occasions, it remains an excellent example of Mediterranean-style architecture, very much in harmony with Santa Barbara's Spanish tradition.

142. El Castillo Building

20 E. Carrillo St.
1926; Wythe, Blaine & Olson

This two-story post-earthquake Andalusian style building with its corner bay tower was constructed for E.J. Peterson and occupied by Southern California Edison Company, which not only provided money and equipment for the earthquake relief effort, but also supported the community's attempt to rebuild in a Spanish style. The tiled walk adjacent to the building, which now leads to the parking structure, was originally constructed as a continuation of Bernhard Hoffmann's "Street in Spain" paseo system, here called Paseo Carrillo or Callejon Carrillo.

143. Recreation Center

100 E. Carrillo St.
1914; J. Corbley Pool
1926 gymnasium; Julia Morgan   SoM (gym)

Although founded in 1907, the Recreation Center did not find permanent quarters until 1914 when this brick building was constructed. Responsible for this much-used public facility were two women. Margaret Baylor, a Cincinnati social worker, realized the need in Santa Barbara for a youth center and housing for unmarried women (see also The Lobero Building, entry #133). She undertook a successful campaign to raise funds, and construction subsequently began in 1913. Bertha Rice directed the center for many years. The architect, J. Corbley Pool, executed the design in a Craftsman-Prairie School mode. Julia Morgan, who designed Margaret Baylor's adjacent inn, was responsible for the gymnasium adjoining the Recreation Center to the east. It replaced a 1918 masonry gym damaged by the 1925 earthquake. The Morgan gymnasium represents one of the city's distinguished versions of the Hispanic tradition—an example which is often missed because of its nearly hidden location.

144.
Towbes Building
(Site of Beard Motor Co.)
222 E. Carrillo St.
(1926; Mary Osborne Craig and
 Ralph Armitage)
1980-81; Edwards-Pitman

The original building on this site, an automobile salesroom, was the product of Mrs. J.A. Andrews and the designer Mary Craig and architect Ralph Armitage, who were also responsible for the Plaza Rubio houses near the Mission (entry #236). In 1973, the property was purchased by Michael Towbes and the original building was demolished. The present large office building was constructed in 1980-81. It has retained the arcaded loggia and low pitched shed roof of the original 1926 design. The Hispanic style of this building should be contrasted with the 1960s and 1970s designs illustrated elsewhere on East Carrillo St.

145.
Southern Counties Gas Co.
(Wells Fargo Bank)
1036 Anacapa St.
1927; Edwards, Plunkett & Howell and
 Marston, Van Pelt & Maybury

Another good example of the Spanish Colonial Revival following the 1925 earthquake, this building features a recessed arcade, wrought iron detailing, and deeply cut window openings. It was built as the Santa Barbara office of the Southern Counties Gas Company.

146.
Offices

(Levy's Furniture Store)
10-18 E. Figueroa St.
1925-26; A.C. Sanders (10 E.)
1927-28; Edwards, Plunkett & Howell
  (14-18 E.)

These two buildings were originally constructed as separate structures and united in 1950. There are many fine architectural details exemplified here, including the recessed arcade, second story corbelling, and wrought iron detailing. These joined buildings show how historic structures can be altered to serve new needs without destroying their original architectural integrity. Notice the picturesque weathervane on the easterly building. In bloom, the Chinese Hibiscus (Hibiscus rosa-sinensis) in the 00 block of E. Figueroa St. boast large showy flowers in a wide range of colors. They were planted in 1965. The majority of street trees in this block, however, are New Zealand Christmas Trees (Metrosideros tomentosa).

147.
Brownsill House #1
   224 E. Figueroa St.
   ca. 1887

This Eastlake-Stick house presents a well-preserved example of the Eastern architectural influence which began to enter Santa Barbara in the 1870s. Decorative patternwork, square bay windows with fixed transoms, fishscale shingle siding, and ornamental gable-end struts suggest affluence. The house was built by Edwin Brownsill, one of many so-called capitalists who came to Santa Barbara during the late 19th century; he lived here only a short while before moving to 1116 Garden Street.

148.
Santa Barbara County Courthouse
   1120 Anacapa St.
   1927-29; William Mooser & Co. and
   J. Wilmer Hersey; Ralph T. Stevens,
   landscape architecture   **NR, L**

Without doubt the most important 20th-century building in Santa Barbara, and second only to the Mission in overall architectural significance, the Santa Barbara County Courthouse can rightly be considered the public monument of the Spanish Colonial Revival in the United States. The present courthouse is Santa Barbara's third. From 1850 to 1872, an adobe on this site was used. The adjoining jail was so impractical, however; that it was joked that the best way to get rid of a troublesome character was to imprison him there from which he would promptly escape and leave town for good. The second courthouse was a classical centrally domed brick building designed by Peter J. Barber. This structure was heavily damaged in the 1925 earthquake, necessitating a new building.

In 1919 the County of Santa Barbara, in cooperation with the City, held a competition for a new County Courthouse, City Hall and Veterans Memorial. This competition was won by Edgar Mathews of San Francisco; the second place design was by Mooser and Simpson, also of San Francisco. Due to financial constraints, no building resulted from this competition. After the earthquake of 1925, the County Supervisors turned to William Mooser and Company for the design of the Courthouse, and a scheme similar to that submitted in the 1919 competition was proposed. This design was not felt to replicate the scale and informal Andalusian character of Santa Barbara. The Architectural Advisory Committee, and other interested individuals, prevailed upon the Supervisors to seek out a new approach to the design of the Courthouse—one which would break the building up into separate units and would be organized around a central courtyard. J. Wilmer Hersey of the Community Drafting Room, in consultation with other Santa Barbara architects, then provided the designs which formed the basis of the working drawings prepared by William Mooser and Co.

The building's most dramatic feature is the Roman triumphal arch—which provides a view of the foothills of Santa Barbara and leads to the central courtyard and sunken gardens. These last consist of the stone foundations of the original 1872 courthouse. Other distinctive features include the many theatrical staircases, decorative sculpture (especially Ettore Cadorin's fountain and statue adjacent the great arch), and open loggia corridors. The interior of the Courthouse is equally ornate; the designers included Dan Sayre Grosbeck, John MacQuarrie, J.B. Smeraldi, and George Hyde. Much of the extensive and colorful tile work was produced in Algiers, North Africa.

The landscaping of the building is equally typical of Southern California at its exotic best. It is so extensive and varied that only a few outstanding specimen trees can be noted here. The Bunya Bunya (Araucaria bidwillii) on the Anacapa St. side is notable for its unusual silhouette and pineapple-shaped cones, each of which can weigh up to ten pounds. Note also the row of California Fan Palms (Washingtonia filifera) on E. Figueroa St. and the sandstone entrances, retaining walls and curbing around the entire block.

149.
Santa Barbara Public Library
40 E. Anapamu St.
1916-17; Henry Hornbostel,
  Francis W. Wilson;
1925; Carleton M. Winslow
1930; Myron Hunt and H.C. Chambers
1979; Jerry A. Zimmer

Although Santa Barbara's first lending library was established in 1870, it did not have a permanent structure until 1892, when the Peter J. Barber-designed library was built at 14 E. Carrillo St. By 1914 a larger facility was needed, so the first building was sold to the Chamber of Commerce and a new property was purchased. Much of the financing for the new building came from the Carnegie Corporation. The design was by the well known Eastern architect, Henry Hornbostel, and the local architect Francis W. Wilson proposed the final working drawings and supervised the construction of the building. The beautiful main portal on E. Anapamu St. was the later post-earthquake work of Carleton M. Winslow. This was originally the main entrance but has now been closed off. The Faulkner Gallery of Modern design, with its gilded Egyptian-like entrances and Art Deco treatment, was added in 1930 and designed by Myron Hunt and H.C. Chambers. The library was considerably remodeled and expanded in 1979. The addition and remodeling were by Jerry A. Zimmer and the landscape design was by Edward Comport. The library remains one of Santa Barbara's most important and beautiful civic institutions. Note the three magnificent eucalyptus trees and the oak trees to the west of the library.

150.
Wall and Pergola
North side of Anapamu St.
between State and Anacapa St.
1981-82; Mahan and Associates
(Henry Lenny)

A bold Churrigueresque-like detached wall, resplendent with a lion's head fountain, hides the automobiles to the north, and looks out formally to the Library across Anapamu St. To the west a piered pergola, acting as the entrance to a paseo, leads into the parking lot.

151.
Victoria Hotel and shops
24-28 E. Victoria St.
1925-26; William A. Edwards

The corbelled course beneath the roofline of the Victoria Hotel gives it the appearance of being three buildings, but it was all constructed at one time to accommodate a 31-room hotel on the second story and three shops on the first. Over the years the shop tenants have changed many times, but the Moorish-influenced Spanish Colonial Revival façade remains unaltered.

152.
Normandy Hotel
(Victoria Building)
27 E. Victoria St.

1888
1980 remodeling; Peter Hunt   SoM

Its age and unusual architectural features, especially the two-story triangular side bays, make this one of Santa Barbara's noteworthy 19th-century buildings. Until the mid-1890s it was the residence of Mrs. C.M. Prince and her two daughters, one an art and embroidery teacher and the other a music teacher. From 1895 until quite recently it was used variously as a rooming house, apartment building, and hotel. Helen Reynolds had the building's front extended in 1912. In 1980 the exterior was restored, decorative features were added, and the interior converted into offices.

153.
MacKellar Court
1318-1324 Anacapa St.
1916   SoM

Whoever designed these four one-story clapboard bungalows may have had English country cottages in mind. Perhaps it was their well-known builder, Alexander MacKellar, himself. The vines, climbing roses, and other old-fashioned plants surrounding the cottages, with their gable roofs of medium and high pitch, certainly suggest the English countryside.

The avocado tree at 1316 Anacapa St. may be the largest in Santa Barbara.

The Brisbane Box trees (Tristania conferta) in the 1400-1600 blocks of Anacapa St. were planted about 1912.

154.
Our Lady of Sorrows Church
21 E. Sola St.
1928-29; Edward A. Eames

The Romanesque-inspired Spanish design of this church is enhanced by the play of light and dark that is achieved through the use of gray stone details against the stucco surface, subtleties that complement the stunning rose window (one of several) above the central portico. The original parish church was located at the corner of State and Figueroa Sts. (see entry #82). When the 1925 earthquake necessitated its rebuilding, the new church was relocated to this spot. It was built upon the site of what, from all accounts, must have been a 19th-century showplace for here, in 1874, John Edwards, a prominent Santa Barbara banker, built a large, two-story wooden residence which featured a sewing room set in a high, 50-foot tower. The basilic tower of the present-day church is certainly no less impressive.

155-a.
MacKellar House
112 E. Sola St.
1921

This quaint Norman Revival cottage is an example of the romantic desire of the 1920s to import rural architectural styles of other places and times to California and the rest of the nation as well. It was constructed by local builder Alex MacKellar for his family.

155-b.
Archer-Spencer Building
116 E. Sola St.
1924; Soule, Murphy & Hastings

This is a relatively straightforward example of Spanish Colonial Revival constructed by the architects for use as their offices. The design combines an arched first-story entrance with a square-bayed and recessed second-story stairway and entrance. Landscape architects Lockwood de Forest and Ralph T. Stevens also had their offices here for several years.

156.
Alameda Plaza
Bounded by Anacapa St., E. Micheltorena St., Garden St., and E. Sola St.
1853   L (part)

Shortly after Santa Barbara became an American town in 1850, the City set aside six blocks in this area for public use. Four of the six blocks, one of which is the present-day Alice Keck Park Memorial Gardens, were eventually lost, apparently because the City did not proceed with its intended park development, and squatters claimed the land. During the 1870s and 1880s, these two remaining blocks were enclosed with picket fences, trees were planted, and a bandstand was erected. Citizens in those decades, however, were more interested in developing, rather than beautifying, the city, and at times the park became overgrown and weed-infested. Finally in 1902 a three-member Park Commission was created with Dr. A.B. Doremus, a dentist, as Park Superintendent. The Park Commission engaged Peter Poole in 1908 to construct the sandstone pedestal-flanked steps located on the corners facing Garden and Santa Barbara Sts. In 1912, Doremus traveled abroad and brought back rare plant specimens and seeds, then personally planted them in the park. Doremus also laid out the walkways that meander diagonally through each block. The wooden bandstand, which dates to 1888, is now a City Landmark.

Among the many specimen trees to be noted here are the three redwoods planted as a group in 1919 by King Albert of Belgium, his wife Queen Elisabeth, and their son Prince Leopold. The seeds of the East African Fern Pines (Podocarpus gracilior) were shot down by Stewart Edward White, a Santa Barbara novelist and big game hunter, and given to Dr. Franceschi by Mrs. White. The one in the eastern block is female, the other to the west is male.

157.
Alice Keck Park Memorial Garden
(Christian and Mary Herter House site)
(El Mirasol Hotel site)
Bounded by E. Micheltorena St., Garden St., E. Arrellaga St., and Santa Barbara St.
1905; Delano & Aldrich
1914
1976; Grant Castleberg, landscape architecture

This block, like those that constitute Alameda Plaza, was part of the six-block area set aside in 1853 for eventual city park development. Unlike the two blocks to the south, however, this block was privately developed. In 1905, Christian and Mary Herter here built their home, the Mission Revival design of which emanated from the New York office of Delano and Aldrich. Later, the house was converted into the famous El Mirasol Hotel. The completed complex consisted of a U-shaped building enclosing a luxurious flower garden with several batten-constructed bungalows scattered alongside the main building. After a fire damaged the hotel's main structure in 1966, the buildings were demolished. Alice Keck Park gave the land to the city in December 1975, and the present garden was created as a memorial to her.

158.
Alameda Court
220 E. Sola St.
1916-17

This bungalow court was originally constructed as a winter retreat for eastern visitors to the city. It provided such amenities as small apartments above the garage at the rear for the chauffeurs of these families. It was later converted to housing. This is one of the most extensive and best preserved of the bungalow courts of the 1910s and 1920s.

159.
University Club
1332 Santa Barbara St.
1880
1922; Soule, Murphy & Hastings

Originally built for J.W. Calkins, vice president of Mortimer Cook's First National Gold Bank, this building was described at the time as "unsurpassed for beauty by any residence in this city" and built "after the Elizabethan style of architecture...with pleasant peculiarities of the style." It was, in fact, peculiar, with battlements, towers, buttresses, drip lintels, multiple gables and everything else the architect could pile on the building to make it appear Elizabethan. By 1922, it was considered a Victorian "horror" and the exterior was remodeled in a suitably genteel if somewhat nondescript Spanish style. The interior retains much of its earlier appearance, including massive redwood beams, oak paneling, and stairway.

160.
Southern California Edison Office
1301 Santa Barbara St.
1931; Edwards & Plunkett

From its construction to 1973, this was the site of the Automobile Club of Southern California office. The architecture, with its peaked chimney hoods, deeply cut and arcaded façade, and stout corner buttresses, is a good example of the Spanish Colonial Revival.

161.
Calder House
206 Equestrian Ave.
1876; possibly Peter Barber

This two-story, L-shaped Eastlake house was built on the corner of Santa Barbara St. and Equestrian Ave.; at that time, it had a porch attached to the front and one side. The house was moved to its present location in 1924. William J. Calder, the original owner, is believed to have been a dentist. The wide shiplap siding, tall double-hung windows, and window molding and sills are typical architectural features of the period, but the elongated oblong decoration on the frieze is distinctive. An interior, octagonal newel post is similar to others found in houses that are known to have been designed by Peter Barber, Santa Barbara's "gentleman architect" who designed several important 19th-century buildings.

162.
Schauer Building
1126 Santa Barbara St.
1930; Edwards & Plunkett
1975-76; Edwards-Pitman

The Schauer Building was constructed for the Schauer Printing Company, its occupant for 45 years. Its architects were among the most prominent in Santa Barbara's Spanish renaissance of the 1920s. Their design is an appropriate foil to the monumental Courthouse across the street.

In 1975-76 Edwards-Pitman remodeled the building for offices, along with the adjacent Storke Building on Anapamu St.

The eleven blocks from 1000-2100 Santa Barbara St. are planted with Queen Palms (Arecastrum romanzoffianum), a Brazilian tree. The portion from Victoria St. to Mission St. was planted in 1929 by Dr. Doremus.

163.
Alhecama Center
914 Santa Barbara St.
1925; Soule, Murphy & Hastings

This complex of buildings was established in 1925 by the Festival Arts School of Santa Barbara. This arts school was a part of the Community Arts Association and had been founded in 1920 to "give instructions in the arts that beautify and enrich life" and "to develop especially the different forms of community festivals, which feature dancing, singing and drama in its many branches." The Community Arts Association, led by such prominent Santa Barbarans as Pearl Chase and Bernhard Hoffmann, played an important role in the Spanish revival of the 1920s, not only in the arts but also in architecture, city planning and landscaping. From the mid-1940s until just recently this was the site of the City College Adult Education Center, an appropriate use since it continued in many ways the ideals of the original Festival Arts School. The Presidio comandancia was located on the front portion of this property until it was demolished following the 1925 earthquake.

164.
Alhecama Theater
914 Santa Barbara St.
1925; Soule, Murphy & Hastings

Located in the former Adult Education Center, this theater was built as a dance and acting studio for the Festival Arts School. Known until 1940 as the Pueblo Theater, it was purchased that year by Alice Schott who changed it to Alhecama, a name derived from the first two letters of her daughters' names—Alice, Helen, Catherine and Mary Lou. The Alhecama Center property was given by Mrs. Schott for adult education use in 1946.

165.
Bonilla House
915 Santa Barbara St.
1887

Visible just in front of this modest late 19th-century cottage are the foundations for the outer defense wall of the Presidio. The house itself was built by Florentino Bonilla, a stage driver and member of José Lobero's orchestra. The house originally had a small front porch and crowning captain's walk.

166.
Moullet House
834 Santa Barbara St.
1896
1955; Jack Boydston

Built on part of the Presidio site by J.F. Moullet for his bride, this brick house, unusual in Santa Barbara, was used as a residence and tamale parlor before becoming the rented headquarters for a branch of the Chinese Nationalist Party in the 1930s. The house was remodeled for commercial purposes in 1955; the changes included replacing paired arched windows with display windows and removing the chimney.

167.
Rochin Adobe
820 Santa Barbara St.
1856   L

Although this adobe was constructed relatively late, in fact after Mexican rule had passed, its history can be traced back to the city's very founding. It was built by a fourth generation niece of Captain José Francisco Ortega, first comandante of the Presidio, using adobe bricks from the then almost entirely destroyed Presidio. Around 1900 the adobe was sheathed in clapboard and the west porch was remodeled. This was also the first example of private land ownership inside the Presidio walls. It is presently owned by a descendant of the original builder. Note just to the north, the smallish Bunya-Bunya tree and, especially, the huge cones it produces.

168.
Sloyd School Site
814 Santa Barbara St.
1893

On this site was Anna Sophia Blake's Sloyd School building. It was a typically fanciful Queen Anne design dominated by a large round tower and dome. Sloyd School, the forerunner of UCSB, was a public school with classes in manual, applied and household arts patterned after the Scandinavian method. The school soon outgrew the building and was moved to a corner of Chapala and Victoria Sts. In 1954 its descendant, UCSB, was finally relocated from the Riviera Campus (1913) to Goleta. The original building was damaged in the 1925 earthquake and demolished in 1930. A plaque now marks its approximate location.

169.
De la Guerra Court
(site of Arrellanes Adobe)
800 Santa Barbara St.
1927; Soule, Murphy & Hastings

The original adobe on this site is believed to have been the first house of significance to have been constructed outside the Presidio walls. It was built in 1795 and was later used as a residence and merchandise store. The Neighborhood House Association purchased it in 1910 and restored and remodeled it. This was one of the first restorations of a historic adobe in Santa Barbara. The adobe was heavily damaged in the 1925 earthquake. It was demolished shortly thereafter and the present structure built in its place by Alexander MacKellar for Associated Charities. The wooden columns along the front porch were originally part of the Aguirre Adobe on East Carrillo St. (see entry #136). They are among the most unusual in Santa Barbara. The headquarters of the Family Service Agency was located here until 1982.

170.
Santa Barbara Schools

   Maintenance and Operations Building
   724 Santa Barbara St.
   1929; Soule, Murphy & Hastings

Here is one of the many Spanish Colonial Revival style buildings designed by this architectural firm following the 1925 earthquake. Because of its use and location close to the center of the block this is regrettably not visited very often. It is in fact one of the most important Spanish Colonial Revival designs in Santa Barbara—for its general proportions and in its detailing.

171.
Covarrubias Adobe

   715 Santa Barbara St.
   1817
   1940; J.J. Plunkett   L, CHL
"Historic" Adobe
   ca. 1825   L

The Covarrubias adobe was built in 1817 by Domingo Carrillo for his bride, Concepción Pico, sister of Governor Pio Pico. José Maria Covarrubias acquired it in 1853, the year after Don José had gone east to deliver California's first electoral vote for Franklin Pierce. The building is a California Historic Landmark. Interesting architectural features of this L-shaped adobe include, on the interior, a 55' long "sala" or main hall, and, on the exterior, massive adobe buttresses and a chimney, which were added in 1940 by the Rancheros Visitadores and give the adobe a monumental appearance. This, with the adjacent "Historic" Adobe and the headquarters building form the Historical Society complex. John Southworth moved the "Historic" Adobe from the 900 block of Anacapa St. in 1921. It was used as a studio, and is now the Rancheros Visitadores headquarters. Note the California pepper trees (Schinus molle) adjacent to the "Historic" Adobe.

172.
Gonzales-Castro House
228 E. De la Guerra St.
1883

Ramon Gonzales built this typical Italianate wood frame home next to an adobe dwelling which extended part way into the De la Guerra St. right-of-way. What appears to be a well casing can be seen at the edge of the hill, where the earlier buildings stood before the streets were graded. The Gonzales family owned portions of several city blocks in this vicinity. A red tile roof was applied to the house in about 1930. Members of the Castro family, long active in Old Spanish Days Fiestas, have lived here for nearly 50 years.

173.
Presidio Springs
705-721 Laguna St.
1977; Kruger-Bensen-Ziemer

The name of this city-built housing complex for the elderly is derived from the nearby Presidio-era springs or De la Guerra wells. It is a recent example of the Spanish Colonial Revival.

174.
Senior Center of Santa Barbara
317 E. De la Guerra St.
1952; Louise Murphy Vhay
1964, 1973; Edwards-Pitman

American Women's Volunteer Service planned these Spanish Colonial Revival cottages as apartments for the low-income elderly. Their designer was Louise Murphy Vhay, who was responsible for much of the development on this block (see entries 175, 176, 177, 178, 180). Since its construction, the complex has been a model for low-cost housing, giving the occupants privacy and a garden setting near the downtown commercial area. The units added in 1964 and 1973 by Edwards-Pitman have continued the Hispanic image of the complex. Elizabeth de Forest was responsible for the lush landscaping.

175.
Vhay Studio
809 Laguna St.
1928; Louise Murphy Vhay
1941; V. Van Akin

As with so many buildings in this area, this house was designed by Mrs. Vhay, a wealthy Santa Barbara benefactor and artist. She planned this Hispanic house as her studio.

176.
Gonzales-Ramirez Adobe
825 Laguna St.
ca. 1825
1923; Louise Murphy Vhay
1956   NHL, NR, L

When this adobe was constructed in the 1820s by Rafael Gonzales for his Italian bride, this area of the pueblo was known as "Las Isletas" due to the many small areas of high ground which were surrounded by swamps, part of the lagoon after which the street is named. Gonzales was the *alcalde* or mayor of Santa Barbara in 1829. The adobe was later owned by Cristobal and Ventura Ramirez, the daughter and son-in-law of Rafael Gonzales. The house was then restored and enlarged by Louise Murphy Vhay. Considered a classical example of California's adobe tradition, the house was one of only six selected in 1937 by the Historic American Building Survey as typifying that tradition.

177.
Pedotti House
>322 E. Cañon Perdido St.
>1926; Louise Murphy Vhay
>1956; Lutah Maria Riggs

The main portion of this residence was built by Louise Murphy Vhay who also built the house to the west. It is said that the bricks and doors for the building came from the second Arlington Hotel after it was demolished following the 1925 earthquake. In 1956 an addition extended the house to the street line. This dwelling represents a delightful Californio-style urban oasis, along with its neighbors to the west and northeast.

178.
Vhay-Hyde House
>312 E. Cañon Perdido St.
>1932-33; Robert M. Hyde
>1952; Barbara Parker Ray

A portion of this authentic appearing apartment was originally constructed as a storage building by Louise Murphy Vhay, owner of much of the block. She was also a writer on Mexican colonial architecture, member of the Community Arts Plans and Planting Committee, creator of the art colony between De la Guerra and Cañon Perdido Sts., and creator of the "El Caserio" complex nearby. In 1933 Robert Hyde constructed a dwelling to the rear, and in 1952 another owner connected the two buildings. Architecturally, this house continues Santa Barbara's adobe tradition.

179.
Grocery Store
(Offices)
301 E. Cañon Perdido St.
ca. 1898   SoM

Originally constructed a block to the west, this wooden building with its semi-circular false front is a rare remaining example of a neighborhood grocery store of the turn of the century. While this area is now almost entirely commercial, it was originally a Hispanic residential area with this building serving as the social and commercial center. It has also been used as a dance hall, a gift shop, and a restaurant. The lush landscaping to the east does much to recapture the almost rural atmosphere of this area a century ago.

The trees in the 200-500 blocks of E. Cañon Perdido St. are Snowy Fleece trees (Melaleuca genistifolia) and Prickly-leaved Paperback trees (Melaleuca styphelioides). The latter are unusual for their white, sponge-like bark.

180.
Tiers-Peake-Schott House
820 Garden St.
1953-54; Louise Murphy Vhay

This secluded, late Spanish Colonial Revival house was designed by Louise Murphy Vhay. It was built for Alex Tiers, a designer, and later owned by Channing Peake, an artist, and Alice F. Schott, an important Santa Barbara benefactor.

181.
Cordero Adobe
906 Garden St.
ca. 1855
1969; Paul Soderburg   L

This adobe, the only one existing of several owned by the large Cordero family, is hidden by board and batten siding and by a garden screening it from the street. Members of the José Cordero family resided in it until about 1940. Mrs. Lyla M. Harcoff restored the house, and the next owners landscaped the grounds. The adobe and garage were converted to offices in 1959, and the siding applied ten years later.

182.
El Caserio
924 Garden St.
1930-37; Louise Murphy Vhay, J.J. Plunkett, Lutah Maria Riggs (various remodelings)

This picturesque grouping of seven Spanish Colonial Revival studios and bungalows has sometimes been called the Greenwich Village of Santa Barbara. Since its construction it has been associated with such artists as John Gamble, Don Freeman, William Hesthal, as well as the designer J.J. Plunkett, the furniture designer Paul Tuttle, and the descendants of Col. W.W. Hollister, who used two of the studios as their townhouses in the 1950s.

183.
Jewel Apartments
(Old Raffour House)
329 E. Carrillo St.
ca. 1887

Originally located on the site of the present City Hall, the Raffour House was built by Louis Raffour, a French diplomat turned restaurateur and hotel keeper. The site was purchased by the city in 1923, and the old Italianate-style hotel was sawn in half. Part of the building was then moved to its present site, stuccoed over, and converted into apartments.

184.
Office and Residential Building
1027 Garden St.
1983-84; Lenvik and Minor

This is a three-story Hispanic design which includes a ground level garage, offices on the second level, and a residence above.

185.
Spiritualist Association Church of the Comforter
1028 Garden St.
1921
1932; J.H. Weston

Originally a print shop and grocery store, this unusual building was remodeled in 1932 into a synagogue by the B'Nai B'Rith Congregation. The spiritualists, whose history in Santa Barbara can be traced back to 1874, purchased the building in 1950. Spiritualism was quite popular in the 1870s, and a newspaper account of a Santa Barbara seance in 1876 describes a typical evening: "A guitar was plained in the air, faces of various kinds appeared at the windows of the cabinet, and nearly every person had some communication with a departed friend, and various phenomena were witnessed that were inexplicable except on the hypothesis of spiritual manifestations." The building is unusual architecturally for its attractive vintage sign and assymetrical false front façade.

186.
Brownsill House #2
1116 Garden St.
1889

Although the first story has been extensively altered, the second still features the fishscale siding and decorated bargeboard on the front gable, characteristic of the Eastlake and Queen Anne styles of the 1880s.

149

187.
Holland Cottage
307 Lloyd Ave.
1883

This is a modest example of the Italianate style with brackets and lintels reduced to a minimum, an L-shaped plan and corner porch. The raised floor level makes it somewhat unusual in the area. This house was built by Arthur Holland, listed as a capitalist in the city directory.

188.
Maguire Bungalows
1122-1126 Garden St.
1916

These three Craftsman bungalows are relatively unaltered examples of the speculative housing of the 1910s. Hundreds of just such modest houses were constructed in Southern California and Santa Barbara during that decade. The trio of bungalows was built by Henry F. Maguire, who lived around the corner in the Italianate house at 307 Lloyd Avenue.

189.
First United Methodist Church
305 E. Anapamu St.
1926; Thomas P. Barber

This church is in a Romanesque style with a campanile and a large rose window over the central entrance. It was constructed in 1926 after the previous church had been destroyed in the earthquake. It is the work of a Los Angeles architect, Thomas P. Barber. Note the huge redwood located in the churchyard and dedicated to Dr. Charles Stoddard.

190.
Wood-Lockhart Cottage
328 E. Anapamu St.
1888

This is a relatively late example of an Italianate cottage. Typical features include the square bay window, the paired brackets, and shiplap siding. Very well maintained, this house has an especially attractive façade. It was built by Mary C.F. Wood, who purchased the lot from Clio Lloyd.

The magnificent rows of Stone Pine trees (Pinus pinea) in the 300-800 blocks of E. Anapamu St. were planted in 1908 and 1929 and derived their name from their edible, stone-like nuts.

191.
Dutton Cottage
1219 Laguna St.
1878

This house is similar to many artisan cottages built for working class families in the 1880s and 1890s. The delicate turned-work on the porch columns and supports is of particular interest. It was built for J.R. Dutton.

192.
Colonial Revival Cottage
1236 Garden St.
1899

Unusual architectural features of this early Colonial Revival cottage include the off-center bay and the tiny Palladian window above in the pedimented gable. Lida Conrad was the first owner.

193.
Hardy House
1332 Garden St.
1886

This is a simple hipped roof house of the 1880s with flattened arches over the windows and an Italianate-inspired square bay window. The side entrance and single column were probably added in the 1890s in an attempt to modernize it in the then-popular Colonial Revival style. It was built for Albert Hardy, a capitalist.

194.
Virginia Hotel
17 W. Haley St.
1916
1922
1926; C.K. Denman

The original Virginia Hotel was a two-story structure constructed in 1916 with Charles Maas as the proprietor. A three-story building was erected in 1922. It was advertised in that year's city directory as the "Headquarters for Commercial Men. Newly Built, Fire Proof, Modern in Every Respect." Although the hotel may have been fireproof, it was not earthquake-proof, as was demonstrated in 1925. Both the east and west walls fell, as well as the cornice. The building was rebuilt in 1926 in the Spanish Colonial Revival style. Unusual features include the twisted columns on the third story and the flanking arched windows.

195.
Salvation Army Building
(Studio)
33 W. Haley St.
(United Pentecostal Church)
35 W. Haley St.
1926; Soule, Murphy & Hastings

This post-earthquake two-story building has many typical Spanish Colonial Revival features of the 1920s including arched windows, wrought-iron detailing, round bullseye windows, and a low-pitched, hipped roof. It concludes a streetscape of substantial commercial buildings illustrating the style. The Salvation Army originally built this structure as an auditorium and gymnasium.

196.
S.B. Tobacco Co. Building
(Auto Services)
317 Chapala St.
1926; Soule, Murphy & Hastings

Unusual details of this shoebox-like building include the double arched façade with engaged Ionic columns and scalloped, corbelling decoration above. It shows how with a minimal effort a basically ordinary building type can be made visually interesting.

BRINKERHOFF AVENUE LANDMARK DISTRICT

The houses at 501, 505 and 509 Chapala Street are located in the Brinkerhoff Avenue Landmark District, centered on Brinkerhoff Avenue in City Block 231. This second landmark district was established in 1982; its earliest houses were constructed in 1887. All of the antique and gift shops, galleries and homes share a turn-of-the-century ambience. Major architectural styles found in the Brinkerhoff district are Italianate, Eastlake (Stick), Colonial Revival, and Queen Anne.

197.
Frank B. Smith House
501 Chapala St.
1895-96   SoM

This relatively ornate house was built in the late nineteenth century by Frank B. Smith, agent for the Pacific Coast Steam Ship Company. Although it has been used for a variety of purposes, the house is relatively unaltered on the exterior and the interior first floor. The octagonal tower and corner square bay are particularly good examples of the Queen Anne style.

198.
Fred Whaley Tire Co.
(Firestone Store)
506 Chapala St.
1930; The Austin Company

The automobile influenced the design of commercial buildings in the 1920s, and led to a wide variety of examples of drive-in architecture. One of the most popular forms was the L-shaped building, placed on a street corner with parking provided between the two arms of the building. In Southern California, drive-in markets and auto stores of one kind or another frequently use this form. The Firestone building is a characteristic example of this form, and in addition it is one of the few examples of Art Deco Moderne in downtown Santa Barbara. Fred Whaley was the Firestone distributor in the early 1930s.

199.
Levy House and Dancaster House
(New House)
505 and 509 Chapala St.
1887; 1888

These houses were constructed during a building boom in Santa Barbara which occurred after the railroad reached the city from Los Angeles. Mrs. Sarah Levy was the original owner of 505. F.H. Dancaster owned 509. Both houses, which were joined in the 1960s, display the typical Italianate style of architecture: 505 has a particularly characteristic off-center bay window; 509 has the more usual cubical massing and low hipped roof associated with that style. New House rehabilitation services for men was established at 509 Chapala in 1955 and was expanded next door three years later.

200.
Dal Pozzo's Tire Corporation
530 Chapala St.
1930; Roland F. Sauter

By 1930, when this building was constructed, Chapala St. was changing from residential to commercial, especially auto-related, uses. The architect, Sauter, designed the building in a stripped-down Spanish Colonial Revival style. Decorative Spanish details include the octagonal tower and the scalloped relief molding. Although essentially Hispanic in design, there is a touch of 1920s Art Deco Moderne in this L-shaped corner building.

201.
C & H Chevrolet
614 Chapala St.
1946; A. Godfrey Bailey,
  Soule & Murphy (associate architects)

This Streamlined Moderne Building was constructed after World War II as a public garage and salesroom for George C. Young, the Chevrolet dealer. It has continued in that function to the present day. Architecturally, the building is a rare example in Santa Barbara of an architectural style—the Streamlined Moderne—which never really caught on. But even here, a vestige of Spanish Colonial Revival architecture survives in the tiled roof.

202.
Sherman House

(Somerset Restaurant)
625 Chapala St.
1877   SoM

Charles E. Sherman, the original owner and builder of this house, was a wholesale and retail butcher with a meat market a block away at 646 State St. Later, in the 1880s, he was Sheriff of Santa Barbara County. His house is a typical L-shaped, story-and-a-half Italianate structure of the mid-1870s. It has been converted into a restaurant.

203.
Shops

(Elkhorn Creamery)
17-21 W. Ortega St.
1905-06

One of Santa Barbara's rare remaining Mission Revival style commercial buildings, this small gem was erected for the owner of the Fithian Building at the corner of State and West Ortega Streets. In the same year R. Barrett Fithian constructed a two-story building to the east, with Francis W. Wilson as architect. It was demolished following the 1925 earthquake, but the creamery building survived. Over the years, several service firms and a tavern have occupied the simple Mission Revival building.

204.
Barclay's Bank

900 Chapala St.
1968; Kruger-Bensen-Ziemer

Although the Brutalist mode of architecture popular in the 1960s is rare in Santa Barbara, this building demonstrates some of the characteristics of that style with its exposed concrete and general heaviness. It does, however, also have a typically Santa Barbara red tile roof.

205.
Hollister Estate Office Building
911 Chapala St.
1931; Edwards & Plunkett

This adobe-like building was built by the descendants of Col. W.W. Hollister in 1930. Although Hollister died in 1886, his family continued to exert considerable influence in Santa Barbara well into the 20th century. Now used as a realty office, the building was occupied by pediatric physicians for several years.

206.
Crawford Building
919 Chapala St.
1936; Soule & Murphy

This miniscule office building boasts two squat Doric columns and a tiny red tiled roof. It was originally constructed for James D. Crawford, a realtor, and has been little altered since.

207.
Old YMCA and Tree of Light
110 W. Carrillo St.
1913; Winsor Soule with Russel Ray

L (tree)

From 1913 to 1960 this building housed Santa Barbara's YMCA. Architecturally, it is an interesting combination of the Mission Revival mode with some elements borrowed from Tuscan architecture of northern Italy. The Norfolk Island Star Pine (Araucaria excelsa) located at the corner is an official City Landmark tree. It was planted in 1878 by Dr. Robert Winchester. Winchester was then living on this site in an adobe which had been constructed in the 1850s by José Lobero, founder of the Lobero Theatre (see #125). The adobe was later used as Col. W.W. Hollister's city residence. It was torn down in 1911 to make way for the present building.

208.
De Riviera Hotel
125 W. Carrillo St.
1915   SoM

This hotel was originally constructed by Norwegian immigrants. Little altered, the building is a good example of the Craftsman ethic with its emphasis on natural materials, sheltering landscaping, and general informality.

209.
St. Vincent's School and Orphanage Knights of Columbus Hall
(Offices)
925 De la Vina St.
1874-75; A. Marquis
1983; Rolly Pulaski and Assoc.   NR, L

The Knights of Columbus Hall is generally considered Santa Barbara's finest surviving Anglo-American building of the 19th century. It was constructed in 1874-75 by the Catholic Order of the Daughters of Charity of St. Vincent de Paul as a girls' school. The Sisters had arrived from their Provincial House in Emmitsburg, Maryland, in 1856 and were originally housed in the Aguirre Adobe (see entry #136). There the predominantly Catholic-Irish Sisters ran a day and boarding school for the Catholic-Hispanic children of the town. In the 1860s the school acquired its present Cieneguitas Ranch site, then beyond the edge ot town. The tuition at the school was $150 per year, payable half-yearly in advance. In 1869-70 a building was constructed downtown, only to burn in 1874. Funds raised from the Mother house in Maryland allowed construction of a new building to begin immediately. This structure was originally three stories and of Italianate design. The third story was removed following the 1925 earthquake. Fortunately, the children had been moved the previous year to a new school on the Cieneguitas Ranch. The local Knights of Columbus lodge occupied the building from 1924 to 1980. The building has undergone renovation and is being used for offices. Architecturally, the edifice is a good example of the Italianate style popular in the 1860s and 1870s. The emphasis is on the vertical with windows recessed beneath segmental and flat hoods, a prominent cornice, and a projecting and pedimented entrance porch. There are two large sandstone hitching blocks on the De la Vina St. frontage, used for tying one's horse in pre-automobile days.

210.
Poor Richard's Pub
(Rusty's Pizza Parlor)
232 W. Carrillo St.
1971; Richard Headley

This unusual building is a close copy of an early 16th-century English farmhouse. Although somewhat out of place in Hispanic Santa Barbara, its fidelity to history and original construction methods makes it an interesting architectural folly, a monument to the aesthetics of its designer.

211.
The Office Mart
222 W. Carrillo St.
1927; G.H. Jacobs

This is an exceptionally late example of the Mission Revival style which flourished in Santa Barbara from the late 1890s through the early 1910s. One of the distinguishing features of this style was the use of Mission-style towers, well exemplified in this building. It was originally constructed for the Knights of Pythias lodge and later became the Carrillo Auditorium.

212.
Carrillo Hotel
31 W. Carrillo St.
1923; Marston, Van Pelt & Maybury

The 200-room Carrillo Hotel opened for business on Christmas day, 1923. It was praised at the time as having "nothing garish, nothing ornate...no ledges laden with gingerbread, no meaningless ornaments, no grinning faces or posing chiseled figures. It's just plain beauty." This was partially because the Pasadena architects "worked in harmony with suggestions outlined by the Community Arts." (The architects also designed the nearby Carrillo Building on State St.). The building's concrete construction enabled it to survive the 1925 earthquake with only minimal damage. It has been converted into a retirement hotel.

213.
Office Building
15 W. Carrillo St.
1930; Edwards & Plunkett

The architects of this building have broken up the relatively long façade through the use of an off-center entry and irregular arch window placement. Attorneys have occupied offices here since the building's construction, and Old Spanish Days had an office here in the 1930s.

214.
All-American Sporting Goods
1025 Chapala St.
1926; Edwards, Plunkett & Howell

Although the first story of this building has been considerably altered, the second story and red tile roof are typical of the 1920s architecture in Santa Barbara. It was occupied by the Hunt Mercantile Co. and a market for five years, then by the Piggly Wiggly grocery.

215.
City Meat Market
1104 Chapala St.
1929-1930; Roland F. Sauter

This is one of the oldest remaining drive-in markets in downtown Santa Barbara. The small scale and slight Spanish touches are typical of a building type which came into being only in the 1920s.

216.
Santa Barbara Club Building
1105 Chapala St.
1903-1904; Francis W. Wilson

The Santa Barbara Club was founded in 1892 by such prominent community leaders as W.W. Hollister, D.W. Thompson, and Joel R. Fithian. Larger quarters were soon needed and the present club building was constructed. It is a neo-classical design with cornice, egg and dart moldings, pilasters and lintels over the windows. This style, derived from Italian Renaissance palazzos, was popularized by the New York architectural firm of McKim, Mead and White, and soon became *de rigueur* for establishments such as this. Note, in particular, the unusual arched entrance with its Palladian-style side windows. The formal entrance porch was removed in the summer of 1925 to provide for widening of Chapala St.

217.
Office Building
1123 Chapala St.
1984; Sharpe, Mahan and Associates

A really grand tiled dome tower looks down on the raised entrance terrace of this Hispanic building. A parking garage occurs on the ground level, and two floors of offices are above.

218.
Office and Residential Building
101 W. Anapamu St.
1983-84; Ketzel and Goodman

Though this Hispanic building is not large, the reduced scale of its parts conveys a feeling that it is of appreciable size. Particularly successful is the treatment of the ground level parking garage on the west side of the building.

219.
San Marcos Garage
(Davis Arcade Building)
25 W. Anapamu St.
1923

Although originally a garage for the adjacent San Marcos building, this structure shows the adherence to the Spanish Colonial Revival in the early 1920s even before the earthquake of 1925.

220.
Wall and Entrance
North side of Anapamu St., between State and Chapala Sts.
1983; Mahan and Associates (William Mahan)

This wall with its arched openings conveys a 19th-century adobe feeling, with its painted brick surfaces. Do note the stone cat peering from the top of the wall. The tile "Anapamu" plaque with Chumash designs was designed by Judy Sutcliffe.

221.
Jordanos'

(El Torre Office Building)
104 W. Anapamu St.
1957; Candreva & Jarrett
1981; Barry Architectural Design Group

The main portion of this building was originally a Jordanos' supermarket. Its design was an exuberant 1950s Modern, with emphasis on the sign and entrance canopy. It has recently been Hispanicized with white stucco, red tile and a square tower. It represents two contemporary trends in Santa Barbara architecture: an office building boom and a new phase of the Spanish Colonial Revival.

222.
City Land Use Controls Office

1235 Chapala St.
1922; H.C. Weeks

Although this building is of some interest architecturally due to its yellowish brick and general Mediterranean styling, its main significance is historical. The building was constructed as the administration building for the Santa Barbara schools, and it served in that capacity for many years. Santa Barbara High School and Junior High School occupied the remainder of the block. The main high school building at De la Vina and West Anapamu Sts. was destroyed in the 1925 earthquake; this, and a similar structure to the rear, are all that remain of the old school facilities. In the mid-1960s the property was acquired by the City of Santa Barbara.

223.
First Baptist Church

(Office Building and Victoria Street Theatre)
1236 Chapala St. and 33 W. Victoria St.
1910, 1921; Norman F. Marsh   **SoM**

This Tudor Revival church complex was constructed in two stages. The rear portion, originally the chapel and kindergarten, exhibits such Tudor elements as half-timbering and steeply pitched roofs. The main portion is dominated by a squat three-story tower with buttresses, lancet windows and stained glass in a Gothic Revival style.

224.
Dr. Myra Sperry House and Office
(Commercial building)
21 W. Victoria St.
ca. 1900

This building was originally a Craftsman house with some Colonial Revival detailing. It has since been stuccoed over and converted into a retail store and restaurant. Note the classical Colonial Revival triple windows on the side. Dr. Sperry, an osteopathic physician, had her office and residence here for 20 years after 1903.

225.
Battistone Foundation Senior Housing
1325 Chapala St.
1983; Edwards-Pitman

This complex is an early 1980s version of the bungalow court tradition of the 'teens and 1920s. A pergola entrance leads into the principal common garden space. Each unit has its own small patio, and to the north the units facing the street hide their patios behind a handsome Spanish stucco wall. These 1982-83 units replace an early Spanish bungalow court which was built in 1917.

226.
The Edgerly Hotel
105 W. Sola St.
1913; Arthur B. Benton

The Edgerly is one of Santa Barbara's oldest and largest residential hotels. It sits on the site of an earlier three-story hostelry known as Harrison House, which was developed in the mid-1880s. When the Edgerly opened, it housed many employees and actors of the American Film Company (see entry #232). Architecturally, the hotel is representative of the late 19th-, early 20th-century interest in wooden structures expressed as skeletons. That effect is achieved on this Craftsman style building chiefly through the half-timbering on the massive overhanging two-story balcony. According to Davis' Commercial Encyclopedia of the Pacific Southwest, Nelson Millett made suggestions to the architect which formed the basis for this design.

227.
Mortimer Cook House
1407 Chapala St.
1872; Peter J. Barber   L

The Cook House, Santa Barbara's finest remaining example of the Italianate style, has a history that reflects, in microcosm, the flamboyant Victorian era. As with many of the larger Italianate houses Barber designed, the Cook House boasts a splendid central cupola. Mortimer Cook, a native of Ohio, lived in Santa Barbara for about a decade, but in that short time he managed to create and also to lose a small fortune. Shortly after he arrived in 1871, he opened a private bank; a year later he established the First National Gold Bank with Amasa Lincoln, owner of the Lincoln House (still standing as The Upham Hotel at 1404 De la Vina St.). In 1874 banker Cook entered politics and was elected town mayor. That same year the First National Gold Bank purchased land on the northwest corner of State and Canon Perdido Sts. and began construction of a three-story Italianate brick bank and office building, completed in 1876. By this time Cook was more interested in real estate development than in banking, and in 1876 he undertook construction of the town's largest building on the corner of Carrillo and State Sts. (the Upper Clock Building). Cook, however, was about to meet his nemesis. Financially overextended, he suffered heavy losses in the 1877 panic. Shortly thereafter he sold his assets and moved to Washington state, where he set up a shingle mill.

In the early 1880s, Joseph W. Cooper, owner of the Santa Rosa Rancho and one-time director of the Commercial Bank, purchased the house. It remained in the Cooper family for about 30 years. Neither Cooper nor subsequent owners, however, has so impressed Santa Barbarans as did the house's heady original owner; and the Mortimer Cook story seems destined to remain as impressive as the house, a City Landmark.

228.
Thompson House
(Santa Barbara Board of Realtors)
1415 Chapala St.
1906

This two-story American Colonial Revival house was constructed for Nancy P. Thompson, widow of Dixey W. Thompson, a prominent 19th-century businessman. Before 1906 the site was part of the Cooper Estate (see entry #227). Except for the first-story window alterations and the added exterior stairway, the house is a good example of its style, which was popular at the turn of the century. Mrs. Thompson lived here until 1927. Since then the house has had only two other owners: the Foursquare Gospel Church (1929-1955) and the Board of Realtors (1956-present).

229.
Medical Arts Building
1421 Chapala St.
1926; Edwards and Plunkett

The handsome tripartite arched arcade and formal landscape of this Spanish Colonial Revival building suggest an elegant residence. The building, however, was designed for use as medical offices for original owner, Dr. Horace F. Pierce. Several additions have been made to the rear since it was built in 1926, but the impressive façade remains unaltered.

230.
Turn-of-the-Century Streetscape
20, 30, 32 and 36 W. Valerio St.
1887-1903

West of State St. along this block sit four, two-story houses that present passersby with a glimpse of one of Santa Barbara's middle-class residential neighborhoods much as it appeared at the turn of the century. A stately and tastefully ornamented Italianate/Eastlake (20 W. Valerio) is followed by two restrained Colonial Revival style houses (30 and 32 W. Valerio); a Queen Anne/Eastlake which stands sentry-like on the west corner (36 W. Valerio) has a fanciful, pagoda-influenced front porch.

For many years the 1887 Lunt House at 20 W. Valerio has been the home of J.J. Callahan, former city councilman and county supervisor. The Herbert House at 30 W. was erected in 1902. The two houses closest to Chapala St. were built for the Eberle family, the house at 36 W. in 1889-90, and the one at 32 W. in 1903.

231.
Modoc Substation
11 W. Mission St.
1930; Russel Ray   SoM

This electrical power substation was specifically designed by the architect, Russel Ray, to project a residential or bungalow image. In so doing, Ray combined two architectural fashions of the 1920s, the Spanish Colonial Revival and Art Deco Moderne. Particularly noteworthy Moderne details are the repeated lightning bolt motif on the building and on the wrought iron gate.

232.
American Film Manufacturing Company site
00 W. Mission St. block
1913; J. Corbley Pool

The Mission Revival building at 34 W. Mission St. (Adams Chair Caning Shop) remains as a reminder of Santa Barbara's leading role in the early days of the film industry. In 1912, the American Film Manufacturing Company, popularly known as the Flying A Studio, purchased an ostrich farm located on this block and proceeded to build an indoor studio and a darkroom. Other buildings were added until the complex spread over the entire block as well as half of the adjacent block to the north. This surviving corner building was used as actors' waiting and dressing rooms. Behind the corner building and fronting on Chapala St. sits another surviving structure, which the film company used as a garage.

The company's production schedule was tight—two films per week. Its first film was shot on July 10, 1912, at the old Dixey Thompson ranch west of the city. Three days later the film crew set a world's record by shooting a 1,000-foot film in two hours and fifteen minutes. The film, "Stranger at Coyote," was shot at Oak Park (Alamar Avenue along Mission Creek) and was described as "a real lurid western drama." American Film producer-director-manager-writer Allan Dwan kept turning out such westerns and thrillers in Santa Barbara for the next decade. By the 1920s, however, the film industry had centralized in Hollywood.

Most of the film company buildings were demolished in the early 1940s. The Spanish Colonial Revival shops and offices at 2001-2007 State St. and 2-4 W. Mission St. were built in 1950. Intimate in scale, the shops gently step up and down the slopes of Mission and State Sts.

233.
St. Mark's Episcopal Church
(Offices)
2020 Chapala St.
ca. 1875; attributed to Peter J. Barber   L

This steeply gabled, board and batten church is Santa Barbara's best remaining example of early Gothic Revival architecture. It is also the city's second oldest extant church, outdated only by the Mission. A particularly noteworthy detail is the stylized cross design of the bargeboards, especially along the façade, where, at the apex, a simple quatrefoil is flanked by two circles. At one time a tall spire rose from the belfry. Presumably it was lost in one of the building's several moves, for in its century-plus existence, the church has served four different congregations in three different locations. In the early 1970s the church was converted into design studios, then in 1984 into offices, but one can hardly tell from the remarkably well preserved exterior and the beautifully landscaped setting. In January 1982 the building was designated a City Landmark.

The Mission area, circa 1890, with three houses in the 2000 block of Anacapa Street shown in the center foreground.

MISSION AREA

In *Two Years Before the Mast,* published in 1835, Richard Henry Dana described Mission Santa Barbara, which he had seen a few years earlier, as standing,

> a little back of the town...a large building, or rather collection of buildings, in the center of which is a high tower with a belfry of five bells. The whole being plastered, makes quite a show at distance, and is the mark by which vessels come to anchor.

With little change, although by 1835 the Mission had two bell towers, the same view met the eyes of all nineteenth-century travelers who arrived at Santa Barbara on seagoing vessels. "The town," Dana continued,

> is composed of one-story houses, built of sun-baked clay, or adobe, some of them whitewashed, with red tiles on the roofs. I should judge that there were about a hundred of them; and in the midst of them stands the presidio, or fort, built of the same material and apparently but little stronger. The town is finely situated, with a bay in front and amphitheater of hills beyond.

This is, without doubt, the image of past idyllic beauty that captivated those who first sought to guide Santa Barbara's twentieth-century architectural and spatial development. The focal points of this image, the Presidio and the Mission, are, of course, symbols of the California lifestyle and culture that made the Southwest regionally distinct.

From 1786 until the mid-nineteenth century, the Mission complex stood alone overlooking the Presidio and dusty pueblo. Fr. Fermin Lasuen, OFM, chose this particular site for the Mission not because of its natural beauty but because it was a sufficient distance from the Presidio to mitigate the corrupting influence of the soldiers yet close enough to enjoy the benefits of their protective sphere. The Mission is located on the former site of a Chumash rancheria, Taynayan; and the Christianized Chumash, who provided the labor necessary to build the religious compound, continued to live in a small village of adobe shelters located west of the Mission entrance. Orchards of fruit and olive trees grew in the area which is now the southern part of Mission Historical Park (entry #235). Workers tended a large garden planted south of the Chumash village, occupying an area now roughly bounded by Mission, Garden, East Los Olivos, and Santa Barbara Streets. And grain fields, mostly wheat, stretched west and north of the Mission.

The orchards and garden were irrigated with water supplied by the Mission water system, a portion of which is now incorporated into Mission Historical Park. A native sandstone dam built in Mission Canyon in 1806 is still standing; it is now a part of the Botanic Garden, located one mile north of the Museum of Natural History. Water from the Mission Canyon dam ran through an aqueduct to a filter house, also still standing, east of the Mission, near the juncture of East Los Olivos Street and Mountain Drive. The filtered water ran into a reservoir located near the intersection of Alameda Padre Serra and East Los Olivos Street, and the reservoir still stores water for the city water system.

After the Mexican government secularized the missions in the 1830s, the Santa Barbara complex ceased to function as a self-sustaining communal society. Mission lands were confiscated and divided up, eventually passing into private ownership. Without land, the Mission community could not carry on its agricultural and related cottage-industry pursuits, but the friars were allowed to continue their religious duties.

In 1874, Messrs. Van Vactor and Myers began to subdivide the area, but the first private residence did not appear until 1880 when Don Gaspar Oreña built a mansion southeast of the Mission, where Roosevelt School is now located. A few years later Lucy Noyes Brinkerhoff, widow of Dr. Samuel Brinkerhoff, built "The Olives" on part of the Mission's former garden site. These elegant dwellings were both demolished many years ago, but their appearance seems to have set the residential character for the area. During the next five decades many of Santa Barbara's socially prominent citizens built homes, and in some cases second or summer homes, in this neighborhood. Between 1890 and 1930 much of the land near the Mission was privately developed. Two of the most architecturally distinguished developments, Crocker Row (entry #252) and Plaza Rubio (entry #236), were undertaken with the Mission setting in mind. Several Mission-related buildings are also located in this area: St. Anthony's Seminary (entry #248), the Monastery of Poor Clares (entry #251), and Junipero Serra Hall (entry #247).

Another group of architecturally notable buildings, the Museum of Natural History complex (entry #240) and St. Mary's Retreat (entry #238), are historically linked. The museum began as the dream of ornithologist William Leon Dawson, who spent his lifetime collecting and studying birds' eggs. Dawson housed his sizable collection in a small cottage north of St. Anthony's Seminary and near Mission Creek. In 1917, he and several other Santa Barbara nature lovers formally associated for the purpose of establishing a natural history museum. Dawson's dream became reality in 1922 when his neighbor, Caroline Hazard, who also sat on the fledgling museum's board, decided that the family estate would be a fitting site. She and her sister-in-law not only donated a portion of the Hazard estate to the cause, but they financed construction of the museum's first buildings as well. The museum is considered to be one of the finest small natural history museums in the United States.

In 1926, Caroline Hazard once again involved herself in an effort to preserve local history when she joined Mrs. Joseph Andrews and several other women to purchase land south of and adjacent to the Mission. Their purpose was to see the spot turned into a park before it could be claimed for residential development. In the same year Anna Blaksley Bliss purchased a parcel of canyon land located further up Mission Canyon in order to prevent developers from proceeding with plans to build houses in that area. She donated the parcel to the public for use as a botanic garden, originally placing it under the aegis of the Museum of Natural History. Thus, through the timely efforts of several Santa Barbara women who had the financial means to demonstrate their civic concerns, Santa Barbara has preserved much of the natural setting and natural history that complement the architecture and cultural history of the Mission.

While the overall character of the Mission area has changed very little since the turn of the century, some older residences have been demolished. Other estates, as well as the convent of the Sisters of Notre Dame de Namur, were homes on smaller lots. Nonetheless, population and building densities remain low here, and many buildings in this neighborhood enhance the city's Hispanic image. Some of the city's most beautiful examples of stonemasonry are also found in this area, including the stone arch bridge over Mission Creek (entry #239) and the Junipero Plaza gates (entry #241).

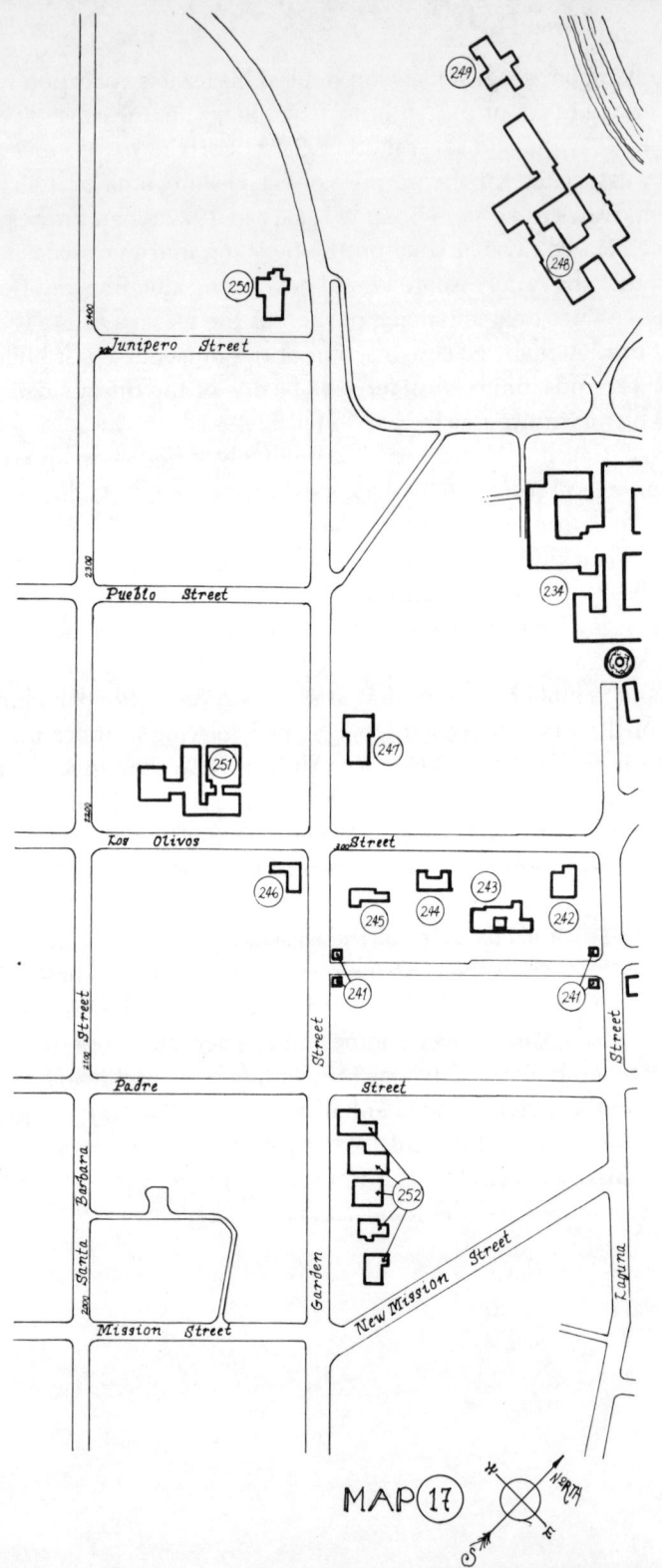

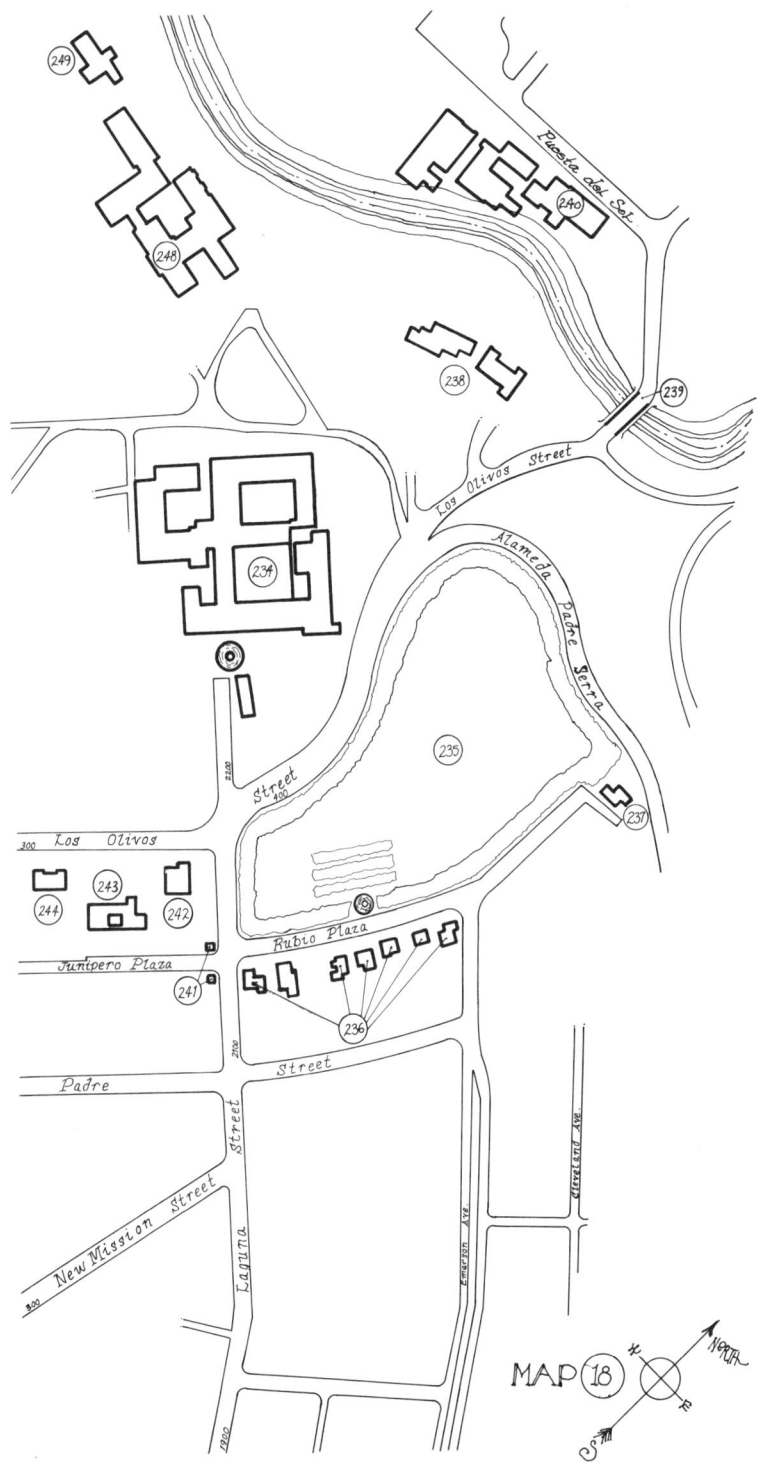

234.
Mission Santa Barbara

Laguna St. at East Los Olivos St.
1815-1820; 1833   NHL, NR, CHL, L

Established in 1786, four years after the Presidio, the Mission was located some distance from the fortress, at the insistence of the padres, in order to mitigate the corrupting influence of the soldiers. The complex was built over a period of 47 years, and the physical development may be divided into three stages: wood, adobe, and stone. The original compound consisted of log buildings surrounded by a wooden stockade. These buildings accommodated the missionaries' needs in the early years, but construction of permanent adobe buildings began as soon as the wooden structures were in place. The first adobe quadrangle was built between 1787 and 1794, the second quadrangle between 1797 and 1811. No sooner had the adobe complex been completed when Santa Barbara was wracked by a severe earthquake in 1812. The complex sustained extensive damage, thus necessitating another cycle of building. The third mission, constructed in part from native sandstone, was built between 1815 and 1820, and Father Antonio Ripoll supervised construction. A second bell tower was added in 1833, the final addition that gave the Mission its present appearance. Its façade, with engaged Ionic columns, a dentilated cornice and frieze, and a crowning pediment, is based upon a plate that appears in an 18th-century Spanish edition of *The Ten Books of Architecture* by Vitruvius, a Roman architect of the 1st century B.C. José Antonio Ramirez, master mason of Mission San Luis Rey, is believed to have been in charge of carpentry and masonry. The labor was, of course, supplied by the Chumash who lived in the mission compound.

Mission Santa Barbara is the only one of California's missions that has been used continuously to the present as a house of worship. In its magnificent setting, so carefully preserved by generations of Santa Barbarans, this building truly deserves its epithet, "Queen of the Missions." It is a City Landmark, a State Historical Landmark, and a National Historic Landmark.

It is said that the two Cota Sycamores (Platanus racemosa) just outside the Mission cemetery were planted by Father O'Keefe to provide shade for the Cota sisters while they did their laundry at the nearby aqueduct.

235.
Mission Historical Park
South and east of the Mission
acquired by the city 1928-1939; 1948

CHL

After the 1925 earthquake, the Franciscan fathers were forced to sell land in order to pay for needed Mission repairs. Mrs. J.A. Andrews, for whom Plaza Rubio was designed, joined with several other socially prominent women to raise money in order to aid the city in its efforts to acquire the open land between the Mission and Plaza Rubio. Their purpose was to keep residential development from obscuring the view of the Mission's impressive southern elevation. The smaller parcel above Alameda Padre Serra was given to the city by the fathers in 1948. This portion of the park contains most of the mission-era ruins: the aqueduct and reservoir (ca. 1827), tannery (1802), gristmill (1827), filter house (1806), and pottery (1808). A lower reservoir, built in 1806 and situated next to the park, still serves the city water system.

236.
Plaza Rubio
South of Mission Historical Park
1925-26; Mary Craig

Architecturally and conceptually, this group of seven Spanish Colonial Revival houses and Mission Historical Park represent a notable early achievement in design and urban planning in Santa Barbara. Mrs. J.A. Andrews commissioned Mary Craig to design the group, giving special attention to the relationship of the individual houses to one another and to the Mission. A publicly owned paseo which was incorporated into the original subdivision design links Plaza Rubio to Padre St.

Plaza Rubio is named after Father Rubio, the last of the California missionaries to come to Santa Barbara. Parishioners so admired Fr. Rubio that they kidnapped him in 1856 in hopes that their aggressive display of affection would dissuade him from leaving the mission. They succeeded, and he lived out his life in Santa Barbara. An 1883 account describes Fr. Rubio as an "accomplished linguist and genial gentleman."

237.
Dardi-Patterson House
530 Plaza Rubio
1927; George Washington Smith

Sandstone and brick steps lead gracefully to the oversized arched entryway which opens into the courtyard of this two-story Spanish Colonial Revival residence. Sited to overlook the village-like grouping of the seven houses below, the hillside house was designed by George Washington Smith for Mrs. J.A. Andrews, who created Plaza Rubio. It was the last of the Plaza Rubio group to be built, and, along with the others, it was built by local contractors Davidson and Maitland. Mrs. Andrews' own home during this period was on Mission Ridge. She also developed property on Plaza Bonita.

238.
St. Mary's Retreat House
(next to the Mission)
505 E. Los Olivos St.
"Mission Hill" 1885
"Dial House" 1916

The one-and-two-story gabled house was constructed in 1885 for Rowland Hazard, a native of Rhode Island, after he bought the land from Dr. S.B.P. Knox. The Hazard family was locally prominent in horticulture, as evidenced by the luxuriously landscaped hill opposite 505 E. Los Olivos St. In 1916, Hazard's son, Rowland G. Hazard, built the large Tudor Revival house. The Hazards called it "Dial House" because it was situated near a sundial which Hazard Sr. had mounted in the aqueduct wall on his property. The Hazards' daughter, Caroline, retired to Santa Barbara after serving as president of Wellesley College from 1899 to 1910. She took a personal interest in community affairs, especially during the 1920s, acting as one of the group of women who assisted the city in purchasing the land that is now part of Mission Historical Park and initiating construction of the Museum of Natural History.

During World War II, Dial House was leased to the American Association of Women, who used it as a shelter for wives of wounded soldiers and for war brides. For a short time in the 1950s both houses were used by University of California, Santa Barbara, sororities. Since 1955 they have been used as a convent and a retreat house by the Anglican Sisters of the Holy Nativity.

239.
Mission Creek Bridge
(visible from creekside in Rocky Nook Park)
North of Mission Santa Barbara on
Mission Canyon Rd. at Mountain Dr.
1891; Dover and Woods

This sandstone bridge is the oldest extant bridge in Santa Barbara County. Joe Dover, the chief builder, learned to cut stone while he was in the Navy. In 1879, at the age of eighteen, he joined the crew on the U.S. Coastal Survey vessel, *McCarthy*. It was during these few years, he told an interviewer in 1922, that "he had studied the fine stonework of naval docks," and later "tried to achieve [a similar] strength and symmetry in his own work." When Dover returned to Santa Barbara in the mid-1880s, he took up stonemasonry, and this became his occupation until he died in 1930.

The nearby water trough at the corner of Mountain Dr. and East Los Olivos St. was commissioned by Mrs. G.S.J. Oliver in 1910, in memory of her husband. George Robson was the stonemason.

240.
Santa Barbara Museum of Natural History
2559 Puesta Del Sol Rd.
1922-23, 1926; Floyd E. Brewster
1927-28, 1932-33, 1934;
  Carleton M. Winslow
1938, 1953, 1956-57; Chester Carjola
1960; Chester Carjola & Frank Greer

SoM

In 1922, Caroline Hazard and her sister-in-law, Mary P. Hazard (see entry #238), gave a portion of their estate to the Museum of Oology (the study of birds' eggs) in memory of Rowland G. Hazard, who died in 1918. Construction began that same year on the original museum, which consisted of a central patio surrounded by a square of single rooms. The first large wing to be added was Indian Hall in 1926. These sections were designed by architect Floyd Brewster. Later additions included Botany Hall, Mammal Hall, and the library, constructed 1927-28; the Junior Nature Center, 1932-33; and Bird Hall and laboratories, 1934. This group constitutes one of Carleton Winslow's largest and most successful projects in Santa Barbara. Fleischmann Lecture Hall, designed by Chester Carjola, was built in 1938 with a bequest from Max C. Fleischmann. Carjola also designed the original Geology and Marine Halls, 1953, and the Gladwin Planetarium, 1956-57. The whole cluster is a beautiful example of Spanish Colonial Revival style of the 1920s. The Chase-Coggeshall Bird Habitat Hall, designed by Carjola and Greer, was added in 1960.

The unusual sandstone wall with the sawtooth top, which fronts the museum entrance and runs along the west side of Mission Canyon Rd., was constructed by Joe Dover in about 1891 (see entry #239). Dover once remarked that he considered this wall to have been his best work.

241.
Junipero Plaza Gates
   2100 block of Laguna and Garden Sts.
   (located mid-block)
   1904-05

This pair of beautiful sandstone gates marks the east and west entrances to a small, exclusive residential street located near the Mission. The Junipero Plaza tract was subdivided in early 1905 by developer Edward F.R. Vail, and the fashionable homes in the tract, along Junipero Plaza and the 300 block of East Los Olivos St., were built in the decade that followed. The stonemason who designed and built these gates is unknown, but many people practiced this craft in Santa Barbara in the late 19th and early 20th centuries. The superior workmanship and the size of these gates make them particularly noteworthy, although sandstone walls, hitching posts, and curbs are abundant in the upper east side and are familiar sights throughout the city.

The Windmill Palms (Trachycarpus fortunei) on Junipero Plaza were originally from China and are characterized by a thick mat of hair-like fiber on their slender trunks.

242.
Edwards House
   340 E. Los Olivos St.
   1911; Bliss and Faville

Although built in the same decade as the other houses along this block of East Los Olivos St., this gambrel-roofed Colonial Revival dwelling stands in contrast to the Hispanic designs of the others. It was built as a honeymoon cottage for John S. Edwards and his wife, Ruth. Edwards, his father, and his brothers were all prominent bankers in Santa Barbara.

243.
Dibblee House
   326 E. Los Olivos St.
   1909; Francis T. Underhill

Partially screened from view by a high wall, the Dibblee House is noteworthy as an early Spanish design by Francis T. Underhill, who, for a period of a decade, practiced architecture and landscape architecture in Santa Barbara. Underhill, who designed this U-plan house for his mother-in-law, Francisca de la Guerra Dibblee, successfully combined Classical and Spanish elements to create a stately and elegantly simple mansion.

244.
Vaughn House
316 E. Los Olivos St.
1914; Russel Ray and Winsor Soule

In 1914, original owners Reginald and Miriam Vaughn engaged Ray and Soule to design this large Hispanic brick and stucco home. Soule was highly accomplished in the style; and this house, which blends nicely with its more classically styled neighbor at 326 East Los Olivos St., reflects his proficiency.

245.
Dennison House
306 E. Los Olivos St.
1916; Russel Ray and Winsor Soule

The Dennison House was the last of these three impressively large Hispanic houses to be built along this block. The original owners were Mary and Charles Dennison, prominent Bostonians who owned the Dennison Paper Company. High stucco walls and wrought iron gates screen the house from view, but they also combine with the luxuriously landscaped surroundings to create a villa-like setting.

246.
Frothingham House
232 E. Los Olivos St.
1922; George Washington Smith

George Washington Smith, Santa Barbara's premier practitioner of the Spanish Colonial Revival style, designed this handsome two-story residence for original owner Brooks Frothingham. A terraced garden is located in back, between the two wings of the L-shaped house.

247.
Junipero Serra Hall
2210 Garden St.
1929-30; Ross Montgomery

This Spanish Colonial Revival meeting hall was designed by Los Angeles church architect Ross Montgomery. He received the second prize in the Plans and Planting Committee's 1929 design competition for this building. Its rectangular plan and low-pitched red tile roof suggest the earlier tradition of adobe building, a design that befits the hall's namesake. Serra Hall is, of course, named after Father Junipero Serra, the Franciscan padre who was placed in charge of all the California missions from the late 1760s until his death in 1784, and who was also present at the founding of Santa Barbara's Presidio in 1782.

The three large olive trees in the garden of Junipero Serra Hall are remnants of the original olive orchard which once occupied this area and from which the name of the street is derived.

248.
St. Anthony's Seminary
2300 Garden St.
1899-1901, Bro. Adrian Wewer, OFM
1923; 1926; 1939
1926 chapel and tower; Ross Montgomery

St. Anthony's is a complex of several elaborately detailed buildings. Spanish Colonial Revival is the dominant style; and the buildings are constructed of native sandstone, stucco over wood frame, and concrete. Ornate towers, arches, pillars, engaged columns and quoins dress the buildings, which are linked together by covered passageways. Gatepost-studded sandstone walls define and enhance the perimeter.

The seminary was founded in 1896 as the Seraphic College of St. Anthony, a boy's preparatory school. It was first located in an unused portion of the Mission, but increasing enrollments soon necessitated a separate structure. The original three-story sandstone building was enlarged in 1923 with a study hall, classrooms, and a dormitory. The 1925 earthquake severely damaged the complex, requiring that the second and third stories be rebuilt. In 1926, another new wing was added, as well as a new chapel and tower. The latter were designed by Ross Montgomery. Several other changes have been made since the 1920s, including a dormitory which was added in 1939-40, and a swimming pool, in 1945. The east kitchen wing was built in 1949.

A concrete wall along the Garden St. boundary of the property was constructed in 1909.

249. Hoffmann House

(St. Anthony's Seminary Library)
2420 Garden St.
1922; James Osborne Craig
   Florence Yoch and Lucile Council,
   landscape architects   SoM

Craig designed "Casa Santa Cruz" for Bernhard and Irene Hoffmann, leaders in the 1920s movement to encourage the creation of an Hispanic image for Santa Barbara's streetscapes. The house is one of Santa Barbara's grandest versions of the Rural Andalusian Tradition. It opens onto south and north terraces, the latter of which is perched at the brink of the hill with an extensive view of Santa Barbara's backdrop of mountains. A fragment of the Spanish gardens laid out by Pasadena landscape architects Florence Yoch and Lucile Council can still be seen west of the house.

Hoffmann, a native of Stockbridge, Massachusetts, was trained as an engineer at Cornell University, after which he held a position with the New York Telephone Company until 1916. He first came to Santa Barbara in 1920; and he and his wife soon established a winter residence here. Like many professional engineers of his generation, Hoffmann had a keen interest in the burgeoning city planning movement, and in the 1920s, he joined with others to institute Santa Barbara's first attempts to control building and development. Among the Hoffmanns' many projects were the restoration of De la Guerra Adobe and the construction of El Paseo which surrounds it, also designed by Craig. Hoffmann's civic leadership earned him the respect and admiration of many Santa Barbarans. He continued to spend part of each year in the city he helped to redesign until he died in 1949 at his summer home in Stockbridge. This house, the Hoffmanns' winter home for many years, was acquired by St. Anthony's in 1940.

250. Boyd House

2401 Garden St.
1929; George Washington Smith

We tend to associate Smith exclusively with Santa Barbara's Hispanic tradition, but he, like other architects of the time, could work as well in a variety of historic modes. The Boyd House is a story and a half French Norman Cottage, similar to others which he designed in Montecito. All of the elements of the French Norman imagery are present, but as in the case with all of his buildings, they have been simplified and highly abstracted. The house was built for Scott Lee Boyd. From 1943 until his death in 1968, Dwight Murphy, a City commissioner, palomino breeder, and Fiesta el presidente, resided here.

251.
Monastery of Poor Clares
215 E. Los Olivos St.
1929-30; Brother Leonard, designer
1956 additions and remodeling: Howell, Arendt and Mosher with Shugart and Mendes

Completing the set of mission-related buildings is the Monastery of Poor Clares. The Order of Sisters of Poor Clare came to Santa Barbara from Oakland in 1928. They purchased two houses at this location, the Stewart Edward White house and the Wingate-Culley house, both built in 1904. White, a well-known writer of Western stories, had lived off and on in Santa Barbara since the 1880s, and he and his wife occupied this house from 1904 to 1916. The following year the small delegation (six nuns) undertook the building of a chapel and monastery. Brother Leonard, who designed the building, chose the Mission Revival style, presumably to complement the architecture of Mission Santa Barbara, even though the style was no longer popular. The scalloped parapet over the chapel entrance and the deeply recessed quatrefoil and stained glass windows are particularly noteworthy details. The complex was enlarged in 1935 when a one-story convent residence was added. A seven-foot adobe wall was built around the property in 1952. In 1956 the last major changes were made. That year the Wingate-Culley house, which the sisters had used as a refectory, kitchen, and workrooms since 1930, was torn down. It was replaced by a large addition to the chapel, and the cloister was substantially altered.

252.
Crocker Row
2010-2050 Garden St.
1894-95; Arthur Page Brown

In the late 19th century, when few homes were located near the Mission, William H. Crocker of San Francisco commissioned the office of Arthur Page Brown in November 1893 to design these five houses. Brown, a San Francisco architect, had earlier designed Crocker's Nob Hill mansion. Before construction of the entire group was finished, a San Francisco newspaper advertisement listed these as "exclusive rentals for affluent winter visitors." The five houses were among the first in Santa Barbara to be designed as a group. Architecturally, they are early and excellent examples of the Mission Revival style, made popular by the California Building at the 1893 Chicago World Columbian Exposition and at the San Francisco Mid-Winter Exposition held at Golden Gate Park in 1894. In addition to the familiar scalloped parapet of the Mission Revival style, window details further distinguish these houses: a quatrefoil (in 2010), a sunburst patterned bullseye (in 2014), and pointed arched windows in four of the houses.

The 300-pound metal dog on the front lawn of 2010 Garden St. has been poised there since 1904, when the Warren Willits family moved it with them from Three Rivers, Michigan. The lifelike, but not life-sized, canine sentry was sculpted in memory of a family pet whose birthdate coincided with that of the Willits daughter. The memorialized pet, contrary to local legend, is not interred within nor buried beneath the sculpture.

SANTA BARBARA'S SURVEY OF ARCHITECTURAL AND HISTORIC RESOURCES

Mary Louise Days

This publication is based on the City of Santa Barbara's Survey of Architectural and Historic Resources. Phase I of the survey, conducted from late 1977 through May, 1979, encompassed the downtown area between U.S. Highway 101 on the west and Laguna Street on the east, and between Sola Street on the north and West Cabrillo Boulevard on the south. The project area also included the oceanfront and East Beach neighborhoods to the easterly city limits. Most of this Phase I project area is within El Pueblo Viejo Landmark District, the original portion of which was first officially recognized by the City in 1959. A number of Santa Barbara's historically and architecturally important buildings and sites are located in the district.

In late 1976, the decision was made to begin systematically recording information about the history of Santa Barbara's buildings. The City Landmarks Committee appointed a survey subcommittee to oversee the survey process. Mary Louise Days of the City Planning Division, Community Development Department, served as staff liaison and resource person. A grant of National Historic Preservation Act funds was received from the State Office of Historic Preservation, California Department of Parks and Recreation, to be matched with locally-generated services. A smaller grant was received from the City's Redevelopment Agency.

Barbara S. Henzell was retained as the survey coordinator, and also performed skillfully as the director of volunteers. Christopher H. Nelson, a graduate student at the University of California, Santa Barbara, and John Chase, then a graduate student at the University of California, Los Angeles, were engaged as assistant consultants.

Information about each building in the project area was recorded on a local form. After screening by the subcommittee, state inventory forms on nearly 300 of the structures and sites were sent to the State Office of Historic Preservation. The inventory data included construction date, designer, builder, style description, and pertinent historical information.

In early 1980, a second grant was received from the State Office of

Historic Preservation, and work commenced on the Phase II survey. Its project area extended northeasterly of the Phase I area, from Sola Street to Oak Park and the Old Mission. The grant enabled the City to contract with Christopher Nelson and Rebecca Conard, coordinator-consultants, and with John Chase, consulting architectural historian.

Using experience gained in the earlier survey, augmented by research methodology devised by the coordinators, the survey was completed in one year with the help of a limited number of volunteers. The survey subcommittee, again led by Louise Boucher, selected 300 resources to be entered on state inventory forms.

Office space was provided gratis by the Santa Barbara Trust for Historic Preservation for both surveys. Matching services in addition to the time of City employees in the Planning Division included voluntary photography services, directed by Louise Boucher, the field work of the volunteer surveyors, and the many hours put in by the survey subcommittee of the Landmarks Committee. Dr. David Gebhard and John Chase, architectural historians, trained volunteers and advised during the discussion stages of the surveys.

The Santa Barbara City Council expressed support of the survey project during both phases, and has urged that the survey continue, recognizing its value as a digest of community resources. Completion reports were written by the coordinators for both surveys and are available for study.

A list of volunteers who contributed to the success of the two Santa Barbara surveys follows:

Lynne Abbey (Mrs. Peter)
Marilyn J. Altman (Mrs. C.W.)
June Anderle (Mrs. Thomas)
Helene Beaver (Mrs. J. William)
Betty Belsher (Mrs. Leslie)
Harvey Bennett
Madeleine Benoit
David Bisol
Hal Boucher
Tom Boucher
Marjorie Boyle (Mrs. Stephen)
Sue Bradbury (Mrs. Wymond)
Kathi Brewster (Mrs. Roger)
Mary Jo Broquedis
Julia Brown

Cathie Butts (Mrs. John)
Joan Canby
Jane Carey
Annette Carrel (Mrs. Robert)
Patricia Cleek (Mrs. Charles)
Annabel Conrado
Linda Davies (Mrs. Glyn)
Phyllis Dodson (Mrs. Edward)
John Douglass
Carolyn Dukes (Mrs. C.K.)
Jan Dunbar (Mrs. William)
Maida Edwards (Mrs. Crandall)
Pat Edwards (Mrs. Blair)
Claire Engel (Mrs. John)
Ann Forrest

Tish Frizzell (Mrs. Kenneth)
Tom Fuller
Keith Gledhill
Norma Green
Paula Hamilton
Felicie Hartloff (Mrs. Paul)
Anne Heard (Mrs. John)
Karen Helgesen (Mrs. Robert)
Marcia Hodges (Mrs. Jamie Contance)
Sharon Hodges Hale
Gary Jensen
Debbie Johnstone
Ernest Jones
Ruth Kallman (Mrs. Robert)
Tom Kelly
Beverly Kirkhart (Mrs. Mark)
Janet H. Larson (Mrs. Glenn)
Henry Lenny
Orris Lewis (Mrs. Cedric)
Judy Lucky (Mrs. M. Charles)
Russ Mackensen
Claudia Madsen (Mrs. William)
Terri McKay
Gail McMahon
Ed Miller
Sherri Montgomery (Mrs. Frederick)
Majorie Nefstead (Mrs. Paul)
Kathy Nelson (Mrs. Christopher)
Vivian Obern (Mrs. George)
George Ogle
Mary Ann Ogle (Mrs. George)
Lilian O'Reilly (Mrs. Thomas)
Judy Orias (Mrs. Eduardo)
Karen Payne
Barbara Peterson (Mrs. Herbert)
Martha Petrie (Mrs. Clifford)
Diana Phillips (Mrs. Roger)
Judy Piper (Mrs. Charles)
Lois Provan (Mrs. Michael)
Cecilia Puppo (Mrs. C.D.)
Russ Pyros
Joann Rodrigue (Mrs. Michael)
Marge Schweinfurth (Mrs. Paul)
Kit Scripps (Mrs. Barry)
Pat Shields (Mrs. Jack)
Mary Standlee (Mrs. Jon)
Marie Anne Strait (Mrs. James Lynn)
Mary Thorson (Mrs. Hugh)
Donald Torbert
Gavin Townsend
Lloyd VanHorsen
Eleanor G. Vignale
Deanne Violich (Mrs. Thomas)
Harriet Von Breton
Suzanne Waldmann (Mrs. John)
Victoria Wallop (Mrs. John)
Richard S. Whitehead
Helene Willey
John Woodward
Marjorie Wurtz

ACKNOWLEDGEMENTS

City of Santa Barbara
Santa Barbara Historical Society
Santa Barbara Trust for Historic Preservation

Interns
Judy Triem   Polly Sturtevant
Paul Israel Susan Jorgensen

STREET NAME GLOSSARY

Mary Louise Days

Santa Barbara's street names are among her most fascinating assets. Most of the earliest named streets commemorate events or persons important to the heritage of the city and the state. A subsequent effort to follow the common Anglo-American policy of numbering streets was nullified. The development of residential subdivisions after both world wars led to a need for many more streets, and a significant number of these subdivisions perpetuated the Spanish-language street names found on the city's first official maps.

In January, 1851, the mayor and Common Council contracted with

Salisbury Haley to make a survey of the city. On February 1, a three-member committee on streets was appointed; its report was presented and accepted the following week. Two weeks later three men, Eugene Lies, Antonio Maria de la Guerra and Joaquin Carrillo, were appointed "a committee to name the streets about to be laid down on the map of Salisbury Haley." Haley presented his map of boundaries on April 7, 1851. The street names proposed by the committee were apparently accepted, as the August 16 minutes refer to State Street.

The Common Council then saw the necessity for an official map of the Haley survey, and in October, 1852, Vitus Wackenreuder, the county surveyor, proposed to perform the work. After delays caused by "want of a drawing board" and by complicated and unclear property ownership titles, Wackenreuder presented his maps in April, 1853. His written title report refers to "the difficult and tiresome task entrusted to me." In return for his efforts, Vitus Wackenreuder was deeded a waterfront corner property as well as City Block 287, bounded by State, Montecito, Yanonali and Anacapa Streets.

Haley-Wackenreuder Map No. 1 encompasses the area between Mission Street and San Buenaventura Street, and between Robbins Street and Canada Street. The more detailed Map No. 2 includes the area surrounded by Vineyard (now De la Vina), Gutierrez, Laguna and Victoria Streets. These are the city's basic official maps, so declared by Ordinance No. 7.

On July, 29, 1854, the Council appointed a committee of two to "correct the orthography of the names of certain streets as laid down on city maps." This could have been the result of confused spelling of some names and difficult pronunciation of others, such as "Enecapap" (Anacapa).

By the 1860s some of the Spanish words had been translated to English in official documents and maps. In 1873 a newspaper editor demanded that the Indian and Spanish names be abandoned in favor of numbers and letters of the alphabet to aid in direction-finding. This was not done; however, in 1873 and 1874 the Van Vactor and Myers subdivisions designated their streets above Mission Street as First, Second, Third, Fourth and Fifth Avenues or Streets. In late 1927 the City Council changed these street names to Padre, Los Olivos, Pueblo, Junipero and Quinto, to match the portions east of State Street. A strong effort was also made at that time to return to the use of "Estado" for State Street.

In 1900 a group of citizens had petitioned the County Board of Supervisors to name the roads leading westward from the city.

These included Ontare Road, Hope Avenue, Cieneguitas Road and Modoc Road, and most of this land is now in the city.

Post World War II subdivisions frequently used saints' names in Spanish, or Spanish words coupled with "calle" (street) or "paseo" (walkway). On Memorial Day 1948, streets at the airport were dedicated to the memory of members of the United States Army Air Force who were killed in World War II. Nine years later the municipal airport area was annexed to the city.

For many years the Planning Commission recommended approval of street names to the City Council. In the late 1960s a street name committee made up of city staff and post office representatives assumed this duty. Attempts were made to establish a policy to prevent mixed Spanish-English street names and to assure correct usage. Since the late 1970s naming of public facilities and streets has been handled by the city administrator and the appropriate departments.

The following street name glossary applies only to streets included in this book. An asterisk indicates an 1851 street.

Anacapa*—The end of the street points to Anacapa Island, one of the Channel Islands, named for the Chumash Indian term for mirage or deception, "Eneapah." Wackenreuder's Map No. 1 spells it "Enecapap" and a later map listed "Enecapa."

Anapamu*—In the Chumash tongue, "anapamu" means "rising place," a high location possessing intense supernatural power.

Arrellaga*—José Joaquin de Arrillaga, a Basque native of Spain, was twice interim governor of the Californias during the Spanish period. He was constitutional governor of Alta California from 1804 to 1814. A dedicated patriot, Arrillaga is buried at Mission Soledad in Monterey County.

Bath*—This street name was anglicized from the Spanish "Baños" shown on the 1853 map. The street led directly to the bathing beach at what is now West Beach. At the turn of the twentieth century the first of a series of public bathhouses or swimming pools named "Los Baños del Mar" was constructed at the end of West Cabrillo Boulevard.

Brinkerhoff Avenue—Dr. Samuel Brinkerhoff, a New York native, arrived in Santa Barbara in 1852 and became the community's first Anglo-American doctor. In 1857 he and Lewis Burton bought Blocks 230 and 231 from the city for twenty dollars in gold. After the doctor died in 1880, Block 231 was sold to Henry Tallant and Edward Harper, who divided it. On the official 1886 subdivision map, Brinkerhoff Avenue was the name given the street bisecting the block in memory of the popular physician.

Cabrillo Boulevard—The beach boulevard is named for Joao Rodrigues Cabrilho, a Portuguese explorer, seaman and navigator. While in the employ of Spain, his two ships discovered Alta California and Santa Barbara Channel in 1542. West Cabrillo Blvd. was developed first, in the 1890s; the eastern extension came a decade later. The two sections became known as the East and West Boulevard, although for a time in the early 1900s the westerly portion in front of the Potter Hotel was called "Esplanade del Mar." The name "Cabrillo Boulevard" with Spanish spelling became official in 1919.

Cañon Perdido*—In the Spring of 1858, the American commanding officer of the Presidio discovered that a cannon was missing from the beach. Suspecting an insurrection, Governor Mason fined the town five hundred dollars. A fiesta held on July 4 raised the money, which was to be returned to the town later. The "lost cannon," spirited away by five boys, reappeared during an 1858 storm, but it was later sold for scrap.

Carrillo*—This intersecting main street is named for the prominent early California family which intermarried with most of the other well-known California families. Its members include a comandante of the Santa Barbara Presidio, Mexican governmental deputies, mayors of Santa Barbara, and the mother of an American governor of California, Romualdo Pacheco.

Castillo*—Another of the streets laid out in 1851, Castillo begins below the hill on which was situated the Presidio's castillo, or defensive gun battery. At other times in its history the high point of land has been the site of Mispu, a Chumash village, and of "Punta del Castillo," the Dibblee family's masonry mansion. Santa Barbara City College is now located on the hill.

Chapala*—This street could be named for Lake Chapala in Mexico, or for the prison from which Governor Micheltorena recruited some of his unruly troops in the late Mexican period.

De la Guerra*—The second prominent California family for whom a street was named was that of de la Guerra ("of the war"). Captain Don José de la Guerra y Noriega was born in Spain and became the fifth comandante of the Santa Barbara Presidio. His son Pablo was a signer of the California State Constitution, a state senator and a judge. Several family members were Santa

Barbara mayors or council presidents. De la Guerra street passes in front of Casa de la Guerra, now part of El Paseo. The former family home faces Plaza de la Guerra.

Equestrian Avenue—This short street commemorates a livery stable or "horse parlors" at 225-27 Equestrian Avenue in operation during the 1890s and 1900s. The building still exists.

Figueroa*—José Figueroa was governor of Mexican Alta California from 1833 to 1835. A native Mexican, he had earlier served as comandante-general of the Sonora-Baja California district. He was sympathetic to the Indians and encouraged establishment of schools. Figueroa is buried at Santa Barbara Mission.

Garden*—Wackenreuder's Map No. 1 shows this street name in both Spanish and English, "Jardines" and "Garden." The street passes through the site of the Presidio's vegetable and fruit gardens, also called de la Guerra gardens, which were in the vicinity of Ortega and Cota Streets.

Haley*—In deference to the sea captain who surveyed the town in 1851, Santa Barbara's street naming committee named Haley Street for Salisbury Haley. Problems with the survey led to later legal and political quarrels, but the central city was developed in accordance with it.

Laguna*—On the 1853 maps a "Laguna" or "lagoon, pond" is shown in the vicinity of Laguna and Ortega Streets. Maps of the 1870s also recorded the lagoon extending from the "estero" or "estuary" to the southeast.

Lloyd Avenue—This block-long street is named for the Lloyd family, which owned property in the block. Its most prominent member was Clio Lloyd, who became mayor in 1909. He held other public positions as well.

Los Olivos—This street, called Second Avenue for many years, was renamed for the graceful olive trees in the vicinity of the Mission. The first olive trees were brought to California by the Franciscans who founded the missions.

Los Patos Way—"Pato" means "duck," and this portion of the historic Old Coast Highway, the former Highway 101, was named in 1968 for the ducks in the nearby Andree Clark Bird Refuge.

Mason*—Richard B. Mason, military governor of California from 1847 to 1849, was the official who assessed the $500 fine for the "lost cannon," so the 1851 street-naming committee christened this street in his honor.

Micheltorena*—Manuel Micheltorena (another Basque name), was Mexican governor of California from 1842 to 1845. He was faced with the unrest prevalent during the period prior to the American takeover. Micheltorena tried to get along with the Californios and to save some of the missions, but events were moving too quickly.

Milpas*—This word is Central American and Mexican usage for a maize field or vegetable garden. In 1851 the street-naming committee recognized the rich soil of the east side, suitable for farms and orchards.

Mission*—Mission Santa Barbara was founded December 4, 1786, by Father Fermin de Lasuen, who succeeded Father Junipero Serra as father president of the missions and is credited with California's major period of mission expansion. The street closest to Mission Santa Barbara on Haley's survey is named for it, although spelled in English, not the Spanish "mision."

Mission Canyon Road—The "Queen of the Missions" sits at the mouth of a beautiful wooded canyon with a rushing creek, originally called Arroyo Pedregoso for its stony terrain. Later the canyon became a popular excursion area, known as "Mission Cañon" or "Mission Canyon."

Montecito*—Another 1851 street, this one points in the direction of Montecito, or "little woods," the suburb to the east. Father Serra had hopes of founding the Mission at Montecito in 1782; this did not happen, but a village of Presidio soldiers' families grew up in the area.

Mountain Drive—Named for the Santa Ynez Mountains, whose foothills and southerly flanks it ascends, Mountain Drive, which begins at the Mission, has been a favorite excursion route since the late 19th century.

Natoma Avenue—This street in the 1924 Ambassador Tract commemorates a Chumash princess in "Natoma," a Victor Herbert opera first performed in Philadelphia in 1911.

Niños Drive—In 1965 the street next to Sycamore Creek, at East Beach, was named "Niños" or "children" to commemorate the city park called A Child's Estate, to which it leads. The park land was previously the John and Lillian Child estate.

Ortega*—José Francisco de Ortega, a native of Mexico, was a founder of the city in 1782 and the first comandante of the Spanish Royal Presidio. Prior to this Ortega had explored Alta California with the 1769 Portola expedition. This is one of a series of streets named in 1851 for well-known California families.

Plaza Rubio—This charming street, part of the 1925 subdivision of the same name, honors Father José Gonzales Rubio, beloved Franciscan missionary of the late Mexican and early American eras.

Por la Mar Drive—In the early 1920s the Cabrillo Park Tract was developed near East Beach, and this street, meaning "by the sea," was included in it.

Puesta del Sol Road—Located partly in the city and partly in unincorporated county area, this road leads to the west where the sun rests; hence the name "sunset."

Punta Gorda*—This 1851 street points toward a promontory or "fat point." It is one of the most easterly of the Haley Survey streets.

Santa Barbara*—The channel, the Presidio, the Mission, and the city are all named for Saint Barbara, patroness of sailors, artillerymen, and protectress against explosion or lightning. This naming sequence began when the sea expedition of Sebastian Viscaino entered the channel waters on December 3, 1602, the eve of Saint Barbara's feastday. In 1851 the city fathers continued the tradition in a street which was aligned with the Presidio.

Shoreline Drive—A blufftop road with an unobstructed view of the Pacific Ocean was developed on the Mesa with the Marine Terrace Subdivisions of the 1950s. Within fifteen years the most southwesterly portion of Cabrillo Boulevard, near the site of Fossil Hill and Punta del Castillo, had been renamed "Shoreline Drive" to join a newly constructed road climbing from Leadbetter Beach to the original blufftop Shoreline Drive.

Sola*—Pablo Vicente Sola served as the last Spanish governor of California, from 1815 to early 1822. Although an opponent of revolution, the haughty Basque native swore allegiance to Mexico in April, 1822, and served as Mexican governor until November.

State*—The city's main street received two names on the 1853 Wackenreuder maps, "Estado" and its English version "State." On the No. 1 map the first four blocks are called "Estado" and the blocks on the other side of the cluster of downtown adobe houses are called "State." The No. 2 map calls the entire main street "State Street," honoring the new State of California. Apparently the latter name was common then, as the council minutes for late 1851 refer to it. In the 1870s parts of the central area of State Street were graded and opened. The street was paved with asphalt in 1887. Official maps used the name "State Street," as did early guidebooks. After the 1925 earthquake, when Hispanic architectural themes were being widely promoted, the City was urged to change the name to "Estado" or "Calle Estado." The old maps were reviewed, and for a time "Estado" received wide usage. Newspaper articles in late 1927 praised the resumption of the name, and business addresses used "Estado" for the next few years. By the 1930s, however, "State" was again appearing in advertisements. The 1924 Olmsted-Cheney plan for the street and park system used "State," but architectural design articles such as the 1926 "New Santa Barbara" used the Spanish version. The 1941 WPA guidebook to Santa Barbara comments "State Street (Calle del Estado) is the main business thoroughfare." A "Paseo Estado" is proposed in the city's General Plan, adopted in 1964: "Particular and special treatment...so that...the principal street in Santa Barbara reflects the character of the town." The Landmarks Committee has recommended that downtown street signs carry the double appellation "Calle del Estado/State Street."

Valerio*—This 1851 street, according to different sources, is named either for an Indian who may have been a mountain cave dweller, living off the land, or for a robber.

Victoria*—Manuel Victoria was a Spanish/Native American military figure who served as Mexican governor of California from 1831 to 1832. He disapproved of secularization of the Missions and took stern measures against wrongdoers. Californio insurgents drove Victoria out of office. This is the final street in our 1851 series named for California governors.

Yanonali*—The great Chumash, Yanonali, was chief of the large village of Syukhtun at West Beach, and leader of the South Coast rancherias. He cooperated in the establishment of the Presidio, and was baptized a Christian several years later. Yanonali (Yanonalit, Yanunali) was memorialized in one of the city's original streets, a street which passes the site of Syukhtun.

BIBLIOGRAPHY

I. GENERAL INTEREST

For those who wish to pursue certain topics further, the following books contain a wealth of information on various aspects of Santa Barbara history and architecture. They were, in addition, written for a wide audience, are amply illustrated, and are available in most local bookstores.

Andree, Herb. *Santa Barbara Architecture, From Spanish Colonial to Modern.* Santa Barbara: Capra Press, 1975; second ed., 1980.

Days, Mary Louise. *A Visit to Santa Barbara's Historical-Architectural Highlights.* Santa Barbara: City of Santa Barbara, 1984.

Gebhard, David. *Santa Barbara—The Creation of a New Spain in America.* Catalogue of an exhibition, November 3-December 12, 1982. Santa Barbara: UCSB Art Museum, 1982.

Geiger, Maynard J. OFM. *Mission Santa Barbara: 1782-1965.* Santa Barbara: Heritage Press for Franciscan Fathers of California, 1965.

Grant, Campbell. *Rock Paintings of the Chumash: A Study of a California Indian Culture.* Berkeley: University of California Press, 1965.

Muller, Katherine K., Richard E. Broder and Will Beittel. *Trees of Santa Barbara.* Santa Barbara: Santa Barbara Botanic Garden, 1974.

Tompkins, Walker A. *Santa Barbara: Past and Present.* Santa Barbara: Schauer Printing, 1975.

II. PUBLISHED SOURCES

Allen, Harris. "The 'Street of Spain', Santa Barbara, California." *Pacific Coast Architect* 27 (March 1925): 23-39.

Andree, Herbert. "The Santa Barbara of Peter J. Barber." *Noticias* 21, no. 2 (Summer 1975): 1-11 and 21, no. 3 (Fall 1975): 3-26.

"Arts Association—Santa Barbara Plans and Planting Branch." *California Southland* 7 (January 1925): 15-31.

Baer, Kurt. *Painting and Sculpture at Mission Santa Barbara.* Washington, D.C.: Academy of American Franciscan History, 1955.

Beittel, Will. *Santa Barbara's Street and Park Trees.* Santa Barbara: Santa Barbara County Horticultural Society, 1972.

Bell, Katherine M. *Swinging the Censer: Reminiscences of Old Santa Barbara.* Santa Barbara, 1931.

Berger, John A. *Fernand Lungren, A Biography.* Santa Barbara: Schauer Press, 1936.

Bissell, Ervanna Bowen. *Glimpses of Santa Barbara and Montecito Gardens.* Santa Barbara: Schauer Printing, 1926.

_____ *The Franciscan Mission of California.* New York: Putnam's Sons, 1941.

Boba, Eleanor, and Weare, Carol Snook, eds. *Studies of a Growing Community: Santa Barbara 1930-1980.* University of California, Santa Barbara, The Graduate Program in Public Historical Studies, 1982.

Bodkin, J.J. *Santa Barbara Mission.* Los Angeles, 1910.

Boegkmann, Henriette. "The Little Street of Spain." *International Studio* 81 (June 1925): 184-188.

Bookspan, Rochelle, ed. *Santa Barbara by the Sea.* Santa Barbara: McNally and Loftin, 1982.

Brainerd, Harry Beardslee. "A Brief for Architectural Control." *Journal of the American Institute of Planners* 4 (1938): 40-44.

Brown, Edward F. "Does Beauty Pay? Exhibition of Designs by the Community Arts Association of Santa Barbara." *The American City Magazine* 30 (February 1924): 165-166.

Caballeria y Collell, Juan. *History of the City of Santa Barbara, California, from its Discovery to Our Own Days.* Santa Barbara: F. de P. Gutierrez, Printer, 1892.

Camarillo, Albert. *Chicanos in a Changing Society: From Mexican Pueblos to American Barrios in Santa Barbara and Southern California, 1848-1930.* Cambridge, Massachusetts: Harvard University Press, 1979.

"Charles H. Cheney will assist the Building Ordinance Committee of the Santa Barbara Chamber of Commerce in framing a new building code for the city." *The Architect and Engineer* 75 (November 1923): 112.

Chase, Pearl. *Bernhard Hoffmann—Community Builder, Santa Barbara 1921-1927.* Reprinted from *Noticias* (Summer 1959) by the Plans and Planting Committee of the Community Arts Association.

———. "Santa Barbara Resurgent." *Survey* 54 (August 1925): 469-472.

Cheney, Charles H. "Architectural Control." *The Octagon, Journal of the American Institute of Architects*, February 1940, 18-19.

———. "Architectural Control in America." *Proceedings, National Conference on Planning.* Chicago, 1940, 125-130.

———. "Architectural Control." *The American Architect* 140 (April 1931): 23, 94.

———. "Building for Permanency." *National Conference on City Planning, 20th Annual Conference.* Dallas, Texas, 1928, 32-46.

———. "California Cities Capitalize Natural Charm—A Symposium." *Western Architect* 40 (March 1931): 11-12.

———. "Progress in Architectural Control." *The Architect and Engineer* 90 (August 1927): 43-47.

———. "Progress in Architectural Control." *National Conference on City Planning, 19th Annual Conference*, Washington, D.C., 1927, 248-265.

Cole, Wiley, comp. *Then and Now.* Santa Barbara: SB Yacht Club, 1978.

Cooligan, James Augustine. *Some Facts About Santa Barbara Mission.* San Francisco: University of San Francisco Press, 1932.

"Community Building in Santa Barbara." *Christian Science Monitor*, October 1, 1925.

"Competition for Santa Barbara County Court House and Memorial." *The Building Review*, 18 (November 1919): 85-87; 95.

Craig, Mary Osborne. "The Heritage of All California." *California Southland* 33 (September 1922): 7-9.

Cullimore, Clarence C. *Santa Barbara Adobes.* Santa Barbara: Santa Barbara Book Publishing Co., 1948.

Curletti, Rosario. *Pathways to Pavements: The History and Romance of Santa Barbara Street Names.* Santa Barbara: Pacific Coast Publ. Co. for County National Bank and Trust Co., 1950; second printing, 1953.

D'Alfonso, Virginia, ed. *Survivors: A Look at Some of the Victorian Architecture of Central Santa Barbara—Cupolas, Witches' Caps, Curlicues and All.* Santa Barbara: Santa Barbara Historical Society, 1979.

Dana, Richard Henry. *Two Years Before the Mast.* Boston: Houghton Mifflin and Co., 1868 (1835).

Days, Mary Louise. *Park Histories.* City of Santa Barbara, Planning Division, Community Development Department, 1977.

Dibblee, Thomas Wilson Jr. *Geology of the Central Santa Ynez Mountains, Santa Barbara County, California.* San Francisco, California Division of Mines and Geology, Bulletin 186, 1966.

Dobyns, Winifred Starr. *California Gardens.* New York: Macmillan and Co., 1931.

Ellison, William Henry, ed. *The Life and Adventures of George Nidever* [1802-1883]. Berkeley and Los Angeles: University of California Press, 1937.

Engelhardt, Zephyrin. *Santa Barbara Mission.* San Francisco: James H. Barry Co., 1923.

Fernald, Charles. *County Judge in Arcady.* Glendale: Arthur H. Clark Co., 1954.

Fillon, Martin. "In a Little Spanish Town." *Progressive Architecture* 58 (November 1977): 72-75.

Finney, M. MacLein. "The Court House Beautiful." *The Architect and Engineer* 98 (July 1929): 35-46.

Forbes, Alexander. *A History of Upper and Lower California.* London: Smith, Elder and Co., Cornhill, 1839.

Franceschi, Dr. F. *Santa Barbara Exotic Flora: A handbook of Plants from Foreign Countries Grown at Santa Barbara, California.* Santa Barbara, 1895.

Franklin, T.J. "The Personality that is Santa Barbara." *Sunset* 57 (July 1926): 42-43.

Gebhard, David and Robert Winter. *A Guide to Architecture in Los Angeles and Southern*

California. Santa Barbara and Salt Lake City: Peregrine Smith, Inc. 1977.

Gebhard, David. "Architectural Imagery: The Missions and California." *Harvard Architectural Review* 1 (Spring 1980): 136-145.

———. *George Washington Smith, 1876-1930*. Catalogue of an exhibition, November 17-December 20, 1964. Santa Barbara: UCSB Art Gallery, 1964.

———. "The Monterey Tradition: History Reordered." *New Mexico Studies in Fine Art* 7 (1972): 10-19.

———. "The Spanish Colonial Revival in Southern California." *Journal of the Society of Architectural Historians* 26 (May 1967): 131-47.

Geiger, Maynard J., OFM. *A Pictorial History of the Physical Development of Mission Santa Barbara from Brush Hut to Institutional Greatness, 1786-1963*. San Francisco: James Barry Co., 1963.

Gidney, C.M., Benjamin Brooks, and Edwin M. Sheridan. *History of Santa Barbara, San Luis Obispo and Ventura Counties, California*. Chicago: Lewis Publishing Co., 1917.

Hannaford, Donald R. and Revol Edwards. *Spanish Colonial or Adobe Architecture of California 1800-1850*. New York: Architectural Book Publishing Co., 1931.

Harrington, John P. "Exploration of the Burton Mound at Santa Barbara, California." *Forty-Fourth Annual Report of the Bureau of Ethnography*. Washington, D.C.: Government Printing Office, 1928.

Hawley, Walter Augustus. *Early Days of Santa Barbara, California*. Santa Barbara: Schauer Printing, 1920.

Hazard, Caroline. *A Precious Heritage*. Peace Dale, R.I.: privately printed, 1929.

Higgins, Sarah Evelina Austin. *La Casa de Aguirre of Santa Barbara, 1841-1884*. Santa Barbara: Press of El Barbareno, 1896.

Hill, Laurance L. and Marion Parks. *Santa Barbara, Tierra Adorada: A Community History*. Santa Barbara[?]: Security First National Bank of Los Angeles, 1930.

Hittell, Theodore H. *History of California*. San Francisco: N.J. Stone & Co., 1898.

Hoffmann, Bernhard. "Architectural Aphorisms." *The Architect and Engineer* 96 (March 1929): 111.

———. "The Rebuilding of Santa Barbara." *Bulletin of the Seismological Society of America* 15 (December 1925): 323-328.

"How Did Santa Barbara Get That Way?" *Sunset* 154 (January 1975): 36-43.

Hudson, Dee Travis. *Chumash Wooden Bowls, Trays, and Boxes* (San Diego Museum Papers, No. 13). San Diego: Museum of Man, November 1977.

Hudson, Dee Travis, Thomas Blackburn, Rosario Curletti, and Janice Timbrook. *Eye of the Flute: Chumash Traditional History and Ritual as told by Fernando Librado Kitsopawit to John P. Harrington*. Santa Barbara: S.B. Museum of Natural History, 1977.

Huse, Charles Enoch; edited by Edith Bond Conkey. *Huse Journal: Santa Barbara in the 1850s*. Santa Barbara: S.B. Historical Society, 1977.

Jackson, Abraham Willard. *Barbariana: Scenery, Climate, Soils and Social Conditions of Santa Barbara, City and County, California*. San Francisco: C.A. Murdock and Co., 1888.

Kirker, Harold. *California's Architectural Frontier*. Santa Barbara and Salt Lake City: Peregrine Smith, 1973 (1960).

Korngold, Piri, *Biography of a Library*. Santa Barbara, 1977.

Larrimore, Wilbur. "Public Aesthetics." *Harvard Law Review* 20 (November 1906): 35-45.

MacKesey, Thomas W. "Aesthetics and Zoning." *Journal of the American Institute of Planners* 5, no. 4 (1939): 95-98.

McIsaac, Colin H. *Santa Barbara Mission: Early Days in California*. Santa Barbara: Schauer Printing, 1929.

McNutt, Rollin L. "Architectural Control Under the Police Power." *Community Builder* 1 (January 1928): 26-28.

Mason, Jesse D. *Facsimile Reproduction of Thompson and West's History of Santa Barbara and Ventura Counties*. With an introduction by Walker A. Tompkins.

Berkeley: Howell-North, 1961 (1883).

Moore, Charles and Gerald Allen. *Dimensions*. New York: Architectural Record Books, 1976.

Moore, Charles, Gerald Allen, and Donlyn Lyndon. *The Place of Houses*. New York: Holt, Rinehart and Winston, 1974.

Morrow, Irving F. Illustration of drawings for State Street. *Pacific Coast Architect* 28 (November 1925): 35-36.

―――― "The New Santa Barbara." *The Architect and Engineer* 86 (July 1926): 42-83.

―――― "A Step in California Architecture." *The Architect and Engineer* 70 (August 1922): 46-103.

Newcomb, Rexford. "The Architecture of Spanish Santa Barbara." *The Western Architect* 30 (December 1921): 129-134 and 31 (February 1922): 25-30.

―――― *The Old Mission Churches and Historic Houses of California*. Philadelphia and London: J.P. Lippincott Co., 1925.

Nickerson, H.C. "The Rise of Santa Barbara." *California South Land* 7 (August 1925): 9-11

Nordhoff, Charles. *California: For Health, Pleasure, and Residence—A Book for Travelers and Settlers*. New York: Harper and Brothers, 1874 (1872).

Nye, Ronald L., ed. *Environmental Hazards and Community Response: The Santa Barbara Experience*. University of California, Santa Barbara: Graduate Program in Public Historical Studies, 1979.

O'Keefe, Rev. Joseph Jeremiah. *The Buildings and Churches of the Mission of Santa Barbara*. Santa Barbara: Independent Job Printing House, 1886.

Old Adobes of Santa Barbara: Spanish, Mexican, and Early American Periods. Santa Barbara: Community Arts Association, Plans and Planting Committee, 1947.

O'Neill, Owen H., ed. *History of Santa Barbara County, Its People and Its Resources*. Santa Barbara: H. McLean Meier, 1939.

Orr, Phil C. *Customs of the Canalino*. Santa Barbara: Museum of Natural History, 1956.

Overman, Caroline L. "Modern Spanish Architecture in California." *The House Beautiful* 5 (April 1899): 33-37.

Phillips, Michael James. *History of Santa Barbara County, California, from its Earliest Settlement to the Present Time*. Chicago: S.J. Clark Publ. Co., 1927.

Richie, C.F. and R.A. Hager. *Chumash Canoe*. Ramona, Ca.: Ballena Press, 1973.

Roberts, Edwards. *Santa Barbara and Around There*. Boston: Roberts Brothers, 1888.

Robinson, Alfred. *The Letters of Alfred Robinson to the De la Guerra Family of Santa Barbara, 1834-1873*. Translated and edited by Maynard J. Geiger, OFM. Los Angeles: Zamorano Club, 1972.

Rogers, David Banks. *Prehistoric Man of the Santa Barbara Coast*. Santa Barbara: S.B. Museum of Natural History, 1929.

Rolle, Andrew F. *California: A History*. New York: Thomas Y. Crowell Co., 1963.

Rouse, Stella Haverland. *Santa Barbara's Spanish Renaissance and Old Spanish Days Fiesta*. Santa Barbara: Schauer Printing, 1974.

Sajous, Edward. "How a Community Arts Association is Raising Architectural Standards." *American City* 29 (July 1923): 39.

Sands, Frank. *Santa Barbara at a Glance*. Los Angeles: Kingsley-Barnes and Neuner Co., 1895.

Santa Barbara [published by the Santa Barbara Chamber of Commerce] 1, no. 7 (July 1906): 11-21.

"Santa Barbara: The Case for a Unified Architecture." *Architectural Forum* 59 (July 1933): 84-85.

Santa Barbara County Courthouse. Santa Barbara: Schauer Printing for Santa Barbara County Board of Supervisors, 1929.

"The Santa Barbara County Courthouse." *California Southland* 10 (January 1928): 11-13.

"Santa Barbara Earthquake." *Bulletin of the Seismological Society of America* 15 (December 1925).

"Santa Barbara Earthquake Number." *Bulletin, Allied Architectural Association of Los Angeles*, no. 10 (August 1, 1925).

"The Santa Barbara, California, Earthquake." *The American Architect* 128 (July 15, 1925): 47-48.

Santa Barbara, A Guide to the Channel City and Its

Environs (compiled and written by the Southern California Writers Project of the Works Progress Administration). New York: Hastings House, 1941.

Santa Barbara Street Names. Santa Barbara: S.B. National Bank, c. 1965

Scott, Mel. *American City Planning.* Berkeley and Los Angeles: University of California Press, 1969.

Seares, M. Urmy. "A Community Approaches its Ideal." *California Arts and Architecture* 37 (June 1930): 19-21, 70-71.

_____ "The Community Arts Association of Santa Barbara, California." *California Southland* 6 (December 1928): 12-13; 22.

Smith, Clifton. *Flora of the Santa Barbara Region, California.* Santa Barbara: S.B. Museum of Natural History, 1976.

Smitheram, Lou Hale. *History of Trinity Church (Episcopal), Santa Barbara.* Santa Barbara, 1973.

Soule, Winsor. "Lessons of the Santa Barbara Earthquake." *The American Architect* 128 (October 5, 1925): 295-302.

_____ "The New Santa Barbara." *American Architect* 129 (1926): 1-10.

_____ "Santa Barbara Architecture." *The Architect and Engineer* 79 (December 1924): 50-73.

Southworth, John R. *Historic Adobes of Santa Barbara.* Santa Barbara: Schauer Press, 1920.

_____ *Santa Barbara and Montecito, Past and Present.* Santa Barbara: Oreña Studios, 1920.

_____ *Viva Santa Barbara.* Santa Barbara, 1946.

Spaulding, Edward Selden. *Adobe Days Along the Channel.* Santa Barbara: Schauer Printing, 1957.

_____ *A Brief Story of Santa Barbara.* Santa Barbara: S.B. Historical Society, 1964.

_____ *Santa Barbara, 1898-1925 as Seen by a Boy.* Pacific Coast Publishing Co., 1974.

_____ *Santa Barbara Club: A History.* Santa Barbara: Schauer Printing, 1954.

Staats, H. Philip, ed. *Californian Architecture in Santa Barbara.* New York: Architectural Book Publishing Co., 1929.

Storke, T.M. with Walker Tompkins. *California Editor.* Los Angeles: Westernlore Press, 1958.

Storke, Yda Addis. *A Memorial and Biographical History of the Counties of Santa Barbara, San Luis Obispo and Ventura.* Chicago: Lewis Publishing Co., 1891.

Tompkins, Walker, A. *A Centennial History of Stearns Wharf.* Santa Barbara: S.B. Wharf Company, 1972.

_____ and Horace A. Sexton. *Fourteen at the Table.* Santa Barbara, 1964.

_____ *Historical Highlights of Santa Barbara.* Santa Barbara: S.B. National Bank, 1970.

_____ and Russell A. Ruiz. *It Happened in Old Santa Barbara.* Santa Barbara: S.B. National Bank, 1976.

_____ *Old Spanish Santa Barbara: "From Cabrillo to Fremont."* Santa Barbara: McNally and Loftin, 1967.

_____ *Santa Barbara History Makers.* Santa Barbara: McNally and Loftin, 1983.

_____ *Santa Barbara Yesterdays.* Santa Barbara: McNally and Loftin, 1962.

Weber, Francis J. *Queen of the Mission: A Documentary History of Santa Barbara.* Los Angeles, 1979.

"What Earthquakes Cannot Destroy." *The Literary Digest* 86 (August 1, 1925): 29-30.

"When Santa Barbara's Dream of 'A Street in Spain' is called into being by Her Peoples." *Santa Barbara Daily News,* May 20, 1922, Special Photogravure Section.

Whitehead, Richard. "Alta California's Four Fortresses." *Southern California Quarterly* LXV, no. 1 (Spring 1983): 67-94.

Williams, James C., ed. *Old Town Santa Barbara—A Narrative History of State Street.* University of California, Santa Barbara: Graduate Program in Public Historical Studies, 1977.

Wilson, Leila Weekes. *Santa Barbara, California.* Santa Barbara: Pacific Coast Publishing Co., 1913; second ed. 1919.

III. UNPUBLISHED SOURCES

Chase, Pearl. "The Reconstruction of State Street." Santa Barbara, ca. 1925.

Kammer, Regina. "St. Anthony's Seminary." Paper for the Santa Barbara County History Fair, University of California, Santa Barbara, May 1, 2, 3, 1981.

Meshot, Mark. "Saint Vincent's: Servant of the People of Santa Barbara for over 100 years." Paper for the Santa Barbara County History Fair, University of California, Santa Barbara, May 1, 2, 3, 1981.

Nelson, Christopher. "Santa Barbara Architecture to 1930." M.A. Thesis, U.C. Santa Barbara, 1980.

Nye, Ronald L. "The Influence of the Chase Family on Santa Barbara History." Paper presented at the West Coast Symposium on Family History, U.C. Santa Barbara, May 1, 1976.

Silver, David. "The History of the Southern Pacific Roundhouse in Santa Barbara." History 195, Professor Carroll Pursell, U.C. Santa Barbara, 1977.

Windolph, M. Ann. "A Case Study of an Outgrowth of Settlement Work: The Department of Recreation of the City of Santa Barbara, California, 1929-1943." M.A. Thesis, U.C. Santa Barbara, 1968.

IV. OFFICIAL DOCUMENTS

Eisner, Stewart and Associates. *Santa Barbara, California: The General Plan.* South Pasadena: Eisner, Stewart and Associates, 1964.

Olmsted and Olmsted. *Major Traffic Street Plan and Boulevard and Park System.* Santa Barbara: Community Arts Association, Plans and Planting Committee, 1924.

Petition in the Matter of Adopting Names for the Roads Lying West of the City of Santa Barbara. Santa Barbara: Board of Supervisors of the County of Santa Barbara. Filed January 7, 1900.

Report of Vitus Wackenreuder. Santa Barbara: County Surveyor to the Common Council. Accompanying the Maps of the City. Filed April 22, 1853.

Robinson, Charles Mulford. *The Report of Charles Mulford Robinson Regarding the Civic Affairs of Santa Barbara, California.* Santa Barbara: printed for the Civic League by the *Independent,* 1909.

Santa Barbara, City of. Minutes of the Common Council, 1851, 1854.

_____ Ordinances of the City Council.

_____ Architectural Board of Review. *Policy for Architectural Control.* August 1958.

_____ City Planning Department. *The General Plan Amended Through 1977.*

_____ Parks and Recreation Departments. *Parks and Recreation Facilities and Programming Master Plan.* March 1978.

V. SERIALS

The Morning Press, 1887-1937.

Noticias, Quarterly publication of the Santa Barbara Historical Society, various issues 1955-present.

Santa Barbara Daily Press, 1872-1885.

Santa Barbara Gazette, 1855-1858.

Santa Barbara News-Press, 1937-present.

Santa Barbara Press, 1886-1887.

VI. ARCHIVES AND OTHER COMMUNITY RESOURCES

American Institute of Architects, Santa Barbara Chapter, Plan Archives.

St. Anthony's Seminary Library.

Santa Barbara City Land Use Controls Division. Building permits.

Santa Barbara City Planning Division. "Street Names" files.

_____ Survey of Architectural and Historic Resources, Phase I (1979) and Phase II (1981). 47 volumes. The *Completion Report* for Phase II, prepared by Christopher Nelson and Rebecca Conard and submitted on March 30, 1981, contains a list of the primary sources (maps, city directories, tax assessment records, census data, etc.) used to document the architectural and historical resources surveyed as part of Phase II. The report also contains a description of the research methods employed.

Santa Barbara Historical Society Library.

Santa Barbara Mission Archive Library.

Santa Barbara Museum of Natural History Library.

Santa Barbara News-Press Photo Archives.

University of California, Santa Barbara,

Library, Special Collections. Community Development and Conservation Collection.

———. Art Department. The Architectural Drawing Collection, University Art Museum.

SPECIAL PHOTOGRAPHS AND ILLUSTRATIONS

126	Aquirre Adobe	Edson Smith Collection, Santa Barbara Public Library.
94	Second Arlington Hotel	Gledhill Library, Santa Barbara Historical Society
142	Arrellanes Adobe	Gledhill Library, Santa Barbara Historical Society
29	Second Bathhouse	Boner-Donald Collection, Santa Barbara City Planning Division
57	Beale-Child House	Gledhill Library, Santa Barbara Historical Society
26	Burton Mound	Santa Barbara Museum of Natural History
133	Old Courthouse	Gledhill Library, Santa Barbara Historical Society
21	Freeway Bridge, proposed	Henry Lenny, Santa Barbara
148	1027 Garden Street	Lenvik and Minor, Architects, Santa Barbara
137	Herter Mansion (El Mirasol)	Gledhill Library, Santa Barbara Historical Society
170	Mission and Mountain View	Gledhill Library, Santa Barbara Historical Society
54	Fess Parker's Hotel	Edwards-Pitman, Architects, Santa Barbara
16	Plaza de la Guerra	Architectural Drawing Collection, University Art Museum, University of California, Santa Barbara
26	Plaza del Mar	Boner-Donald Collection, Santa Barbara City Planning Division
102	Presidio Plan	The Bancroft Library, University of California, Berkeley
142	Sloyd School	Gledhill Library, Santa Barbara Historical Society
60	800 Block State Street 1887	Gledhill Library, Santa Barbara Historical Society
60	800 Block State Street 1926	Community Development Collection, Special Collections, Library, University of California, Santa Barbara
80	Thompson Adobe	Gledhill Library, Santa Barbara Historical Society
104	United States Coast Survey Map	Map and Imagery Laboratory, Library, University of California, Santa Barbara
157	Old Y.M.C.A. Building	Gledhill Library, Santa Barbara Historical Society

Line drawings by Henry Lenny, A.I.A., and Lawrence Auchstetter, illustrator, Planning Division, Santa Barbara City Community Development Department

BIOGRAPHIES

REBECCA CONARD, co-author, holds a Ph.D. in history from the University of California, Santa Barbara (1984). In 1980-1981, she and Christopher Nelson coordinated the Santa Barbara Architectural and Historic Resources Survey, Phase II. Ms. Conard is a partner of PHR Associates, a historical and information consulting firm.

CHRISTOPHER H. NELSON, co-author, is a 1985 recipient of the Ph.D. degree in history at the University of California, Santa Barbara. He has performed services for the U.S. Department of the Interior, the State of Maryland, the City of Santa Barbara, and U.C.S.B., specializing in cultural history. The author of "Pre-Earthquake Santa Barbara" in *Environmental Hazards and Community Response,* published by the U.C.S.B. Public Historical Studies program, he has also written articles on architecture in Santa Barbara and the West.

MARY LOUISE DAYS, staff to the Survey and Book Subcommittee of the City Landmarks Committee, is a native Santa Barbaran and fourth generation Californian. A member of the City of Santa Barbara Planning Staff since 1961, she has staffed the Landmarks Committee since 1975. She has worked on numerous historical research activities for the Committee and the City including *Park Histories, City of Santa Barbara* and an architectural highlights brochure. Outside of her duties as City Staff, she has served as president of the Santa Barbara Trust for Historic Preservation, a grand officer of the Native Daughters of the Golden West, and has completed several articles of historic interest.

LOUISE BOUCHER, subcommittee chairman, has resided in Santa Barbara since 1933 and is a graduate of U.C.S.B. A member of the Landmarks Committee for several years, she also serves on the City Sign Committee. Mrs. Boucher is president of the Citizens Planning Association of Santa Barbara County and member of a number of civic organizations.

DAVID GEBHARD, vice chairperson of the Landmarks Committee, is the author or co-author of books, guides, articles, and exhibition catalogs on architecture and planning, the most recent being his co-authorship of *Architecture in Los Angeles: A Compleat Guide* (1985). He is a professor of architectural history at the University of California, Santa Barbara, and was director of the University Art Museum from 1961 to 1980; is a past president of the Society of Architectural Historians and of the Citizens Planning Association of Santa Barbara County.

JAMES EDWARD MORRIS, subcommittee member, is an architect and is past president of the Santa Barbara Chapter of the American Institute of

Architects. He has been active in the design of structures at Birnam Wood Golf and Country Club in Montecito. Mr. Morris became a member of the Landmarks Committee in 1979.

HENRY LENNY, map artist, is an architect who studied at the Autonoma de Guadalajara, Mexico, and at the California Polytechnic State University, San Luis Obispo, School of Architecture. He came to Santa Barbara in 1968 and has been associated with an engineering firm and an architectural firm, where he has produced audio-visual presentations on architecture and art. Mr. Lenny is 1985 president of the Santa Barbara Chapter of the American Institute of Architects, and a member of the Landmarks Committee.

FREDERICK A. USHER, book designer, is an industrial designer with wide experience in museum exhibit work, graphics, publications, architecture, world exhibitions, and interior design. He taught at the University of Southern California School of Architecture, and is currently consultant to the State of Washington for its participation in EXPO-'86. Mr. Usher is a member of the Santa Barbara City Landmarks Committee and of the Sign Committee.

Cover—Santa Barbara County Courthouse
End Papers—"A Typical Block of State Street" schemes for reconstruction 1925, Lutah Maria Riggs, George Washington Smith.

INDEX

NOTE: Those buildings in El Pueblo Viejo listed on the National Register of Historic Places are designated: NR; those which are California Historic Landmarks are designated: CHL; Those which are Landmarks of the City of Santa Barbara are designated: SBLM; those which are City of Santa Barbara Structures of Merit are designated: SBSM.

A

Adams Chair Caning Shop, 168
Adobes
   Aguirre, 126, 142, 158
   Arrellanes-Kirk (SBLM), 105, 142
   Buenaventura Pico (SBLM), 105
   Burton Mound, 27, 43, 105
   Canedo-Whittaker (SBLM), 123
   Cordero (SBLM), 147
   Covarrubias (CHL; SBLM), 143
   De la Guerra (NR; CHL; SBLM), 15, 16, 61, 79, 80, 103, 105, 116, 117, 118, 184
   Gonzales-Ramirez (NR; SBLM), 145
   Guard House (SBLM), 119
   Hill-Carrillo (CHL; SBLM), 127
   "Historic" (SBLM), 143
   Leyva, 78
   Lugo (SBLM), 16, 119, 120
   Magdalena Cota, 115
   Masini (Ortega-Masini), 127
   Miranda (SBLM), 119
   Orella, 61, 87
   Oreña (SBLM), 15, 118
   Pico (SBLM), 105, 125
   Rochin (SBLM), 141
   Santiago de la Guerra (SBLM), 119
   Thompson, 61, 80
   Trussell-Winchester (CHL, SBLM), 27, 39
   Yorba-Abadie, 15, 16, 117
Adler, David (with Chester Carjola)
   Santa Barbara Museum of Art, 1941 (85), 90
Adobe Antiques, The, 115
Adult Education Center, City College, 140
Advisory Landmark Committee, 20
Agricultural Park, 27, 28
Aguirre Adobe, 126, 158
Aguirre, Jose Antonio, 126
Aiken, W.H. (Aiken Block), 81
Airport, Santa Barbara Municipal, 192
Alameda Court, 138
Alameda Plaza (& Bandstand) (SBLM), 137
Albert, King of Belgium, 137
Aldrich, Chester (see Delano & Aldrich)
Alexander Building, 76, 77
Alhecama Theater and Center, 140
Alice Keck Park Memorial Gardens, 137
All-American Sporting Goods, 160
Allen, Harris, 23
Allied Architectural Association of Los Angeles, 15
Alpha Floral, 96
Ambassador Ball Room, 44
Ambassador Bungalows, 49, 51
Ambassador by-the-Sea, 44
Ambassador Hotel, 29, 43
Ambassador Park, 43, 48

Ambassador Tract (district), 48, 195
American Association of Women, 179
American Film Company, 165, 168
American House, 74
American Institute of Architects, 207, 208
American Institute of Planners, 9
American Women's Volunteer Service, 144
Amtrak Station, 70
Anacapa Island, 39, 192
Anacapa Street (see individual entries by address in Presidio and Pueblo chapter), 192
"Anapamu" plaque, 162
Anapamu Street (see individual entries by address in Presidio and Pueblo chapter), 192
Andree Clark Bird Refuge, 41, 57, 194
Andrews, Mrs. J.A., 130, 173, 178, 179
Andria's Seafood Restaurant, 70
Antique Market Place, 114
Archer-Spencer Building, 136
Architectural Advisory Committee, 17, 68, 69, 132
   Alexander Building, 1925 (58), 76
   State Street Dry Goods, 1925 (70), 83
Architectural Board of Review, 17, 19, 21, 23
Arendt, Wallace; Mosher, Glen D.; Grant, Robert S.; Pedersen, Leo R.; Phillips, Roger A.
   Arlington Center, 1976 alt. (94), 94
Arlington Center for the Performing Arts (see Fox Arlington Theater), 18
Arlington Hotel, 28, 55, 62, 93, 94, 95, 96, 146
   (Garden Arch) (SBSM), 94, 95
Arlington Hotel Company, 94
Arlington Jockey Club, 28
Arlington Paseo, 93
Arlington Silk Oak, 93
Armitage, Ralph
   Beard Motor Company, 1926 (144), 130
Army Redistribution Headquarters, 55
Arrillaga, Jose Joaquin, 192
Arrellaga Street, 192
Arroyo Pedregoso, 195
Asian-Americans, 106
Asian community, 123
Associated Architects
   Los Banos del Mar, 1938 (4), 40
   Hunt's China Shop, 1926-27 (140), 128
Associated Charities, 142
Audax
   Santa Barbara Clinic, 1978 remod. (102), 98
Austin, Company, The
   Fred Whaley Tire Co., 1930 (198), 154
Austin, John C.
   Potter Hotel, 1902 (9), 43
   Potter Hotel Annex, 1920 (20), 48
Australia, 47

209

Automobile Club of Southern California, 138
Auto Show Rooms, 72
Avery, A.H.
   Avery Garden Court, 1923 (106), 101
   Avery Garden Court, 101

B

Bagley, J.W.
   Hotel Neal, 1905-06 (47), 71
Bailey, A. Godfrey (with Soule & Murphy)
   C&H Chevrolet, 1946 (201), 155
Bank of Montecito, 85, 87
Barbara Hotel, 74
Barber, Peter J., 53, 105, 128, 132, 133, 139
   Faith Mission, 1888-89 (50) (attrib), 72
   Upper Hawley Building, 1887 (87), 91
   Arlington Hotel, 1875 (94), 94
   Mortimer Cook House, 165
   St. Mark's Episcopal Church, 1875 (233) (attrib), 168
Barber, Thomas P.
   First United Methodist Church, 1926 (189), 150
Barry Architectural Design Group, 52
   Jordanos', 1981 remodel (221), 163
Barry, Gilbert F. (see above)
Bartoli, Douglas, 79
Bath Street (see individual entries by address in Oceanfront), 192
Battistone Foundation Senior Housing, 164
Baylor, Margaret, 125, 129
Beale, John and Lillian, 57
Beard Motor Company, 130
Bellosguardo, 58
Belvedere Apartments, 45
Belvedere Hotel, 43
Bensen, Donald H. (see Kruger-Bensen-Ziemer)
Benton, Arthur B.
   Arlington Hotel, 1910 (94), 94
   Edgerly Hotel, 1913 (226), 165
   Lou Rose, 1922 (attrib.) (93), 94
Berkeley, 90
Bicentennial, City's, 78
Biltmore Hotel, 54, 55
Bird Refuge, Andree Clark, 57
Birnam Wood Golf and Country Club, 208
Blake, Anna Sophia, 142
Blevins, Mel (see Holewinski and Blevins)
Bliss and Faville
   Edwards House, 1911 (242), 181
Bliss, Anna Blaksley, 173
Bliss, Walter D. (see Bliss & Faville)
Blyth, Eastman, Dillon & Co., 84
B'Nai B'Rith Congregation, 149
Boegkmann, Hennriette, 23
Bonilla, Florentino, 140
Bonilla House, 140
Botanic Garden, Santa Barbara, 172, 173
Bothin Building(s), 78, 81
Bothin Helping Fund, 72, 78, 81
Bothin, Henry, 72, 73
Boucher, Louise, 188, 207
Boyd House, 184
Boyd, Scott Lee, 184
Boydston, Jack
   Moullet House remodel, 1955 (166), 141
Bradley's Race Track, 27, 57
Breakwater and Harbor, 41
Bregante, Lisa
   Russ' Camera, 1983 (77), 86

Brewster, Floyd E.
   Museum of Natural History, 1922-23, 1926 (240), 180
Brinkerhoff Avenue, 153, 192, 193
Brinkerhoff Avenue Landmark Dist., 153
Brinkerhoff, Lucy Noyes, 172
Brinkerhoff, Dr. Samuel, 172, 192
Brinks Grocery, 99
Brooks Building, 124
Brooks, Clayton (with Wahlquist, Lawrence, Richards)
   Brooks Building, 1982-84 (130), 124
Brown, Arthur Page
   Crocker Row, 1894-95 (252), 185
Brown, Edward F., 23
Brownsill House #1, 105, 132
Brownsill House #2, 149
Buddhist Temple site, 123
Buick Automobiles, 71
Burgos, Spain, 78
Burton Adobe, 43
Burton, Lewis T., 42, 192
Burton Mound (CHL), 26, 27, 28, 43, 57, 105

C

C & H Chevrolet, 155
Cabrillo Ball Park, 54
Cabrillo Boulevard (see individual entries by address in Oceanfront chapter), 53, 193
Cabrillo, Joao Rodrigues (Cabrilho), 27, 193
Cabrillo Park Tract, 196
Cabrillo Pavilion, 55
Cadorin, Ettore, 120, 133
Caesar's Alley, 78
Calder House, 139
Calder, William J., 139
California—A Book for Travelers and Settlers, 27
California Dept. of Parks & Recreation, 187
California Highway Patrol, 59
Californian, Hotel, 68, 71
California State Employment Building, 115
Calkins, J.W., 138
Callahan, J.J., 167
Callahan, Neal, 71, 74
Callahan, Neal Building, 74
Calle Estado, 197
Candreva, Peter Jack & Jarrett, William C.
   Jordanos', 1957 (221), 163
Canedo, Jose Maria, 123
Canedo-Whittaker Adobe (SBLM), 123
Canon Perdido Street (see individual entries by address in Presidio and Pueblo chapter), 193
Carjola, Chester L.
   Santa Barbara Museum of Art, 1941 (with David Adler) (85), 90
   State Department of Motor Vehicles, 1936 (40-a), 59
   Little Town Club, 1936 & 1937 addtns. (135), 126
   Museum of Natural History, 1938, 1953, 1956-57 (240), 1960 (with Frank Greer), 180
Carmichael, Michael
   Shop and office building, 1979 (90), 93
Carnegie Corporation, 133
Carrillo Auditorium, 159
Carrillo Building, 159
Carrillo, Domingo, 143
Carrillo, Francisca, 80
Carrillo, Guillermo and Joaquin, 127, 191
Carrillo Hotel, 159

Carrillo Street (see individual entries by address in Presidio and Pueblo chapter), 193
Casa de la Guerra (NR; CHL, SBLM), 61, 80, 103, 105
"Casa Santa Cruz", 184
Castleberg, Grant
    Alice Keck Park Memorial Garden, 1976 (157), 137
Castillo Street (see individual entries by address in Oceanfront chapter), 193
Castro family, 144
Central Bank, 79
Chamber of Commerce, 28, 29, 128, 133
Chambers, H.C. (see Hunt & Chambers)
    San Marcos Building, 1925-26 (84), 90
Channel Islands Surfboards, 68, 69
Chapala Street (see individual entries by address in Oceanfront, Presidio & Pueblo chapters), 193
Chapel, Presidio, 123
Chapman, Joseph, 43
Charity of St. Vincent de Paul, Sisters of, 126
Chase Building, 85, 86
Chase Commercial Building, 47
Chase, Harold Stuart, 53, 86
Chase, Hezekiah G., 86
Chase, John, 187, 188
Chase Palm Park, 53
Chase, Pearl, 4, 17, 22, 23, 53, 86, 140
Cheesman, Roy W.
    Kerry's Restaurant, 1947 (88), 92
    Christian Science Reading Room, 1950-51 (89), 92
Cheney, Charles H., Back cover, 10, 11, 12, 13, 14, 22. 29, 30, 53
Chicago World Columbian Exposition, 185
Child's Estate, A., 57, 58, 195
Child, Mr. and Mrs. John, 57, 195
Chinese community, 106, 121
Christian Science Monitor, 22
Christian Science Reading Room, 89
Christie, Mr., 53
Chumash, 27, 43, 57, 61, 105, 171, 176, 192, 193, 195, 197
Churrigueresque, Spanish, style, 14
Cicero, C., 49
Cieneguitas Ranch, 158
Citizens Planning Association, 20, 207
City Charter, 20
City Commerce Bank, 125
City Council, 20, 188, 191, 192
City Hall, 16, 105, 116, 117, 122, 132, 148
City Hall Plaza, 78
City Land Use Controls Office, 163
City Meat Market, 160
City Nursery, 99
City Planning Division, 187, 188, 207
City Recreation Department, 55
City Redevelopment Agency, 187
City Sign Committee, 207, 208
Civic League, 12
Civil War, 119, 124
Clark, Andree, 57
Clark Estate, 53, 58
Clark, Huguette, 57
Clark, William A., 58
Coast Federal Savings and Loan, 97
Colonial Revival Cottage, 151
Commercial Bank, 165
Common Council, City, 190, 191
Community Arts Association, Santa Barbara, 13, 15, 16, 87, 40, 53, 69, 122, 124, 140, 159
Community Drafting Room, 15, 53, 69, 132

Comport, Edward, 133
Conard, Rebecca, 188, 207
Conrad, Lida, 151
Congregational Church, 97
Contract Design Limited
    Hotel Neal, 1979 remodel (47), 71
Cook, Mortimer, house (SBLM), 75, 84, 138, 165
Cooke, Noel; Frost, Walter H.; Greer, Frank L; & Schmandt, Charles K.
    Santa Barbara Yacht Club, 1966 (7) 42
Copper Coffee Pot, 62, 87
Cordero Adobe (SBLM), 147
Cordero, Jose, 147
Corrigan, G.W., 53
Coolidge, Calvin, 9
Cooper, Colin Campbell, 120
Cooper Estate, 166
Cooper, John
    La Arcada Court, 1926 (82), 89
Cooper, Joseph W., 165
Copeland's Sporting Goods, 92
Copeland Stationers, 83
Cota-Knox Building, 124
Cota, Francisca, 124
Cota sisters, 176
Council, Lucile
    Hoffmann House, 1922 (249) (with F. Yoch), 184
County National Bank, 85
County Savings Bank, 91
Courtyard offices, 100
Covarrubias Adobe (CHL; SBLM), 143
Covarrubias, Jose Maria, 143
Crabb, Alonzo and Charles, 47
Craig, James Osborne, 15
    El Paseo, 1922-24 (64-a), 79
    Orena Adobes, 1919-20 rest. (118), 118
    Hoffmann House, 1922 (249), 184
Craig, Mary, 22
    El Paseo, 1922-24 (64-a), 79
    Beard Motor Co., (with Ralph Armitage), 1926 (144), 130
    Plaza Rubio houses, 1925-26 (236), 178
Crane Company, 69
Crawford Building, 157
Crawford, James D., 157
Crocker Row, 172, 185
Crocker, William H., 185
Cunningham (Robert) Design Inc.
    La Casa del Mar Motel, 1983-84 (26), 51
    Patio de las Aves, 1984 (40-b), 59
Curletti, J.L.
    Mission Theatre alt., 1929 (55), 75
    Hitchcock Building, 1926 (86), 91

D

Daily Independent, 114
Daily News, 16, 118
Daily Press, Santa Barbara, 10
D'Alfonso, Alex
    La Playa Motel, 1936-37 (24), 50
    Alpha Floral, 1940 (97), 96
Dal Pozzo's Tire Corporation, 155
Dana, Richard Henry, Jr., 80, 171
Dancaster, F.H., 154
Dancaster House, 154
Dardi-Patterson House, 179
Daughters of Charity, 158

Davidson and Maitland, 179
Davis Arcade Building, 162
Davis, Eldon C. (with Richard B. Taylor)
    City Commerce Bank, 1975 (134), 125
Dawson, William Leon, 172-173
Days, Mary Louise, 187, 207
de Forest, Elizabeth, 144
de Forest, Lockwood Jr., 90, 136
De la Guerra Adobe (NR, CHL, SBLM), 15, 16, 79, 80, 116-118, 184, 194
De la Guerra, Antonio Maria, 119, 191
De la Guerra Court, 142
De la Guerra family, 73, 80, 193
De la Guerra, Francisco, 73
De la Guerra gardens, 194
De la Guerra, Jose, 80, 118, 193
De la Guerra, Pablo, 193
De la Guerra Plaza, 15, 16, 116, 194
De la Guerra, Santiago Adobe (SBLM), 119
De la Guerra Street (see individual entries by address in Presidio and Pueblo chapter), 193-194
De la Guerra Wells, 144
Delano, William Adams & Aldrich, Chester
    Herter House, 1905 (157), 137
de Neve, Felipe, 103
Denman, C.K.
    Virginia Hotel, 1926 remodel (194), 152
Dennison, Charles and Mary, 182
Dennison House, 182
Dennison Paper Company, 182
Department of Motor Vehicles, State, 59
Depot Park, 70
De Riviera Hotel, 158
Designworks
    Upper Hawley Building, 1978 (87), 91
"Dial House", 179
Diamond Apartments, 101
Dibblee, Francisca de la Guerra, 181
Dibblee House, 181, 193
Diedrich Auto Parts, 73
Diehl's Grocery Store, 81
Doremus, Dr. A.B., 40, 97, 137, 139
Dover and Woods, 180
Dover, Joe, 180
Douglas Dauntless Divebombers, 72
Dutton Cottage, 151
Dutton, J.R., 151
Dwan, Allan, 168
Dwight Murphy Field, 56

E

Eames, Edward A.
    Our Lady of Sorrows Church, 1928-29 (154), 135
Earthquake, the 1925, 17, 62
East Beach, 28, 29, 53, 54, 56, 195, 196
East Boulevard Improvement Assn., 29, 53, 54, 56
Eastern Star Home, Brentwood, 56
Eastlake style, 14
Eberle houses, 167
Ecole des Beaux Arts, 125
Edgerly Hotel, 165
Edison Electric Co., 40
Edwards House, 181
Edwards, John, 135, 181
Edwards, Peter; Pitman, John
    Nature Conservancy building and Museum of Natural History Sea Life Center, 1984 (27), 52

Fess Parker's Red Lion, 1985-86 (30), 54
Coast Federal Savings (with Holewinski and Blevins), 1980-81 (99), 97
Towbes Building, 1980-81 (144), 130
Schauer Building, 1975-76 remod. (162), 139
Senior Center, 1964, 1973 (174), 144
Battistone Foundation Senior Housing, 1983 (225), 164
Edwards, William A. and Plunkett, Joseph, 18, 120
    Alexander Building, 1934 (58), 76
    Chase Commercial Building, 1940 (16), 47
    Fox Arlington Theatre, 1930-31 (94), 94, 95
    Hollister Estate Office Building, 1931 (205), 157
    Medical Arts Building, 1926 (229), 166
    Moore Building, 1933 & 1935 (105), 100
    Office Building, 1930 (213), 160
    Salisbury Field Building, 1925 (139), 128
    Santa Barbara Savings, 1930 (79), 87
    Schauer Building, 1930 (162), 139
    Shop and office building, 1934 (91), 93
    Southern California Edison Office (Auto Club) 1931 (160), 138
    Van Dyke House, 1941 remod. (107), 101
Edwards, Plunkett & Howell, Henry W., 59
    All-American Sporting Goods, 1926 (214), 160
    Blyth, Eastman, Dillon & Co., 1927 (72), 84
    El Centro Building, 1929 (124), 121
    Little Town Club, 1928 addtn. (135), 126
    Los Arcos Antique Center, 1925 (111), 115
    Lou Rose, 1926 add., (93), 94
    Moore Building, 1927 (remod.) (105), 100
    Offices, 1927-28 (146), 131
    Orella Adobe, 1927 (78), 87
    Southern Counties Gas Co., (with Marston, Van Pelt & Maybury) 1927 (145), 130
Edwards, Stanley
    State Street Dry Goods, 1925 (70), 93
Edwards and Wade
    News-Press Building, 1951 addtn. (116), 117
Edwards, William A. (see Edwards & Plunkett and Edwards, Plunkett & Howell and Edwards & Wade)
    Shops and Office, 1925 (51), 73
    Victoria Hotel and shops, 1925-26 (151), 134
Eisen, Percy A. (see Walker and Eisen)
Eisenberg's, 76
Eisner, Simon, 20
Eisner-Stewart Associates, 20, 23
El Camino Motor Car Company, 72
El Caserio, 146, 148
El Castillo Building, 129
El Centro Building, 106, 121
El Cuartel (SBLM), 122
Elisabeth, Queen of Belgium, 137
Elkhorn Creamery, 156
Elks Club Building, 88
Elliott, J.V., 81
El Mirasol Hotel, 19, 137
El Paseo (NR; SBLM), 15, 16, 17, 79, 80, 118, 119, 120, 184, 194
El Paseo Restaurant, 15, 79
El Presidio Building (SBSM), 119
El Presidio de Santa Barbara State Historic Park, 123
El Pueblo Viejo District, 20, 21, 86, 120, 187
El rancho de la playa, 27
El Torre Office Building, 163
Episcopal congregation, 100
Equestrian Avenue, 139, 194
Erro, Josefa, 86
Estado, 62, 191, 196, 197

Estado Court Apartments, 101
Estero Race Track and Agricultural Park, 57
Estudillo, Francisca, 126
EXPO-'86, 208

F

Faith Mission (NR; SBLM), 72
Family Service Agency, 142
Farallone Fisheries, 70
Faville, William B. (see Bliss & Faville)
Faulkner Gallery, 133
Fernald, Charles and Hannah, 39
Fernald House (SBLM), 39
Festival Arts and Arts School, 80, 124, 140
Figueroa, Governor Jose, 194
Figueroa Street, 194
Field, E. Salisbury, 86, 128
Field, Salisbury and Co., 84
Fiesta, 80, 87, 184
Firestone Store, 154
First Baptist Church (SBSM), 163
First Church of Christ, Scientist, 92
First Congregational Church Site, 115
First Federal Savings Building, 84
First National Gold Bank, 138, 165
First United Methodist Church, 150
Fithian Building (SBSM), 62, 75, 156
Fithian, Joel Adams, 75
Fithian, Joel R., 161
Fithian, R. Barrett, 156
Fitzhugh, Thornton and Teal
 Pierce Block, 1925 (54), 74
Fleischmann, Max C., 41, 127, 180
Fleischmann Yeast Company, 41
Flying A Studio, 168
Forbush, Roswell, 39
 Fernald House, 1862 (2), 39
Ford Motor Co., 55
Fossil Hill, 196
Foursquare Gospel Church, 166
Fox-Arlington Theatre (SBLM), 18, 94, 95, 96, 119
Fox West Coast Theatres, 95
France, 11
Franceschi Flame Tree, 72
Franceschi, Dr. Francesco, 137
Franciscan Fathers, 178, 194
Frank B. Smith House, 153
Franklin, T.J., 22
Fred Whaley Tire Co., 154
Freeman, Don, 148
Freeway Advisory Committee, 21
Fremont, Lt. Col. John, 80
French Second Empire style, 62
Frohman, Philip Hubert and Harold Martin
 Trinity Church, 1912 (104), 100
Frost, Walter H. (see Cooke, Frost, Greer & Schmandt)
Frothingham, Brooks, 182
Frothingham House, 182

G

Gebhard, David, 22, 188, 207
General Plan, City, 197
Geneva, 53
Gervasoni's My Florist and offices, 96
Gidney Building, 128

Gledhill, Carolyn and Edwin, 46
Gledhill Studios, 46
Galley coffee shop, 52
Gamble, John, 148
Garcia, Gilbert
 Chase Commercial Building, 1974 (16), 47
Garden Street (see individual entries by address in Presidio & Pueblo and Mission chapters), 194
Garretson House, 114
Garretson, J.M., 114
Goldfish Cafe, 86
Goleta Slough, 41
Gonzales-Castro House, 144
Gonzales, Rafael, 145
Gonzales-Ramirez Adobe (NR, SBLM), 145
Gonzales, Ramon, 144
Goodhue, Bertram Grosvenor, 14, 15, 98
Goodman, Jerry (see Ketzel-Goodman)
Gothic Cottage, 116
Goycochea, Felipe de, 122
Graham Estate, 58
Granada Building, 19
Grand Hotel, 73
Grant, Robert S., (see Arendt, Mosher, Grant, Pedersen and Phillips)
Gray, David and Martha Platt, 55, 126
Gray, Paul (see Warner and Gray), 90
Gray Pavilion, 55
Great Depression, 30, 53, 56, 62
Greer, Frank L. (see Cooke, Frost, Greer & Schmandt)
 (with Chester Carjola) Museum of Natural History, 1960 (240), 180
Gregg Motors Ltd., 71
Grocery Story, 147
Grosbeck, Dan Sayre, 133
Guard House (SBLM), 119
Gutierrez, Benigno, 75
Gymnasium, Recreation Center, 129

H

Haley, Salisbury, 191, 194
Haley Street, 194
Haley Survey, 195, 196
Haley-Wackenreuder Map #1, 191, 192, 194, 196
Haley-Wackenreuder Map #2, 191, 196
Harbor Restaurant, 52
Harbor View Inn, 51
Harcoff, Mrs. Lyla M., 147
Hardy, Albert, 152
Hardy House, 152
Harper, Edward, 192
Harrington, J.K., 26
Harrison House, 165
Hastings, T. Mitchell (see Soule, Murphy & Hastings)
Hawley, John, 90
Hawley, Walter N., 91
Hazard, Mary P., 180
Hazard, Caroline, 173, 179, 180
Hazard, Rowland, 179
Hazard, Rowland G., 179, 180
Headley, Richard
 Poor Richard's Pub, 1971 (210), 159
Henzell, Barbara S., 187
Herbert House, 167
Herbert, Victor, 195
Hersey, J. Wilmer 18, (with William Mooser & Co.)
 Santa Barbara County Courthouse, 1927-29 (148), 132

Herter, Albert, 46
Herter, Christian and Mary, 137
Herter House site, 137
Hesthal, William, 148
Higginson, Augustus B.
    Gledhill Studios, 1907 (14), 46
Hill-Carrillo Adobe (CHL; SBLM), 127
Hill, Daniel, 127
Hispanic/Mediterranean style, 14, 15
"Historic" Adobe (SBLM), 143
Historic American Building Survey, 145
Hitchcock Building, 63, 91
Hitchcock, Mrs. Herbert R., 91
Hitchcock Motor Company, 69
Hoffman Associates, 54
Hoffmann, Bernhard, 13, 16, 17, 21, 22, 23, 79, 120, 129, 140, 184
Hoffmann House (SBSM), 184
Hoffmann, Irene, 79, 120, 184
Holewinski, Peter J. and Blevins, Mel (with Edwards-Pitman)
    Coast Federal Savings, 1980-81 (99), 97
Holland, Arthur, 150
Holland Cottage, 150
Hollander Buildings, 46
Hollander, L.P. and Co., 46
Hollister Estate Office Building, 157
Hollister, W.W., 62, 90, 91, 148, 157, 161
Holmes, Rachel, 127
Holy Nativity, Sisters of, 179
Home Federal Savings, 84
Home Savings and Loan, 99
Homolka, Frank Jr., and Assoc.
    Home Savings and Loan, 1972 and 1982-83 alterations (103), 99
Hoover, Herbert, 9
Hornbostel, Henry (with Francis W. Wilson)
    Santa Barbara Public Library, 1916-17 (149), 133
Hotels
    Ambassador, 29, 43
    Arlington, 28, 55, 62, 93-96, 146
    Barbara, 74
    Belvedere, 43
    Californian, 68, 71
    Edgerly, 165
    El Mirasol, 19, 137
    Fess Parker's Red Lion, 54
    Grand, 73
    Harrisòn House, 165
    Lincoln House, 165
    Mar Monte (Vista Mar Monte), 55, 71
    Mascarel, 74
    Neal, 71
    Occidental (American House), 74
    Potter, 28, 29, 43, 46, 47, 50, 51, 55, 98, 193
    San Carlos, 80
    San Marcos, 91
    Upham, 165
Howard-Canfield Building, 81
Howell, Henry (see Edwards, Plunkett & Howell; Howell and Arendt; Howell, Arendt, Mosher and Grant; Howell, Arendt and Mosher)
Howell, Henry; and Arendt, Wallace
    Mason Apartments, 1946 (25), 51
    Shop and office building, 1954 (91), 93
Howell, Henry; Arendt, Wallace; and Mosher, Glen L. (with Shugart and Mendes)
    Monastery of Poor Clares, 1956 add., 185

Howell, Henry; Arendt, Wallace; Mosher, Glen L.; and Grant, Robert S.
    Welch-Ryce remod., 1956 (100), 97
Hoyt, Robert Ingle, 63
    Santa Barbara Historical Society Museum, 1964-65 (122), 120
    State Street Drive through Plaza, 63
Hunstable, Edward E., 49
Hunstable Houses, 49
Hunt, Myron; and Chambers, H.C.
    Lou Rose, 1934 remod. (93), 94
    Santa Barbara Public Library, 1930 addtn. (149), 133
Hunt Mercantile Co., 160
Hunt, Myron (see Hunt & Chambers)
    County National Bank, 1919-21 (74), 85
    La Arcada Court, 1926 (82), 89
    San Marcos Building, 1925-26 (84), 90
Hunt, Peter (with Steven Handelman)
    Normandy Hotel, 1980 remodel (152), 134
Hunt's China Shop, 128
Hyde, George, 133
Hyde, Robert W.
    Mihran Studio, 1922 (137), 127
    Vhay-Hyde House, 1932-33 (178), 146

I

International Style, 63
Italianate style, 14
Italy, 11

J

Jacobs, G.H.
    The Office Mart, 1927 (211), 159
Janssens, Augustin, 87
Japanese community, 106
Jarrett, William C. (see Candreva and Jarrett)
Jefferson, Thomas, 61
Jensen, A.C., 99
Jewel Apartments, 148
Johnson House, 59
Johnson, Reginald D.
    Clark Estate, 1932-36 (38), 58
    United States Post Office, 1936-37 (123), 121
Johnson, W.H., 59
Jones, A. Quincy Jr.
    California State Employment Building, 1952 (110), 115
Jordanos' Market, 99, 163
Junior Chamber of Commerce, 57
Junior, Frederick E., 46
Junipero Plaza gates, 173, 180
Junipero Serra Hall, 172, 183

K

Keith-Orpheum Circuit, 75
Kerry, Reginald, 92
Kerry's Restaurant, 92
Ketzel, Raymond; Goodman, Jerry
    Office and Residential Building, 1983-84 (218), 162
King Carlos III, statue of, 78
King, Owen
    Sand Castle Motor Lodge, 1952, (8), 42

Ambassador by-the-Sea and Pacific Park Motels, 1951 (10), 44
Kirker, Harold, 22
Knights of Columbus, 158
Knights of Columbus Hall, 158
Knights of Pythias Lodge, 159
Knox, Dr. Samuel B.P., 124, 179
Kramer, Sam E., 56
Kruger, Kenneth C.; Bensen, Donald H.; Ziemer, Donald
  Presidio Springs, 1977 (173), 144
  Barclay's Bank, 1968 (204), 156

L

La Arcada Court, 89
La Casa del Mar Motel, 51
Laguna Street (see individual entries by address in Presidio & Pueblo and Mission chapters), 194
Lake Chapala, 193
Lancers Cavalry Unit, 119
Landmarks Committee, City, 20, 63, 83, 187, 188, 197, 207, 208
La Placita Building, 78
La Playa Motel, 50
La Purificacion Rancho, 87
Larco, Andrea, 70
Larco Fish Market, 70
Larco, Sebastian, 70
Larkin, Thomas Oliver, 80, 127
La Ronda Apartments, 45, 49
"Las Isletas", 145
Las Tiendas Building, 79
Lasuen, Fr. Fermin, 171, 195
Lataillade, Caesar, 78
La Vies, William, 114
Leadbetter Beach, 196
Leifer-Marter
  El Paseo Restaurant remodel, 1984 (64-a), 79
Leifer, Vincent E. (see Leifer-Marter)
Lenny, Henry, 134, 208
Lenvik, Edwin A.; and Minor, Kenneth O.
  La Casa del Mar Motel, 1983-84, (26), 51
  Office & Residential Building, 1983-84 (184), 148
Leonard, Brother
  Monastery of Poor Clares, 1929-30 (251), 185
Leopold, Prince of Belgium, 137
Letsch, Beulah, 48
Letsch Duplex, 48
Levy's Furniture Store, 131
Levy House, 154
Levy, Michel, 82
Levy, Sarah, 154
Levy Shoes, 82
Leyva Adobe, 78
Lies, Eugene, 191
Lincoln, Amasa, 165
Lincoln House, 165
Little Town Club (SBSM), 126
Lloyd Avenue, 150, 194
Lloyd, Clio, 151, 194
Lloyd family, 194
Lloyd's Bank, 88
Lobero Building, 125, 129
Lobero, Jose, 122, 124, 157
Lobero Theatre (CHL; SBLM), 17, 18, 121, 122, 157
Lockard, E. Keith (see Sauter and Lockard)
  La Ronda Apartments, 1930 (13), 45
  Cabrillo Pavilion, 1926 (32), 55

Neal Callahan Building, 1926-27 (53), 74
Lockard and Sauter (see Sauter and Lockard), 16
Lockheed Aviation Company, 68
Logan and Bryan, 84
Los Arcos Antique Center, 115
Los Banos del Mar, 40, 192
Los Olivos Street (see individual entries by address in Mission chapter), 194
Los Patos Way (see individual entries by address in Oceanfront chapter), 194
Los Patios (SBSM), 56
Loughead, Allan and Malcolm, 66
Lou Rose Annex, 93
Lou Rose, 94
Lower Clock Building, 75
Lower Hawley Building, 62, 91
Lugo Adobe (SBLM), 16, 119, 120

M

Maas, Charles, 152
MacKellar, Alexander, 135, 136, 142
MacKellar Court, 135
MacKellar House, 136
MacKesey, Thomas W., 9
MacQuarrie, John, 133
Magdalena Cota Adobe, 115
Magnin, I. and Company, 94, 98
Maguire Bungalows, 150
Maguire, Henry F., 150
Mahan, William and Associates
  Wall and Pergola, 1981-82 (150), 134
  Wall and Entrance, 1983 (220), 162
Mahan, William (see Mahan and Associates and Sharpe, Mahan and Associates), 162
Maher, Patrick, 55
Marchbanks, Glenn Jr.
  First Federal Savings, 1963 (73), 84
Margaret Baylor Inn, 125
Marine Terrace Subdivisions, 196
Mar Monte Hotel, 55, 71
Marquis, Alexander W.
  St. Vincent's School and Orphanage, 1874-75 (209), 158
Marsh, Norman F.
  First Baptist Church, 1910, 1921 (223), 163
Marston, Sylvanus; Van Pelt, Garrett, Jr.; & Maybury, Edgar
  Carrillo Hotel, 1923 (212), 159
  Southern Counties Gas Co., 1927 (145) (with Edwards, Plunkett & Howell), 130
Marter, Howard (see Leifer-Marter)
Martin, Harold (with P.H. Frohman)
  Trinity Church, 1912 (104), 100
Mascarel Hotel, 74
Mason Apartments, 51
Mason, Governor Richard B., 193, 194
Masonic Order, 128
Masonic Temple, 128
Mason Street (see individual entries by address in Oceanfront chapter), 194
Mathews, Edgar A., 15, 132
Maybury, Edgar (see Marston, Van Pelt & Maybury)
Medical Arts Building, 166
Medico-Dental Arts Building, 73
Meridian Studios (SBLM), 16, 120
Mesa fault zone, 61
Metropolitan Theatres, 75
Mexico, 11, 12, 15, 17, 19, 61, 120, 193, 195, 196.

215

Micheltorena, Gov. Manuel, 193, 194-195
Micheltorena Street, 194-195
Mihran Studio (SBSM), 127
Miller, Herman, 92
Miller, J.C.F., 46
Millett, Nelson, 165
Milpas Street (see individual entries in Oceanfront chapter), 195
Minor, Kenneth O. (see Lenvik and Minor)
Minton, H.A.
    Retail Store, 1931-32 (81), 88
Miranda Adobe (SBLM), 119
Miramar Hotel, 55
Mispu, 193
Mission area, 170
Mission Church (see Santa Barbara Mission)
Mission Canyon, 61, 172, 173, 195
Mission Canyon Road, 195
Mission Creek, 61, 173
Mission Creek Bridge, 180
Mission fault zone, 61
"Mission Hill", 179
Mission Historical Park, 171, 172, 178, 179
Mission lands, 43
Mission Revival Style, 11
Mission San Luis Rey, 176
Mission Santa Barbara, 14, 20, 27, 61, 62, 80, 105, 120, 130, 132, 168, 171-177, 178, 180, 185, 188, 194, 195, 196
Mission Soledad, 192
Mission Street, 195
Mission Theatre, 75
Mississippi River, 14
Moby Dick coffee shop, 52
Modern style, 12, 18, 19
Modoc Substation, 167
Monastery of Poor Clares, 172, 185
Montecito Street (see individual entries by address in Oceanfront chapter), 195
Monterey, California, 14, 80, 127
Monterey Greek Revival style, 39
Montgomery, Ross
    Junipero Serra Hall, 1929-30 (247), 183
    St. Anthony's Seminary, 1926 add. (248), 183
Montgomery Ward store, 88
Moore Building, 100
Moore, Henry W., 100
Mooser and Simpson, 15, 132
Mooser, William, and Co., 18
    Los Patios, 1930 (34), 56
    Santa Barbara County Courthouse, 1927-29 (148) (with J. Wilmer Hersey), 132-133
Moreton Bay Fig Tree (SBLM), 47
Morgan, Julia
    Margaret Baylor Inn, 1926-27 (133), 125
    Gymnasium at Recreation Center, 1926 (143), 129
Morris, James Edward, 207-208
Morrow, Irving F., 22, 23
Mosher, Glen D. (see Arendt, Mosher, Grant et al)
Motel, 49
Moullet, J.F., 141
Moullet House, 141
Mountain Drive, 195
Municipal Soccer Field, 56
Murphy, John Frederic (see Soule & Murphy; Soule, Murphy & Hastings)
Murphy, Dwight, 56, 184
Museum of Natural History, Santa Barbara (SBSM), 172, 173, 179, 180
Museum of Oology, 180

Mc

"McCarthy," U.S. Coastal Survey vessel, 180
McKay Building, 78
McKim, Mead and White, 161
McNitt, Roland, 22

N

Nardo Building, 83
National Historic Preservation Act, 187
National Horse Show, 40
Native Daughters of the Golden West, 207
"Natoma", 195
Natoma Apartments, 49
Natoma Avenue (see individual entries by address in Oceanfront chapter), 195
Naval Reserve Armory, 41
Naval Reserve Training Center, 41
Neal Callahan Building, 74
Neal Hotel, 71
Neighborhood House Association, 142
Nelson, Christopher H., 187, 188, 207
Nelson, Richard Bliss
    Santa Barbara Yacht Club, 1966, (7), 42
    Mar Monte Hotel, 1977 remodel (33), 55
New Deal, 30
New House, 154
News-Press, 16
News-Press Building, 117, 122
New York's Central Park, 29
New York Telephone Company, 184
Nichols, E.C., 53
Niños Drive, 195
Nixon, Thomas
    Fernald House, 1880 (2), 39
    Fithian Building, 1895-96 (56), 75
Nordhoff, Charles, 27
Normandy Hotel (SBSM), 134
Notre Dame de Namur, Sisters of, 173

O

Oak Park, 168, 188
Occidental Hotel, 74
Oceanfront, 27
Office Building, 160, 161
Office Mart, The, 159
Office and Residential Building, 148, 162
Offices, 131
O'Keefe, Father, 176
Old Spanish Days Carriage Museum, 40
Old Spanish Days Fiesta, 80, 87, 144, 160
Oliver, Mrs. G.S.J., 180
Olmsted and Olmsted, 13, 29, 53
Olmsted-Cheney Plan, 197
Ordinance No. 7, 191
Orella Adobe, 61, 87
Orella Building, 62, 76
Orella Family, 86, 87
Oreña Adobes (SBLM), 15
Oreña, Gaspar, 118, 172
Oreña Store, 118
Ortega, Jose Francisco, 103, 141, 195
Ortega-Masini Adobe, 127
Ortega, Rafaela Luisa, 127
Ortega Street (see individual entries by address in Presidio and Pueblo chapter), 195

Osborne's Book Store, 82
Our Lady of Sorrows Church, 89, 135
Overman, Caroline L., 11, 22
Owl Drug Store, 88

P

Park, Alice Keck, 137
Park Superintendent, 137
Parker, J.Y., 71
Parker Way, 71
Parkinson, John (see Parkinson & Parkinson)
  Howard-Canfield Bldg., 1903 (66) 81
Parkinson, John; & Parkinson, Donald
  Elks Club Building, 1926 (80) 88
Parma Brothers, 77
Parma Building, 77
Parma, G.B., 77
Pasadena, 90
Paseo Carrillo or Callejon Carrillo, 129
Paseo de la Guerra, 79
Patio de las Aves, 59
Peake, Channing, 147
Pedersen, Donald E.
  Hitchcock Building, 1982 remodel (86) 91
Pedersen, Leo R. (see Arendt, Mosher, Grant, Pedersen, Phillips)
Pedotti House, 146
Pershing Park, 40
Peterson, E.J., 129
Pfleuger, Timothy L.
  I. Magnin and Company, 1946-47 (101), 98
Phillips, Roger A. (see Arendt, Mosher, Grant, Pedersen, Phillips)
Piccadilly Square, 80
Pico, Anita, 125
Pico, Buenaventura, Adobe, 105, 125
Pico, Concepcion, 143
Pico, Pio, Governor, 143
Pico, Santiago, 125
Pier One, 62, 83
Pierce Block, 62, 74
Pierce Brothers, 73
Pierce, Charles, 74
Pierce, Franklin, 143
Pierce, Dr. Horace F., 166
Piggly Wiggly Super Market, 160
Pinkham, Walter H., 101
Pitman, John, (see Edwards-Pitman)
Pitman, Richard H. (also see Carleton M. Winslow)
  La Casa del Mar Motel, 1947-49 (26), 51
Planning Commission, City, 192
Plans and Planting Committee, 13, 16, 19, 20, 53, 69, 146, 183
Plaza del Mar, 26, 29, 40, 55
Plaza Rubio, 130, 172, 178, 179, 196
Plunkett, Joseph (see Edwards and Plunkett), 95
  El Presidio Building, 1945-46 (119), 119
  Covarrubias Adobe alter., 1940 (171), 143
  El Caserio (with others), 1930-37 (182), 148
Por la Mar Drive, 196
Pool, J. Corbley
  Auto Show Rooms, 1911, 1913 (49), 72
  Levy Shoes, 1919 (68), 82
  Osborne's Book Store, 1914 (69), 82
  San Marcos Building, 90
  Recreation Center, 1914 (143), 129
  American Film Mfg. Company, 1913 (232), 168
Poole, Peter, 70, 137

Poole, William
  Larco Fish Market, 1911 (46), 70
  Diedrich Auto Parts, 1926-27 (52), 73
  Russ' Camera, 1916 (77), 86
  Daily Independent, 1926 (108), 114
Poor Richard's Pub, 159
Portola expedition, 195
Portola Theatre, 77
Post Office, Santa Barbara (NR), 74, 90, 126
Potter Art Gallery, 46
Potter Hotel Annex, 48
Potter Hotel, 26, 28, 29, 43, 46, 47, 50, 51, 55, 98, 193
Potter, Milo M., 43
Presidio Avenue, 119
Presidio and Pueblo, 103
Presidio, Santa Barbara (NR; CHL), 14, 20, 61, 78, 80, 89, 102, 103, 105, 106, 118, 119, 120, 122, 123, 125, 140, 141, 142, 144, 171, 176, 183, 193, 194, 195, 196, 197
Presidio Springs, 144
Pries, Lionel
  Auto Show Rooms and Seaside Building, 1926 (49), 72
  Bothin Building, 1925-26 (62), 78
  Bothin Building, 1925 (67), 81
Primavera Festival, 40
Prince, Mrs. C.M., 134
Pueblo Theater, 140
Puesta del Sol Road, 196
Pulaski, Rolly and Assoc.
  Knights of Columbus Hall, 1983 rehab. (209), 158
"Punta del Castillo" 193, 196
Punta Gorda Street (see individual entries by address in Oceanfront chapter), 196
Pure Gold Vintage Clothing, 77
P.W.A., 40
Pacheco, Romualdo, 193
Pacific Coast Steam Ship Company, 153
Pacific House, 127
Pacific Park Motel, 44
Packard automobiles, 69
Padre's Quarters, Presidio, 123
Palm Park, 53
Panama-California Exposition, San Diego, 14
Park, Dr. C.C., 58, 75
Park Commission, 56, 137
Parker, Fess, 53
Parker, Fess, Hotel, 54

Q

Queen Anne style, 14

R

Raffour House, 148
Raffour, Louis, 148
Ramirez, Cristobal and Ventura, 145
Ramirez, Jose Antonio, 176
Rancheros Visitadores, 143
Ray, Barbara Parker
  Vhay-Hyde House, 1952 addtn. (178), 146
Ray, Russel, 29
  Auto Show Rooms and Seaside Building, 1917 (49) attrib., 72
  YMCA, Old, 1913 (207) (with Winsor Soule), 157
  Modoc Substation, 1930 (231), 167

Vaughn House, 1914 (244) (with Winsor Soule), 182
Dennison House, 1916 (245) (with Winsor Soule), 182
Recreation Center (Gymnasium SBSM), 129
Restaurants (96), 63, 96
Retail Store, 88
Reynolds, Helen, 134
Rice, Bertha, 129
Riffle, Stanley R. Jr.
    Gervasoni's, 1976 (98), 96
Riggs, Lutah Maria, 15, 16, 122
    El Paseo State Street arcade, 1960s (64-a), 79
    Pedotti House, 1956 addtn. (177), 146
    El Caserio remodels, 1950s (182), 148
Ripoll, Fr. Antonio, 176
Rivers and Harbors Act of 1935, 41
Riviera Campus, 142
Robbins, Thomas, 43
Robinson, Charles Mulford, 12, 22
Robinson, Frank D.
    Presidio Padre's Quarters, 1977-81 (128), 123
Robson, George, 180
Rochin Adobe (SBLM), 141
Rogers, E.F., 83
Rogers Furniture Building, 83
Rojko, Melvin A.
    First Federal Savings, 1963 (73), 84
Roosevelt School, 172
Rosenthal, A.B., 19
"Royal Ordinances Concerning the Laying Out of New Towns", 103
Rubio, Father Jose, 178, 196
Russ' Camera, 86
Russell, John Robert, 63
Rusty's Pizza Parlor, 159

S

Sajous, Edward, 22
Salisbury Field Building, 128
Salt Pond, 57
Salvation Army building, 73, 152
San Carlos Hotel, 80
Sanchez, Gilbert
    Presidio Chapel, 1982-84 (128), 123
Sanders, A.C.
    Las Tiendas Building, 1925 (63), 79
    Offices, 1925-26 (146), 131
    Town House Restaurant, 1926 (95), 96
Sand Castle Motor Lodge, 42
San Diego Exhibition, 1915, 98
San Francisco's Golden Gate Park, 29, 185
San Francisco Mid-Winter Exposition, 185
San Marcos Building, 90, 162
San Marcos Garage, 162
San Marcos Hotel, 91
Santa Barbara Abstract Co., 86
Santa Barbara Associated Charities, 58
Santa Barbara Beautiful, 20, 95, 96
Santa Barbara Board of Realtors, 166
Santa Barbara City College, 193
Santa Barbara Clinic (SBSM), 98
Santa Barbara Club, 161
Santa Barbara Club Building, 161
Santa Barbara College, 62, 90
Santa Barbara Community Arts Assn., 13
Santa Barbara County, 27, 132, 156

Santa Barbara County Board of Supervisors, 18, 132, 191
Santa Barbara County Courthouse (NR, SBLM), 18, 90, 105, 115, 120, 126, 132-133, 139
Santa Barbara Datsun, 68, 69
Santa Barbara Elks Club, 88
Santa Barbara Foundation, 57, 127
Santa Barbara Herald Weekly, 73
Santa Barbara High School, 163
Santa Barbara Historical Society, 39, 120, 143
Santa Barbara Historical Society Museum, 120
Santa Barbara Improvement Company, 78
Santa Barbara Junior High School (SBLM), 163
Santa Barbara Land and Improvement Co., 57
Santa Barbara Mission (NR; CHL; SBLM), 14
Santa Barbara Morning Press, 73
Santa Barbara Museum of Art, 89, 90, 121
Santa Barbara Museum of Natural History (see Museum of Natural History)
Santa Barbara Mutual Building, 85
Santa Barbara News-Press, 78, 117
Santa Barbara Post Office (see Post Office)
Santa Barbara Presidio (see Presidio)
Santa Barbara Public Library, 89, 133, 134
Santa Barbara Savings, 87
Santa Barbara Schools Maint. Building, 143
Santa Barbara Street (see individual entries by address in Presidio & Pueblo section), 196
Santa Barbara Trust for Historic Preservation, 20, 78, 80, 118, 123, 188, 207
Santa Barbara Wharf, 27
Santa Barbara Yacht Club, 42, 52
Santa Rosa Rancho, 165
Santa Ynez Valley, 87
Santiago de la Guerra Adobe (SBLM), 119
Sauter, Roland F. (also see Sauter and Lockard)
    Cabrillo Pavilion, 1926 (32), 55
    Neal Callahan Building, 1926-27 (53), 74
    Dal Pozzo's Tire Corp., 1930 (200), 155
    City Meat Market, 1929-30 (215), 160
Sauter, Roland F.; and Lockard, E. Keith
    Hotel Neal, 1925 (47), 71
    Neal Callahan Building, 1926-27 (53), 74
    Fithian Building, 1925 (56), 75
    Tomlinson Building, 1925 (57), 76
    City Hall, 1923 (115), 117
Savoy Hotel, 72
S.B. Tobacco Co. Building, 153
Schauer Building, 139
Schauer Printing Co., 139
Schmandt, Charles K. (see Cooke, Frost, Greer & Schmandt)
Schott, Alice, daughters, 140, 147
Scott, Mel, 22
Sears, M. Urmy, 22
Seaside Hotel Company, 28
Seaside Oil Company, 72
Seaside Oil Co. Building (SBSM), 72
Seckels, L.J., 41
Second World War, 19, 51
Senior Center of Santa Barbara, 144
Seraphic College of St. Anthony, 183
Serra, Fr. Junipero, 103, 183, 195
7-Up Bottling Company, 47
Seville, 53
Sharpe, Donald G. (see Sharpe, Mahan and Associates)
    Santa Barbara Clinic, 1978 remod. (102), 98
Sharpe, Donald G.; Mahan, William; and Associates
    Wharf kiosk, 1981 (27), 52
    Mar Monte Hotel (Sheraton), 1982-83 (33), 55

Office Building (Barcelona Building), 1984 (217), 161
Sheraton Hotel and Spa, 55
Sherman, Charles E., 156
Sherman House (SBSM), 156
Shop and office building, 93
Shops, 89, 156
Shops and Office, 73
Shore Acres, 54
Shoreline Drive, 196
Shugart and Mendes, 185
Shugart, Don, 58
Sisters of Charity, 126
Sisters of the Holy Nativity, 179
Sisters of Notre Dame de Namur, 173
Sisters of Poor Clare, 185
Sloyd School, 142
Smeraldi, J.B., 133
Smith, Frank B., 153
Society of Architectural Historians, 207
Sola, Governor Pablo, 196
Sola Street, 196
Somerset Restaurant, 156
Sonora-Baja California district, 194
Soule, Winsor; and Murphy, John Frederic
   Veterans Memorial Building, 1927 (11), 44
   Restaurants, 1946 (96), 96
   C & H Chevrolet (with A. Godfrey Bailey), 1946 (201), 155
   Crawford Building, 1936 (206), 157
Smith, George Washington, 15, 16
   Lobero Theatre, 1924 (125), 122
   Meridian Studios, 1923 (121), 120
   News-Press Building, 1922 (116), 117
   Little Town Club, 1923-24 (135), 126
   Dardi-Patterson House, 1927 (237), 179
   Frothingham House, 1922 (246), 182
   Boyd House, 1929 (250), 184
Snook and Kenyon, 44, 126
Soderburg, Paul
   Cordero Adobe alter., 1969 (181), 147
Soule, Winsor (see Soule & Murphy; Soule, Murphy & Hastings)
   Naval Reserve Armory, 1941 (6), 41
   Old YMCA (with Russel Ray), 1913 (207), 157
   Vaughn House (with Russel Ray), 1914 (244), 182
   Dennison House (with Russel Ray), 1916 (245), 182
Soule, Winsor, 22
Soule, Winsor; Murphy, John Frederic; & Hastings, T. Mitchell
   Alhecama Theater, 1925 (164), 140
   Alhecama Center, 1925 (163), 140
   Archer-Spencer Building, 1924 (155-b), 136
   Chase Building, 1926 (77), 86
   Crane Company, 1926 (44), 69
   De la Guerra Court (Associated Charities) 1927 (169), 142
   Orella Building, 1925 (59), 77
   Rogers Furniture, 1925 (71), 83
   Salvation Army Building, 1926 (195), 152
   Santa Barbara Mutual Building, 1924 (75), 85
   Santa Barbara Schools Maintenance and Operations Building, 1929 (170), 143
   Santa Barbara Tobacco Co. Building, 1926 (196), 153
   Studio Building, 1928 (129), 124
   University Club, 1922 (159), 138
Southern California Acclimatizing Association, 72
Southern California Edison Co., 129, 138
Southern Californians, 11

Southern Counties Gas Co., 130
Southern Pacific Eating House, 71
Southern Pacific Railroad, 53, 70, 100
Southern Pacific Railroad Depot (SBLM), 70, 71
Southern Pacific Roundhouse Site, 53, 54
Southern Pacific Transportation Co., 47
Southworth, John, 143
Spain, 12, 15, 17, 103, 120, 192, 193
Spanish Colonial Revival style, 12, 62, 63
Sperry, Dr. Myra House and Office, 164
"Spirit of the Ocean", 120
Spiritualist Association Church of the Comforter, 149
Standard Oil Company, 59
State Office of Historic Preservation, 187
State Street (see individual entries by address in State Street Plaza chapter), 15, 60, 61, 196-197
   400 and 500 blocks, 73
State Street Dry Goods Store, 83
Stearns, John P., 52
Stearns Wharf, 27, 41, 42, 52, 53, 59
Stevens, Ralph T., 132, 136
Stevenson, Robert Louis (Mrs.), 82
Stewart Edward White house, 185
Stoddard, Dr. Charles, 150
Storke Building, 139
Storke Plaza, 78
Storke, Thomas M., 78, 117, 121
"Stranger at Coyote", 168
Street in Spain, 15, 79, 129
Street Name Glossary, 190-197
Studio, 152
Studio Building, 124
Survey of Architectural & Historic Resources, 187-189, 207
Sutcliffe, Judy, 162
Syukhtun, 43, 61, 197
St. Anthony's Seminary, 172, 173, 183, 184
Saint Barbara, 128, 196
St. Mark's Episcopal Church (SBLM), 168
St. Mary's Retreat House, 172, 179
St. Vincent's School (NR; SBLM), 62, 158

T

Tallant, Henry, 192
Taylor, Richard B., 63
   Mar Monte Hotel, 1956, (33), 55
   City Commerce Bank (with Eldon C. Davis), 1975 (134), 125
Taynayan, 171
Thomas, George M. Studio
   Villa Rosa, 1930-31 (12), 45
Thompson (Alpheus B.) Adobe (later San Carlos Hotel), 61
Thompson (Alpheus B.) Adobe Site, 80
Thompson, Alpheus B., 80
Thompson, Dixey W., 161, 166, 168
Thompson House, 166
Thompson, Nancy P., 166
Tiers, Alex, 147
Tiers-Peake-Schott House, 147
Tomlinson Building, 76
Tomlinson, George, 76
Towbes Building, 106, 130
Towbes, Michael, 130
Town House Restaurant, 95
Tree of Light (SBLM), 157
Trenwith's, 81

219

Trinity Church, 100
Trussell, Capt. Horatio Gates, 39
Trussell-Winchester Adobe (CHL, SBLM), 27, 39
Turn-of-the-Century Streetscape, 167
Tuttle, Paul, 148
Twin Palms, 42
Two Years Before the Mast (1840), by Richard Henry Dana, Jr., 80, 171

U

Underhill, Francis T.
    Dibblee House, 1909 (243), 181
Union Oil office building, 42
United Pentecostal Church, 152
United States Coast Guard, 69
United States Coast Survey Map, 104
United States Highway 101, State Street Bridge, 21
United States Army Air Force, 192
United States Post Office & Federal Building, 90, 121
University Club, 137
University of California, Santa Barbara, 142, 179, 207
University of California, Santa Barbara, University Art Museum, 207
Upham Hotel (SBLM), 165
Upper Clock Building, 62, 84, 165
Upper Hawley Building (SBSM), 91
Urton, Charles, 42
Usher, Frederick A., 208

V

Vail, Edward F.R., 181
Vaile, Harold John
    V.E. Wood Auto Building, 1946 (48), 71
    Little Town Club, 1948 addtn. (135), 126
Valenzuela, Jose Jesus, 122
Valerio Street (see individual entries by address in Presidio & Pueblo chapter), 197
Van Akin, V.
    Vhay Studio, 1941 alt. (175), 145
Van Dyke House, 101
Van Dyke, Sidney S., 101
Van Horn House, 48
Van Horn, J.A., 48
Van Pelt, Garrett Jr. (see Marston, Van Pelt and Maybury)
Van Vactor and Myers Tract, 172, 191
Vaughn House, 182
Vaughn, Reginald and Miriam, 182
Vega Mar, 57
Verhelles' City Nursery, 99
Veterans Memorial, 132
Veterans' Memorial Building (SBSM), 44
Vhay-Hyde House, 146
Vhay, Louise Murphy
    Gonzales-Ramirez Adobe, 1923 & 1956 alt. (176), 145
    Pedotti House, 1926 (177), 146
    Senior Center, 1952 (174), 144
    Tiers-Peake-Schott House, 1953-54 (180), 147
    Vhay Studio, 1928 (175), 145
    El Caserio, 1930-37 (with others) (182), 148
Vhay Studio, 145
Victoria Building, 134
Victoria Court, 91
Victoria, Governor Manuel, 197

Victoria Hotel and shops, 134
Victoria Street (see individual entries by address in Presidio and Pueblo chapter), 197
Victoria Street Theatre, 163
Village Fair, The, 95
Villa Rosa, 45
Virginia Hotel, 152
Viscaino, Sebastian, 196
Vista del Mar Ball Room, 44
Vista Mar Monte Hotel, 55
Vitruvius (Marcus Vitruvius Pollio), *Ten Books of Architecture*, 176
Volunteers, Historic Resources Survey, 188-189

W

WPA, 41
Wackenreuder, Vitus, 191
Wade, William (see Edwards & Wade)
Wahlquist, Carl D.; Lawrence, Richards
    Brooks Building (with Clayton Brooks), 1982-84 (130), 124
Walker, Albert; and Eisen, Percy A.
    Vista Mar Monte, 1927, 1935 (33), 55
    Wall and Entrance, 162
    Wall and Pergola, 134
Ward, F.S.
    Hotel Californian, 1925 (42), 68
Warner Bros., 75
Wass, H.L.
    Osborne's Book Store, 1925 (69), 82
Warner, Jack; and Gray, Paul
    Santa Barbara Museum of Art, 1983 (85), 90
Washington Cathedral, 100
Watering Trough and Fountain (SBLM), 58
Weber, Kem
    Christian Science Reading Room, 1950-51 (89), 92
Weeks, H.C.
    City Land Use Controls Off., 1922 (222), 163
Weitze, Karen, 22
Welch-Ryce Corporation, 97
Welch-Ryce-Haider Mortuary, 97
Wellesley College, 179
Wells Fargo Bank, 130
Wenderoth, Oscar
    Santa Barbara Museum of Art (with Francis W. Wilson), 1914 (85), 90
Werner, Carl W.
    Masonic Temple, 1923-24 (141), 128
West Beach, 28, 30, 42, 48, 192, 197
Weston, J.H.
    Synagogue (Church of the Comforter), 1932 (185), 149
Wewer, Brother Adrian
    St. Anthony's Seminary, 1899-1901 (248), 183
Whaley, Fred, 154
White House of Santa Barbara, 76
White, Mr. & Mrs. Stewart Edward, 137, 185
Whittaker, Elmer H., 123
Willits, Warren family, 185
Wilson, Francis W., 156
    Southern Pacific Railroad Depot, 1905 (45), 70
    McKay Building, 1903-04 (62), 78
    Santa Barbara Museum of Art (with Oscar Wenderoth), 1914 (85), 90
    Santa Barbara Public Library (with Henry Hornbostel), 1916-17 (149), 133
    Watering Trough and Fountain, 1911 (39), 58

Santa Barbara Club, 1903-04 (216), 161
Wilson, John D. and Ramona, 127
Winchester Adobe, 39
Winchester family, 39
Winchester, Robert, 157
Winchester, Sarah, 39
"Winfield Scott", 39
Wingate-Culley house, 185
Winslow, Carleton Monroe (some with Richard H. Pitman)
    Auto Show Rooms and Seaside Oil Building, 1937 (49), with R.H. Pitman, 72
    El Paseo, 1928-29 (64-a), 79
    Santa Barbara Clinic, 1920, 1927, 1929-30 (102), 98
    Brinks Grocery, 1933 (103), 99
    Meridian Studios, 1925 addition (121), 120
    Santa Barbara Public Library, 1925 alterations (149), 133
    Museum of Natural History, 1927-28, 1932-33, 1934 (240), 180
Woman's World, 96
Wood's Garage, 73
Wood-Lockhart Cottage, 151
Wood, Mary C.F., 151
Wood, V.E. Auto Building, 71
Wood, Vincent E., 71
Work Inc. and shops, 72
World War I, 52
World War II, 19, 30, 44, 54, 55, 62, 72, 92, 106, 115, 119, 179, 192

Wythe, Joseph Henry, Blaine & Olson
    El Castillo Building, 1926 (142), 129

Y

Yacht Club, 42, 52
Yanonali, 197
Yanonali Street (see individual entries by address in Oceanfront chapter), 197
YMCA, Old, 157
Yoch, Florence
    Hoffmann House (with Lucile Council), 1922 (249), 184
Yorba-Abadie Adobe, 15, 16, 117
Young, George C., 155

Z

Ziemer, Donald (see Kruger-Bensen-Ziemer)
Zimmer, Jerry
    Santa Barbara Public Library, 1979 addtn. & remodel (149), 133
Zimmerman, James J.
    Harbor Restaurant, 1980-81 (27), 52
    Patio de las Aves, 1984 (40-b), 59
Zoning Ordinance, Santa Barbara City, 19